D0567230

EXTERNAL FINANCING FOR LATIN AMERICAN DEVELOPMENT

EXTERNAL FINANCING FOR LATIN AMERICAN DEVELOPMENT

Published for the
General Secretariat of the
Organization of American States
by
The Johns Hopkins Press
Baltimore and London

338.98
O68e

Copyright © 1971 by The Johns Hopkins Press
All rights reserved
Manufactured in the United States of America

The Johns Hopkins Press, Baltimore, Maryland 21218
The Johns Hopkins Press Ltd., London

Library of Congress Catalog Card Number 74-119109

ISBN 0-8018-1208-9   FH

Contents

JAN 2 '73

HUNT LIBRARY
CARNEGIE-MELLON UNIVERSITY

Foreword

This study on external financing derives from a report which the OAS Secretariat presented to the VI Annual Meeting of the Inter-American Economic and Social Council (known as CIES, from its Spanish initials), in Port of Spain in June 1969.

That year, the last of the First Development Decade, saw several important events take place in inter-American political and economic relations. The first of these was the Latin American governments' accord on the objectives to be achieved in their future economic relations with the United States. Their forum was CECLA (Special Committee for Latin American Coordination), and their statement was the Consensus of Viña del Mar. Latin American unity was, in fact, a notable element of the Port of Spain meeting.

During 1969, also, several studies were begun, the single purpose of which was to set the framework—through the lessons of past experience—for future development activities. Thus, the Pearson Report was to fulfill this promise within a global framework, as was the Prebislı Report for Latin America, the Jackson Report for the United Nations and the Peterson Report for the United States. The CIAP (Inter-American Committee on the Alliance for Progress, which is the Permanent Executive Committee of the CIES), in a more concentrated way, also felt a need to assess the 1960's and the eight-year experience of the Alliance for Progress, concentrating mainly on trade and finance.

With specific reference to finance, following CIAP's recommendations we set about evaluating as objectively as possible the contribution that external financing had made in Latin America during the sixties and the aid component in the capital flows. We also hoped to make a preliminary determination of future financing prospects and requirements, in order to draw attention to the magnitude of the task ahead for the decade about to begin.

The result of our study—in a broad sense—was to reaffirm our conviction that Latin America's development will depend basically on the will of, and the decisions taken by, the countries themselves. The external sector, that is, trade—especially the expansion of export capacity—will play a vital role in this development strategy. External financing, for its part, can play only a temporary role, which is not to imply that it is of lesser importance. For it to be really effective, however, it must be forthcoming in greater amounts and on better terms.

It is with satisfaction and pride that we commend this study to print. The attempt to measure the real aid component of capital flows represents, we believe, an innovation in the traditional examination of financial assistance. We sincerely hope that it is a useful contribution to all who are equally dedicated to solving the problems which impede the rapid development of the less-developed countries.

WALTER J. SEDWITZ

Executive Secretary for Economic
and Social Affairs

Organization of American States

Introduction

The purpose of this report is to analyze the external financing received by Latin America in the period covered by the Alliance for Progress; to examine future needs and availabilities of external resources, with special reference to the next decade; and to suggest a course of action compatible with the dual objectives of accelerating the development of the region and gradually reducing, and eventually eliminating, the dependence on external financial cooperation on which that development is now based—and will be based for some time yet.

The conclusion reached here is that, if the target of no less than 2.5 percent increase in the per capita product is to be achieved, Latin American countries must receive during the period 1970-75, external cooperation in substantially greater amounts and on more adequate terms than during the present decade. According to the assumption adopted in this report, that increase in external cooperation to Latin America would, in the years ahead, have to be channeled through hemispheric financial cooperation mechanisms, primarily through the Inter-American Development Bank and, to a lesser extent, through the bilateral financial assistance programs—AID and P.L. 480—of the United States government. According to tentative estimates, the development of Latin America would require these institutions to provide the countries of the region in the period 1970-75 with an average of some $1.5 billion each year, a figure which represents for that period the external resources gap of Latin America which is unlikely to be covered by any other sources of financing.

The proposal made in this report implies a substantial multilateralization of the Alliance for Progress, since under it the IDB would provide total credits of approximately $1.3 billion yearly in the period 1970-75. For that purpose the IDB would need to increase substantially its operations, adapting them to the new and broader responsibilities that would be assigned to it, and also have the full coordinated support of all the other mechanisms of the Inter-American System.

In order to be able to substantiate the findings—albeit still tentative—contained herein and thus implement various resolutions of the Inter-American Economic and Social Council, the Secretariat began to plan this report more than a year ago. Much of the necessary information was obtained during the last cycle of the CIAP country reviews, and some of the procedures used in this report were already introduced in selected cases. Use was made also of data and estimates submitted by the CIAP Panel of Experts in its recent report on *La Brecha Externa de la América Latina, 1968- 73.*

The analysis of financing received by Latin America during the period 1961-68, as shown in this report, is limited to that obtained from the United States and from international agencies headquartered in Washington. Included also, with respect to financing from official sources, is an analysis of the credits and grants given by the Agency for International Development, the Export-Import Bank, and the United States Food for Peace Program, as well as, in some cases, those provided by the International Monetary Fund and the United States Treasury. No separate analysis is made of the operations and prospects of the financial institutions operating on the subregional level—the Central American Bank for Economic Integration and, for the future, the Andean Development Corporation; included, however. are the contributions made to the Central American Bank by the United States government and the Inter-American Development Bank.[1]

As to private financing, the only aspect analyzed is that of the background data on capital flows and financial services originating in direct private United States investment in Latin America.

This limitation of analysis is due primarily to two reasons. On the one hand, the incomplete and fragmentary information available on other financial flows has made it impossible to analyze them in sufficient depth and on comparable bases, in view of which it has been considered appropriate to omit them from this study. On the other hand, transactions analyzed herein are, on a net basis, the most important ones in quantitative terms for examining the flow of external resources to Latin America and analyzing the change of structure and the external financing provided during past years, as shown in the accompanying table.

As this table shows, most of the overall capital transactions and financial services of the present decade—excluding changes in international reserves—have been negative. This has been due to the combined effect of a substantial increase in the inflow of official capital, net of amortizations and interest and a high net outflow—except for 1967—on account of direct investment and yield on United States private capital, plus flows of capital and financial services from other sources.

The net total shown under "other sources" for flows of capital and financial services in the table evidently covers up the various different charac

---

[1]The analysis of financing on the subregional level will be incorporated into the second stage of this study.

teristics and trends of diverse types of financial flows, of both official and private foreign capital, and of Latin American capital as well. These items, though not analyzed herein, are also important, and it is the Secretariat's purpose to continue this study in order to include, in the next stage, an analysis of these other transactions.

Latin America: Structure of the Capacity to Import, 1956–67 (in Percentages)

		*Net Capital Flows and Financial Services**				
Year	Exports of Goods and Services	Official Capital[a]	Direct U.S. Investment[b]	Investment from Other Sources[c]	Net Totals (5=2+3+4)	Capacity to Import
	(1)	(2)	(3)	(4)	(5)	(6)
1956	98.7	0.8	0.1	0.4	1.3	100.0
1957	91.9	3.7	4.2	0.2	8.1	100.0
1958	103.9	6.1	2.2	−12.2	−3.9	100.0
1959	100.9	3.8	−2.6	−2.1	−0.9	100.0
1960	102.5	3.1	−3.6	−2.0	−2.5	100.0
1961	101.4	6.0	−3.1	−4.3	−1.4	100.0
1962	105.0	6.3	−5.1	−6.2	−5.0	100.0
1963	102.4	6.9	−5.4	−3.9	−2.4	100.0
1964	102.6	6.1	−4.8	−3.9	−2.6	100.0
1965	99.5	5.9	−3.2	−2.2	0.5	100.0
1966	98.7	6.0	−3.8	0.9	1.3	100.0
1967	93.7	4.8	−4.7	6.2[d]	6.3	100.0

[a]For 1961–67, figures include inflows due to utilization of AID credits and grants and to P.L. 480 (except in 1956–59), IDA, IDB, IBRD, and EXIMBANK, net of amortizations and interest. Figures for 1956–60 include U.S. Development Loan Fund, EXIMBANK, IBRD, and P.L. 480, also net of amortizations and interest.
[b]Net investment of profit transfers.
[c]All inflows of capital, both public and private, long- and short-term, not included in (3) and (4), net of amortizations, including errors and omissions.
[d]Includes substantial repatriation of capital for countries that made progress in their stabilization policies, particularly Argentina.
*Does not include flows of monetary reserves.

Source: OAS, *Problems and Perspectives of Economic and Social Development* (CIES/1380), chap. II.

Due also to some deficiencies in existing information and to delays in processing data, it has not been possible to present in this report an analysis of the rate of disbursement of official credits granted by external agencies cooperating with the Alliance for Progress. This work, which is already under way, will be reported in a separate study.

The findings so far obtained through this study have been arranged in six chapters as follows.

Chapter I discusses the main characteristics of the development of official external financing in the period 1961–68, the various sources of financing, the recipient countries, and the sectors for which the financing was intended.

In chapter II an attempt is made to calculate the aid component of that official external financing, from the standpoint of both the cost to the United States and the benefit to Latin America.

Chapter III briefly examines the evolution of foreign private investment in the recent past, especially with respect to the balance of payments.

In chapter IV alternative projections are made of the gaps in the real and financial resources of Latin America for the period 1970–85, together with an indication of some of the requirements that would have to be met if the targets indicated in the initial paragraphs of this introduction are to be reached.

The problems arising from the use by the United States of tied loan procedures and of the principle of additionality are analyzed in detail in chapters V and VI. The former also includes an examination of the relations between external financing and national priorities in development policy, with special attention to the case of program loans.

The summary and conclusions in chapter VII bring together the recommendations stemming from the analysis made in the previous chapters and arrange them in the framework of what is intended to be a coherent scheme that squares the attainment of external resources in the years ahead with the main features of a Latin American development strategy based on the fundamental principles of the Charter of Punta del Este.

Furthermore, it should be emphasized that it is advisable to consider the analysis and suggestions made herein together with those which, in other fields of action, are presented in the general report of the Secretariat to the IA-ECOSOC on the problems and perspectives of Latin America's development process[2] and in other studies also prepared for this occasion, in fulfillment of previous resolutions of the IA-ECOSOC.[3] Thus, for example, the strategy of external financing set forth in the general report of the Secretariat emphasized the need to intensify domestic development efforts—particularly those directed at promoting exports—and to generate and utilize properly domestic savings, in order to overcome gradually the basic factors that limit the chances for economic growth. The report also pointed out the urgent need for the industrialized nations to adopt trade policies designed to promote the increase of new Latin American exports.

---

[2] *Problems and Perspectives of Economic and Social Development* (CIES/1380).

[3] See also the following documents: *Self Help, Performance Criteria and Aid Allocation* (CIAP/297); and F. Pazos, *Increasing Latin America's Share in the United States Market* (CIES/1376).

Finally, in presenting this report to the consideration of the Inter-American Economic and Social Council, the Secretariat wishes to express its gratitude to the governments and financial institutions who provided the necessary information for preparing it.

EXTERNAL FINANCING FOR LATIN AMERICAN DEVELOPMENT

CHAPTER I

Main Characteristics of the External Financing Received in the Period 1961-68

This chapter examines the general characteristics of the flow of official capital to those Latin American countries that have been members of the OAS from the beginning of the Alliance for Progress program. First, the amounts authorized are analyzed by agency, sectoral composition, and distribution by country; next an analysis is made of the amounts disbursed, the size of the amortizations and official external debt service, and the consequent net flow of capital in the period; and, finally, the conditions governing official external financing are analyzed.

AUTHORIZED EXTERNAL FINANCING

Amounts and Sources

The total amount of authorized funds, including project and program loans, compensatory credits and grants from the United States government and international agencies, amounted to $16,556 billion in the period 1961-68 (see table I-1).

Credits and grants from the United States accounted for 42.9 percent of that sum, or $7,114 billion of which 14.8 percent consisted of grants; 16.2 percent was financed under P.L. 480; 43 percent were loans from AID; and the remaining 26.1 percent represented loans from EXIMBANK, which are expressly intended to promote United States exports and are repayable in dollars and at almost commercial interest rates.

Loans authorized by the World Bank and IDB accounted for 32.6 percent of the total financing, or $5,409 billion.

For IBRD operations and the ordinary operations of the IDB, interest rates are higher and periods of grace and amortizations shorter than for AID operations. The profitability of the projects and the debt capacity of the borrower are taken more into account because the funds come from contributions of member countries and the sale of bonds on the capital markets. However, loans made by the Special Operations Fund and the Social Progress Trust Fund of the IDB have been awarded on more flexible repayment terms and the administrative procedures have been less exacting than usual, so that,

Table I-1. Latin America: Authorized External Financing, 1961–68 (in Millions of $)

Source	1961	1962	1963	1964	1965	1966	1967	1968	1961–68 Absolute	1961–68 Relative
Credits and Grants	1,171.6	1,506.0	1,338.1	1,697.8	1,507.3	1,644.3	1,711.4	1,947.2	12,523.7	75.6
U.S. Government	605.1	827.0	769.9	1,261.7	750.9	906.4	1,051.6	941.7	7,114.3	42.9
AID, total	371.8	440.6	508.2	817.2	478.8	618.8	464.4	403.5	4,103.3	24.8
AID, donations[a]	84.0	170.3	181.6	212.2	142.7	108.5	71.7	80.0c	1,051.0	6.3
AID, development	205.3	134.1	244.1	292.5	183.6	220.0	177.4	115.6	1,572.9	9.5
AID, programs	82.5	141.7	82.5	312.5	152.5	290.0	215.3	207.9	1,484.9	9.0
EXIMBANK	139.4	183.9	86.4	239.1	160.8	150.7	470.5	428.2	1,859.0	11.2
P.L. 480, Titles I and IV	71.8	145.2	105.8	126.6	24.3	94.2	70.7	60.0c	698.6	4.2
P.L. 480, Titles II and III	22.1	57.3	69.5	78.8	87.0	42.7	46.0	50.0c	453.4	2.7
World Bank	276.5	348.8	307.2	135.4	384.0	342.1	166.5	578.5	2,539.0	15.3
IBRD	206.8	328.0	303.6	103.3	371.1	322.6	156.8	551.4	2,343.6	14.1
IFC	10.7	9.4	–	9.1	9.4	12.0	7.7	18.0	76.3	0.5
IDA	59.0	11.4	3.6	23.0	3.5	7.5	2.0	9.1	119.1	0.7
Inter-American Development Bank	290.0	330.2	261.0	300.7	372.4	395.8	493.3	427.0	2,870.4	17.3
Ordinary Capital	127.1	83.5	179.2	167.5	120.4	100.6	167.9	189.7	1,135.9	6.9
Special Operations Fund	47.3	41.8	34.7	47.3	196.6	291.3	313.0	210.1	1,182.1	7.1
Social Progress Trust Fund	115.6	204.9	47.1	85.9	51.2				504.7	3.0
Others					4.2	3.9	12.4	27.2	47.7	0.3

Compensatory Credits									
U.S. Treasury	*1,254.5*	*348.9*	*352.6*	*312.1*	*476.1*	*467.9*	*391.4*	*428.8*	*4,032.3*	*24.4*
IMF	147.0	125.0	60.0	96.3	69.8	12.5	75.0	4.8	590.4	3.6
EXIMBANK[b]	456.2	221.3	166.2	142.7	258.0	331.5	316.4	424.0	22,316.3	14.0
	651.3	2.6	126.4	73.1	148.3	123.9	—	—	1,125.6	6.8
TOTAL	*2,426.1*	*1,854.9*	*1,690.7*	*2,009.9*	*1,983.4*	*2,112.2*	*2,102.8*	*2,376.0*	*16,556.0*	*100.0*

[a]Obtained by difference. Grants by fiscal year are: (1961) 109.6; (1962) 126.5; (1963) 164.3; (1965) 149.2; (1966) 165.2; and (1967) 111.3.

[b]EXIMBANK compensatory credits include debt refinancing as follows:
1961: US$298.4 million (Brazil); US$92.1 million of one credit and US$206.3 million of several credits, merged into one in that year.
1962: US$2.6 million (Costa Rica)
1963: US$91.3 million (Argentina: US$72.0; Brazil: US$19.3)
1964: US$73.1 million (Brazil)
1965: US$58.3 million (Argentina: US$15.4; Costa Rica: US$2.5; Chile: US$40.4)
1966: US$33.9 million (Bolivia)

[c]Estimate by the secretariat.

Sources: IDB: *Statement of Loans Approved,* December 1961–68; IBRD: *Statement of Loans,* December 1961–68; EXIMBANK: *Statement of Authorized Loans and Credits,* December 1961–68; AID: *Statement of Agreements and Loans,* December 1962–68; IDA: *Statement of Development of Credits,* December 1961–68; IMF: *International Financial Statistics,* February 1962–69; U.S. Treasury: *Treasury Bulletin,* April 1962–68; P.L. 480; information provided by AID. Numbers in italics are totals.

as a whole, the operations of that institution are usually much more favorable. The same might apply to the operations of the IBRD and its affiliate, the IFC, but the latter institution has made very few loans to Latin America and its share in the total is therefore very small.

Finally, in the period 1961–68, compensatory financing, which completes the general picture, represented 24.4 percent of the total loans approved for the region and amounted to $4,032 billion. Of that amount 14.6 percent was loaned by the U.S. Treasury; 57.4 percent by the IMF; and the remaining 27.9 percent by EXIMBANK.

Most of the credits (66.6 percent) authorized in the Alliance for Progress period have been earmarked for projects. Authorized program loans represented 9 percent, and the remaining 24.4 percent consisted of compensatory credits. Of the external financing agencies only AID has made program loans, while compensatory credits were awarded by EXIMBANK and the IMF.[1]

The apparent preference for project financing is due to several factors, including: (1) the possibility of earmarking loans for activities that have already been thoroughly studied and whose economic and social effect is measurable and identifiable; (2) the greater ease of control and supervision of the various financial aspects and of project operations; (3) greater control by the lender over the technology to be used and in certain cases over the economic side-effects, such as designation of the country in which the funds loaned or pledged to the project will be spent; and (4) the psychological and political benefit of carrying out a project, especially if its impact is immediately visible to the population of the recipient country.

A year-by-year analysis of the financing authorized (table I-1) shows that in the Alliance period total authorizations declined between 1961 and 1963, especially in 1962 in the wake of a sharp reduction in EXIMBANK loan authorizations which in 1961 had reached a high level, owing in part to operations for the refinancing of the external debt; thereafter a gradual climb took place up to 1968, even though the amount of credit authorized in 1961 was not exceeded in any one year. If compensatory credit authorizations are excluded, it is to be noted that loan authorizations and donations increased substantially relative to 1961, although they fluctuated sharply throughout the period.

The share of institutions in authorized development loans—excluding compensatory financing, grants, and operations under P.L. 480—also considered on a year-to-year basis, has tended to vary very little over the period. Table I-2 shows that, for the entire period, the resources of IDB, excluding its

---

[1] No reliable information is available about bilateral credit authorizations from countries other than the United States.

Table I-2. Latin America: Loans Authorized by International Institutions, 1961–68

Institution	1961	1962	1963	1964	1965	1966	1967	1968	1961–68
				(In Millions of $)					
IDB	290.0	330.2	261.0	300.7	372.4	395.8	493.3	427.0	2,870.4
Ordinary Capital	127.1	83.5	179.2	167.5	120.4	100.6	167.9	189.7	1,135.9
Special Fund	47.3	41.8	34.7	47.3	196.6	291.3	313.0	210.1	1,182.1
Trust Fund	115.6	204.9	47.1	85.9	51.2	–	–	–	504.7
Others	–	–	–	–	4.2	3.9	12.4	27.2	47.7
AID	287.8	275.8	326.6	605.0	336.1	510.3	392.7	323.5	3,057.8
IBRD	206.8	328.0	303.6	103.6	371.1	322.6	156.8	551.4	2,343.6
IDA	59.0	11.4	3.6	23.0	3.5	7.5	2.0	9.1	119.1
EXIMBANK[a]	139.4	183.9	86.4	239.1	160.8	150.7	470.5	428.2	1,859.0
Total	983.0	1,129.3	981.2	1,271.4	1,243.9	1,386.9	1,515.3	1,739.2	10,249.9
				(In Percentages)					
IDB	29.5	29.2	26.6	23.7	29.9	28.5	32.6	24.6	28.0
Ordinary Capital	12.9	7.4	18.3	13.2	9.7	7.3	11.1	10.9	11.1
Special Fund	4.8	3.7	3.5	3.7	15.8	21.0	20.7	12.1	11.5
Trust Fund	11.8	18.1	4.8	6.8	4.1	–	–	–	4.9
Others	–	–	–	–	0.3	0.3	0.8	1.6	0.5
AID	29.3	24.4	33.3	47.6	27.0	36.8	25.9	18.6	29.8
IBRD	21.0	29.0	30.9	8.1	29.8	23.3	10.3	31.7	22.9
IDA	6.0	1.0	0.4	1.8	0.3	0.5	0.1	0.5	1.2
EXIMBANK	14.2	16.3	8.8	18.8	12.9	10.9	31.0	24.6	18.1
Total	100.0	100.0	100.0	100.0	100.0	100.0	100.0	100.0	100.0

[a]Does not include compensatory credits.

Source: Table I-1.

ordinary capital resources, together with AID, and IDA—i.e., the resources granted under more favorable conditions—accounted for 47.9 percent of the authorized total. IBRD, EXIMBANK, and IDB in its ordinary capital resources—with harder loan conditions—provided the remaining 52.1 percent.

However, there is a general tendency to give increasing importance to the IDB Special Operations Fund, while, on the other hand, a decline is observed in the relative importance of loans both from the IDB Social Progress Trust Fund—which has virtually ceased to operate—and from IDA.

Sectoral Allocation of Authorized Project Loans[2]

The sectoral allocation of the development loans authorized in the period shows that most of them have been made to the economic infrastructure sectors of transportation and electric power. Next in importance are loans to the productive sectors of agriculture and industry, followed by multisectoral funds earmarked primarily for agriculture and industry. And, finally, but to a lesser extent, loans have been made to social sectors such as water supply, sewage disposal, and housing[3] (see table I-3).

The allocation of loans to infrastructure sectors has been as follows: from 1961 to 1965 the allocation of loans to transport as a percentage of the total rose to 26.7 percent of the sectoral credits authorized. In 1966 and 1967, however, that proportion declined considerably since it amounted to about 14 percent in both years. The electric power sector, which was the most privileged sector in the allocation of external credits during the period, maintained its considerable importance with 21.5 percent on the average in the period 1961–67, although showing considerable fluctuations.

As for the main trends of the loans made to economic sectors, there was an upturn in the authorization of loans to the industrial sector, which accounted in 1964 for 18.5 percent but in the years 1965–67 fluctuated from 13 to 16 percent of total loans made. The agricultural sector, which received approximately 15 percent of the credits awarded during the period, received increasing attention during the first three years of the Alliance, as allocations of loans to that sector rose from 9.2 percent to almost 22 percent of the total. However, in 1964, allocations fell sharply to 10.9 percent, only to increase from year to year back to 22 percent in 1967, when the agricultural sector received the highest share of credit authorizations.

Most important among the social sectors are water supply and sewerage, housing, and education. The funds assigned to water supply and sewerage

[2]Excluding compensatory financing, grants, funds under P.L. 480, and IFC funds.
[3]Program loans have represented a considerable part of the loans authorized in the period, but no information is available about the sectoral allocation of these loans.

Table I-3. Sectoral Structure of Development Loans Authorized by International Institutions (in Percentages)[a]

Sector	1961	1962	1963	1964	1965	1966	1967	Total 1961–67
Agriculture	9.2	10.3	21.7	10.9	10.9	16.8	21.6	14.8
Mining	1.8	5.2	2.7	4.4	0.0	1.2	15.8	4.9
Industry	10.6	8.0	13.3	18.5	13.0	11.9	16.3	13.2
Transportation	29.3	9.5	20.2	24.5	26.7	14.9	13.3	19.4
Communications	0.1	0.0	1.5	0.0	3.8	0.2	2.5	1.3
Electric power	9.5	30.9	21.4	22.1	26.9	25.6	14.6	21.5
Multisectoral	16.5	6.2	7.8	5.4	4.7	10.9	4.9	7.8
Water supply and sewerage	9.2	10.6	4.4	4.5	7.4	7.6	4.5	6.8
Housing	11.0	12.6	5.4	5.8	3.8	4.9	1.6	6.1
Education	0.0	1.3	0.8	2.0	1.4	3.7	4.1	2.0
Public health	0.0	0.0	0.1	0.7	0.6	0.6	0.2	0.3
Government	0.0	0.1	0.2	0.0	0.0	0.0	0.2	0.1
Unclassified	2.7	5.4	0.5	1.1	0.9	1.6	0.5	1.7
Sectoral totals	100.0	100.0	100.0	100.0	100.0	100.0	100.0	100.0

[a]Does not include grants, credits of the IFC, or P.L. 480 funds.

Source: Chap. I, app. table A-1.

averaged 6.8 percent during the period but showed no definite trend. The housing sector, which at the beginning of the Alliance was receiving about 11 percent of total loans, has continued to lose importance in the allocation of the external loans and, in 1967, obtained only 1.6 percent of the sectoral loans. Finally, mention must be made of the behavior of loans in relation to the educational sector, because of the crucial importance of that sector for development. Of the total external funds authorized in the period 1961–67, that sector's allocation was only 2 percent. However, there is evidence that its importance is increasing, even though in 1967 the proportion of loans it received was still only 4.1 percent.

Sectoral Priorities of Financing Agencies

Table I-4 shows the sectors which have received the highest proportion of the project loans authorized in the period of the Alliance, as well as the lending institutions and the year-by-year evolution of the loans. This arrangement brings out the priority assigned to the main economic sectors by external financing agencies in the distribution of their loans.[4]

Table I-4 shows that most of the loans authorized for the agricultural and social sectors were awarded by the IDB. Most of the loans awarded to the industrial sector came from EXIMBANK, followed, in order of importance, by the IDB. For economic infrastructure sectors, such as transportation and power, external loans originated primarily with the IBRD, which awarded to transportation 30 percent and to power 63 percent of all loans authorized. Finally, it will be seen that AID authorized more than 50 percent of the multisectoral loans, which have been mainly channeled toward productive sector projects. It is evident that the IDB has also been one of the main lenders for multisectoral projects, contributing about 38 percent of all loans to the latter.

It is difficult to detect any clear-cut trends indicating changes in the order of priorities in the sectoral allocation of loans authorized by international agencies, but an examination of the figures indicates that, in the industrial sector, EXIMBANK funds are increasing as a proportion of the whole. Further, the IDB and EXIMBANK have increased their participation in the transportation sector, and AID has done the same in the electrical power sector, while that of the IBRD has declined. Finally the educational sector, which, as noted above, received only 2.0 percent of the total loans authorized in the period 1961–67, is receiving increasing attention from IDB and AID; according to repeated statements of senior officials of AID, IBRD, and IDB,

[4]Table I-4 also includes the educational sector because of its increasing importance in the allocation of loans.

Table I-4. OAS Member Countries: Development Loan Authorizations of International Institutions by Sectors (in Percentages)

Item	1961	1962	1963	1964	1965	1966	1967	1961–67
Agriculture	100.0	100.0	100.0	100.0	100.0	100.0	100.0	100.0
IDB-I	24.8	13.4	43.0	35.4	0.0	10.0	9.4	18.7
IDB-II	14.2	17.2	0.6	13.7	22.2	33.2	52.0	26.0
IDB-III	15.7	37.0	7.4	13.9	5.9	0.0	0.0	8.1
IDB (Total)	(54.7)	(67.6)	(51.0)	(63.0)	(28.1)	(43.2)	(61.4)	(52.8)
AID	26.9	29.4	25.3	35.4	18.1	31.5	10.0	23.0
IBRD	18.1	0.0	20.0	0.0	53.5	19.3	26.2	21.2
EXIMBANK	0.4	2.9	1.9	1.6	0.3	1.8	1.8	1.6
IDA	0.0	0.0	1.8	0.0	0.0	4.1	0.7	1.2
Industry	100.0	100.0	100.0	100.0	100.0	100.0	100.0	100.0
IDB-I	39.4	48.2	34.2	35.9	42.2	24.2	27.7	34.6
IDB-II	11.4	0.0	0.0	5.2	5.5	5.8	9.8	5.9
IDB-III	0.0	0.0	0.0	0.0	0.0	0.0	0.4	0.1
IDB (Total)	(50.8)	(48.2)	(34.2)	(41.1)	(47.7)	30.0	(37.9)	(40.6)
AID	3.2	10.6	16.0	10.9	2.8	18.3	5.7	9.4
IBRD	3.2	0.0	25.1	0.0	0.0	19.2	0.0	6.1
EXIMBANK	43.0	41.1	24.7	48.1	49.5	32.5	56.5	44.0
Transport	100.0	100.0	100.0	100.0	100.0	100.0	100.0	100.0
IDB-I	0.0	4.4	5.5	2.6	10.3	0.0	7.5	4.5
IDB-II	0.9	0.0	0.2	0.2	27.7	16.8	15.3	9.4
IDB-III	0.0	0.0	0.9	1.7	1.0	0.4	0.0	0.7
IDB (Total)	(0.9)	(4.4)	(6.6)	(4.5)	(39.0)	(17.2)	(22.8)	(14.6)
AID	9.7	10.6	30.2	46.7	7.3	19.4	13.7	19.8
IBRD	50.9	52.5	45.8	18.8	25.3	9.8	11.6	30.0
EXIMBANK	16.1	23.7	17.5	26.6	27.2	53.6	51.9	29.6
IDA	22.3	9.0	0.0	3.4	1.2	0.0	0.0	5.6

(Continued)

Table I-4. Continued

Item	1961	1962	1963	1964	1965	1966	1967	1961–67
Electric power	100.0	100.0	100.0	100.0	100.0	100.0	100.0	100.0
IDB-I	19.5	5.8	10.2	10.0	9.5	7.3	29.9	11.6
IDB-II	0.2	0.1	7.5	1.7	1.1	3.2	6.8	2.8
IDB (Total)	(19.7)	(5.9)	(17.7)	(11.7)	(10.6)	(10.5)	(36.7)	(14.4)
AID	0.0	0.0	12.8	26.3	23.4	6.4	23.0	13.5
IBRD	63.4	91.5	62.2	27.9	66.0	79.9	25.1	62.8
EXIMBANK	16.7	2.5	7.3	27.1	0.0	3.2	15.2	8.4
IDA	0.0	0.0	0.0	7.1	0.0	0.0	0.0	1.0
Multisectoral	100.0	100.0	100.0	100.0	100.0	100.0	100.0	100.0
IDB-I	19.5	0.0	12.6	11.7	0.0	16.8	15.6	13.1
IDB-II	11.9	16.1	15.4	16.0	17.2	50.2	25.8	23.3
IDB-III	0.0	0.0	0.0	0.0	2.3	2.7	5.5	1.4
IDB (Total)	(31.4)	(16.1)	(28.0)	(27.7)	(19.5)	(69.7)	(86.9)	(37.8)
AID	68.5	83.9	40.7	43.1	80.7	30.2	46.5	54.9
IBRD	0.0	0.0	31.4	0.0	0.0	0.0	0.0	3.9
EXIMBANK	0.1	0.0	0.0	29.2	0.0	0.0	6.6	3.4
Water and sewerage	100.0	100.0	100.0	100.0	100.0	100.0	100.0	100.0
IDB-I	28.4	9.6	12.9	11.5	3.2	11.9	0.0	11.4
IDB-II	0.0	13.4	8.1	26.6	69.7	56.2	77.2	36.0
IDB-III	48.8	60.8	26.3	61.9	25.5	0.0	0.0	32.8
IDB (Total)	(77.2)	(83.8)	(47.3)	(100.0)	(98.4)	(68.1)	(77.2)	(80.2)
AID	4.2	0.0	52.7	0.0	1.6	6.5	16.5	8.3
IBRD	0.0	0.0	0.0	0.0	0.0	25.4	0.0	4.3
EXIMBANK	18.7	13.4	0.0	0.0	0.0	0.0	6.4	6.8
IDA	0.0	2.9	0.0	0.0	0.0	0.0	0.0	0.6

10

Housing							
	100.0	100.0	100.0	100.0	100.0	100.0	100.0
IDB-II	0.0	0.0	0.0	0.0	22.0	86.9	65.7	15.7
IDB-III	62.8	73.8	33.0	48.7	51.0	0.0	0.0	49.1
IDB (Total)	(62.8)	(73.8)	(33.0)	(48.7)	(73.0)	(86.9)	(65.7)	(64.8)
AID	37.2	26.2	67.0	51.3	27.0	13.1	34.3	35.1
EXIMBANK	0.0	0.0	0.0	0.0	0.0	0.0	0.0	0.0
Education		100.0	100.0	100.0	100.0	100.0	100.0	100.0
IDB-II	—	0.0	0.0	0.0	30.2	72.2	59.8	44.1
IDB-III	—	91.7	56.9	67.9	18.1	0.0	7.5	24.3
IDB (Total)	—	(91.7)	(56.9)	(67.9)	(48.3)	(72.2)	(67.3)	(68.4)
AID	—	8.3	43.1	14.5	24.8	27.8	32.6	26.5
IBRD	—	0.0	0.0	0.0	18.8	0.0	0.0	1.9
EXIMBANK	—	0.0	0.0	17.6	8.1	0.0	0.0	3.1

Note: IDB-I = Ordinary Capital Resources.
IDB-II = Special Operations Fund.
IDB-III = Social Progress Trust Fund.

Source: Chap. I, app. table 2.

11

in the future this sector is to receive a much higher proportion of the total financing provided by those agencies.

Table I-5 shows the sectoral allocation of credits authorized by external financing agencies during the period under review, reflecting the scale of priorities used by the agencies in assigning loans. Thus, it is noted that (1) IDB concentrated on the productive sectors of agriculture and industry and also on the water supply and sewerage sector; (2) AID concentrated on program loans multisectoral credits, agriculture, and transportation; (3) IBRD and IDA concentrated on the economic infrastructure and on the agricultural sector; and (4) EXIMBANK did so on financing for industry, mining, and transport.

Allocation of Financing by Country

Finally, it is of interest to examine the allocation of resources by country, bearing in mind also the characteristics of noncompensatory loans and the sectoral allocation in each case.

Table I-6 shows the total value of loans authorized by country, in absolute and relative terms, and the per capita amount authorized in the period. The countries are arranged roughly according to their per capita product. Thus, the first country is Haiti, with the lowest per capita product, and the last is Venezuela, with the highest per capita product figure. This arrangement gives an additional perspective when analyzing the distribution of loans made by the United States government and international agencies. It will be seen in table I-6 that the seven most highly populated countries were those that received the largest proportion of the credits authorized: Brazil (21.3 percent); Mexico (13.9 percent); Chile (14.4 percent); Colombia (11.3 percent); Argentina (8.9 percent); Venezuela (7.0 percent); and Peru (5.2 percent), which all together account for 82 percent of the authorized loans. The remaining 14 countries (table I-6, col. 3) received 18.0 percent of the loans.

Finally, the authorized amount of loans per capita is shown in col. 4. If we bear in mind the distribution of countries by per capita product, it will be seen that there is no clear relationship between the per capita loans and the level of development, although a relationship does exist with respect to the aid component of that financing, as noted below.

Of the countries that received the highest per capita financing, six are among the nine countries with the highest per capita product. Of these, those receiving the highest per capita loans were Chile ($142.18); Panama ($104); Costa Rica ($93); Nicaragua ($71); and Venezuela ($70).

As noted above, bearing in mind total funds authorized, the main type of financing has been project financing. For Bolivia, Chile, Costa Rica, Ecuador,

Table I-5. Latin America: Structure of Non-Compensatory Loan Authorizations by International Institutions, 1961–67 (in Percentages)

Sector	IDB-I	IDB-II	IDB-III	IDB (Total)	AID	IBRD	EXIMBANK	IDA
Agriculture	21.1	28.6	16.5	23.1	9.0	12.7	1.2	11.9
Mining	4.2	1.2	0.0	2.1	0.6	0.0	20.0	0.0
Industry	34.9	5.8	0.2	15.8	3.3	3.2	29.4	0.0
Transportation	6.7	14.2	1.8	8.6	10.1	23.5	29.0	71.7
Communications	0.3	0.0	0.8	0.3	0.0	3.5	1.4	0.0
Electric power	19.0	4.5	0.0	9.2	7.7	54.5	9.2	13.6
Multisectoral	7.8	13.6	1.5	8.8	11.4	1.2	1.3	0.0
Water and sewerage	5.9	18.2	30.8	16.2	1.5	1.2	2.3	2.7
Housing	0.0	7.2	41.5	11.8	5.7	0.0	0.0	0.0
Education	0.0	6.7	6.8	4.2	1.4	0.2	0.3	0.0
Public health	0.0	0.0	0.0	0.0	0.6	0.0	0.4	0.0
Government	0.0	0.0	0.0	0.0	0.2	0.0	0.0	0.0
Unclassified	0.0	0.0	0.1	0.2	1.8	0.0	5.4	0.0
Program loans	0.0	0.0	0.0	0.0	46.7	0.0	0.0	0.0
Total all sectors	100.0	100.0	100.0	100.0	100.0	100.0	100.0	99.9

Note: IDB-I = Ordinary Capital Resources.
IDB-II = Special Operations Fund.
IDB-III = Social Progress Trust Fund.

Source: Chap. I, app. table 3.

HUNT LIBRARY
CARNEGIE-MELLON UNIVERSITY

Table I-6. Latin America: Per Capita Development Loans Authorized, 1961-67

Country	Amount Authorized		In Percentages (Excluding Large Countries)	Amount per Capita [b]
	In Millions of $	In Percentages		
	(1)	(2)	(3)	(4)
Haiti	10.6	0.1	0.1	2.45
Bolivia	201.4	2.4	2.4	64.48
Paraguay	100.8	1.2	1.2	51.06
Honduras	107.3	1.3	1.3	48.42
Brazil	1,786.3	21.3	—	22.74
Ecuador	175.4	2.1	2.1	35.15
Colombia	943.7	11.3	—	53.93
El Salvador	97.4	1.2	1.2	37.94
Dominican Republic	186.2	2.2	2.2	53.09
Guatemala	90.0	1.1	1.1	20.87
Peru	439.6	5.2	—	38.83
Nicaragua	114.0	1.4	1.4	70.98
Chile	1,209.5	14.4	—	142.18
Costa Rica	128.7	1.5	1.5	92.86
Mexico	1,168.0	13.9	—	28.24
Trinidad and Tobago	61.2	0.7	0.7	64.69
Panama	126.0	1.5	1.5	104.30
Uruguay	106.5	1.3	1.3	39.72
Argentina	750.2	8.9	—	33.77
Venezuela	590.0	7.0	—	69.81
Total	8,392.8 [a]	100.0	18.0 [c]	

[a] Does not include regional credits, grants, or P.L. 480 funds.
[b] Based on average population in the period 1961-67.
[c] Sum of percentages.

Sources: Statements of operations of the agencies and population data published by ECIA.

Guatemala, Honduras, Mexico, Panama, Paraguay, Peru, Trinidad and Tobago, and Venezuela this type of financing accounted for at least 60 percent of the funds authorized for each country in the period 1961-67 (table I-7).

Financing by means of compensatory credits awarded by EXIMBANK, IMF, and the United States Treasury occupies second place in order of magnitude, with 30 percent of the loans authorized for the region in the period 1961-67.[5] These loans represent a substantial part of the financing authorized for two of the largest countries in Latin America, Brazil (38.6 percent) and Argentina (42.6 percent), with both countries receiving a larger proportion than the region as a whole. Compensatory financing represented more than 30 percent of the credits authorized for Bolivia, Costa Rica, El Salvador, Guatemala, Haiti, Nicaragua, Dominican Republic, and Uruguay. It must be pointed out that, for Brazil, Argentina, Bolivia, and Costa Rica, part of the compensatory financing awarded by EXIMBANK included the refinancing of external debt. For the period 1961-67 refinancing represented $390.8 million for Brazil, $87.4 million for Argentina, $33.9 million for Bolivia, and $5 million for Costa Rica.

Finally, program loans received by the countries, including budget assistance credits, have been substantial, representing the following share of the total authorized in each case: Colombia (26 percent); Dominican Republic (20 percent); Brazil (19 percent); Chile (17 percent); Ecuador (13 percent); Argentina (7 percent); Panama (5 percent); and Honduras (2 percent).

The sectoral distribution of development loans[6] does not show, over the years, a clear relationship to their relative level of development. Classification of the funds authorized by productive sectors, economic infrastructure sectors, social sectors, and others (table I-8), shows that for thirteen out of the twenty countries listed the external funds authorized for economic infrastructure projects were greater than those for the productive and social sectors and eight of these countries are among the ten with low per capita product.

Although the figures indicate that generally speaking loan authorizations for the relatively less developed countries reflect a certain preference for economic infrastructure sectors, the funds authorized for large countries such as Mexico, Argentina, Brazil, Peru, Colombia, and Venezuela also show the same preference.

[5] In table I-1 this proportion was 24.4 percent. The difference is due to the fact that the analysis in table I-7 is limited to the period 1961-67, since the necessary information is not available for each country for 1968 and, furthermore, it does not include AID donations, funds under P.L. 480, IFC funds, and regional loans that are included in table I-1 to give a complete picture of authorized financing.

[6] Excluding grants, IFC Credits, and P.L. 480 funds.

Table I-7. Latin America: Country Distribution of Credits Authorized for Latin America by International Agencies, 1961–67

Country	Millions of $				Percentages			
	Project	Program	Compensatory[b]	Total	Project	Program	Compensatory	Total
Argentina	710.2	40.0	557.4	1,307.6	54.3	7.2	42.6	100.0
Bolivia	201.4	–	125.4	326.8	61.6	–	38.4	100.0
Brazil	1,236.3	550.0	1,122.5	2,908.8	42.5	18.9	38.6	100.0
Chile	944.5	265.0	342.5	1,552.0	60.9	17.1	22.1	100.0
Colombia	638.7	305.0	226.4	1,170.1	54.6	26.1	19.3	100.0
Costa Rica	128.7	–	73.3	202.0	63.7	–	36.3	100.0
Dominican Republic	103.5	82.7	236.3	422.5	24.5	19.6	55.9	100.0
Ecuador	150.4	25.0	25.0	200.4	75.0	12.5	12.5	100.0
El Salvador	97.4	–	75.0	172.4	56.5	–	43.5	100.0
Guatemala	90.0	–	57.4	147.4	61.1	–	38.9	100.0
Haiti	10.6	–	43.4	54.0	19.6	–	80.4	100.0
Honduras	105.3	2.0	22.0	129.3	81.4	1.5	17.0	100.0
Mexico	1,168.0	–	460.0	1,628.0	71.7	–	28.3	100.0
Nicaragua	114.0	–	90.0	204.0	55.9	–	44.1	100.0
Panama	118.7	7.3	22.4	148.4	80.0	4.9	15.1	100.0
Paraguay	100.8	–	7.0	107.8	93.5	–	6.5	100.0
Peru	439.6	–	17.5	457.1	96.2	–	3.8	100.0
Trinidad and Tobago	61.2	–	–	61.2	100.0	–	–	100.0
Uruguay	106.5	–	75.0	181.5	58.7	–	41.3	100.0
Venezuela	590.0	–	25.0	615.0	95.9	–	4.1	100.0
Total	7,115.8[a]	1,277.0	3,603.5	11,996.3	59.3	10.6	30.0	100.0

[a]Does not include $114.7 million in regional credits; $971 million in AID donations; $638.6 million under P.L. 480, Titles I and IV; $4.034 billion under P.L. 480, Titles II and III; and $58.3 million from the IFC.
[b]Includes EXIMBANK, U.S. Treasury, and IMF.

Source: Data obtained from statements of operations of each agency.

Table I-8. Latin America: Sectoral Distribution of Development Funds Authorized, 1961–67 (in Percentages)

Country	Productive Sectors	Multisectoral	Subtotal: Productive Sectors[a]	Economic Infrastructure	Social Sectors and Global Credits	Total
Haiti	2.8	32.7	35.5	29.9	34.6	100.0
Bolivia	24.9	15.1	40.0	45.4	14.7	100.0
Paraguay	31.3	3.7	35.0	60.1	4.9	100.0
Honduras	10.4	13.1	23.5	53.9	22.6	100.0
Brazil	27.9	2.4	30.3	55.2	14.5	100.0
Ecuador	18.3	10.2	28.5	37.0	34.7	100.0
Colombia	33.8	1.4	35.2	48.1	16.7	100.0
El Salvador	21.4	2.6	24.0	40.3	35.7	100.0
Dominican Republic	21.4	14.2	35.6	30.2	34.2	100.0
Guatemala	15.3	19.1	34.4	44.8	20.9	100.0
Peru	28.6	7.1	35.7	41.6	22.7	100.0
Nicaragua	40.4	5.9	46.3	28.0	25.9	100.0
Chile	50.5	19.9	70.4	17.5	12.1	100.0
Costa Rica	35.8	18.8	54.6	26.1	19.4	100.0
Mexico	43.8	0.8	44.6	50.0	5.4	100.0
Trinidad and Tobago	8.2	—	8.2	76.3	15.5	100.0
Panama	25.5	7.3	32.8	22.4	44.8	100.0
Uruguay	40.2	7.1	47.3	21.2	31.4	100.0
Argentina	32.5	4.5	37.0	42.0	20.9	100.0
Venezuela	20.8	0.7	21.5	49.6	28.9	100.0
Regional	—	97.2	97.2	—	2.8	100.0

[a]Includes multisectoral, since most of the multisectoral loans are earmarked for the productive sectors.

Source: Chap. I, app. table 4.

EXTERNAL FINANCING RECEIVED

Gross and Net Flows

Table I-9 summarizes the flow of the development loans from the United States government and international development financing institutions in the period 1961–68. Examination of this table shows the total gross flows received by the region and the disbursements by the following institutions: AID (27.6 percent); EXIMBANK (20.3 percent); IBRD (13.9 percent); IMF (12.9 percent); IDB (11.9 percent); P.L. 480 (10.5 percent); United States Treasury (2.1 percent); and IDA (0.9 percent).

If payments abroad for amortizations and interest are considered the picture is substantially changed; the inflow of EXIMBANK loans, because of a relatively short amortization period and high interest rates and commissions, becomes a net outflow of funds from the region. The relatively hard terms of the IBRD loans also helped to reduce the contribution of that institution, since although its disbursements represented 13.9 percent of the gross inflow, the net flow less interest on the loans of that agency only represented 10.4 percent of the total in the period 1961–68. In the case of IDB, AID, P.L. 480, and IDA the opposite trend is visible, as their contributions increased to 18.1, 51.6, 20.4, and 1.7 percent, respectively.

The third part of table I-9 shows the flows of amortization and interests and the net flows as percentages of the total disbursed by each of the financing agencies. The net flow less interest on loans (col. 5) represented only 49.5 percent of the total gross disbursements for the region in the period 1961–68. With respect to individual agencies the highest proportions were those of IDA[7] and P.L. 480. In the case of IDA this was due to long grace periods, as a result of which no amortizations are yet being received; in the case of P.L. 480, it was due to the high component represented by grants. The respective ratios for the other agencies were 92.7 percent for AID, 75.8 percent for IDB, 37.1 percent for IBRD, and −14.1 percent for EXIM-BANK.[8] In the case of the EXIMBANK the net flow reflects an outflow of funds from the region because of amortization and interest payments substantially greater than the funds disbursed by the institution in that period. Table I-10 shows the evolution of gross disbursements made by the agencies in the period 1961–68.

---

[7]However, that very small volume of the IDA loans to Latin America, as shown in table I-9, should be kept in mind.

[8]The IMF and the U.S. Treasury are not mentioned in connection with this analysis, since no complete information is available on interest payments to those agencies.

Table I-9. Latin America: Loan Contracts and Grants by International Institutions, 1961–68 (in Millions of $ and Percentages)

Institution	Gross Disbursements	Amortizations	Net Flow	Interest	Net Flow Less Interest
IDB	1,331.0	168.1	1,162.9	154.1	1,008.8
AID[a]	3,096.6	95.8	3,000.8	130.6	2,870.2
P.L. 480[b]	1,174.1	28.2	1,145.9	10.7	1,135.2
IBRD	1,562.3	492.1	1,070.2	489.9[e]	580.3
IDA	97.5	–	97.5	2.4	95.1
EXIMBANK[c]	2,285.0	1,889.2	395.8	717.0	–321.2
U.S. Treasury[d]	235.2	256.6	–21.4	–	–21.4
IMF[d]	1,444.7	1,229.1	215.6	–	215.6
Total	11,226.4	4,159.1	7,110.1	1,504.7	5,562.6
	(As a Percentage of the Total)				
IDB	11.9	4.0	16.4	10.2	18.1
AID	27.6	2.3	42.2	8.7	51.6
P.L. 480	10.5	0.7	16.1	0.7	20.4
IBRD	13.9	11.8	15.1	32.6	10.4
IDA	0.9	–	1.4	0.2	1.7
EXIMBANK	20.3	45.4	5.6	47.7	–5.8
U.S. Treasury	2.1	6.2	–0.3	–	–0.4
IMF	12.9	29.6	3.0	–	3.9
Total	100.0	100.0	100.0	100.0	100.0
	(As a Percentage of Gross Disbursements)				
IDB	100.0	12.6	87.4	11.6	75.8
AID	100.0	3.1	96.9	4.2	92.7
P.L. 480	100.0	2.4	97.6	0.9	96.7
IBRD	100.0	31.5	68.5	31.4	37.1
IDA	100.0	–	100.0	2.5	97.5
EXIMBANK	100.0	82.7	17.3	31.4	–14.1
U.S. Treasury	100.0	109.1	–9.1	–	–9.1
IMF	100.0	85.1	14.9	–	14.9
Total	100.0	37.0	63.3	13.4	49.5

[a]Includes grants.

[b]Disbursements under Title I of P.L. 480 have been considered as grants. In order to figure amortizations and interests on P.L. 480 loans under Title IV, the information used was obtained from the loan contracts, since no data were available on the real flow of amortizations and interest. Finally, the assumption has been made that disbursements under Titles II and III of P.L. 480 correspond to the yearly authorized sums, since not enough information is available regarding real disbursements.

[c]Includes compensatory credits.

[d]No information is available on the flow of funds to cover commissions and interest.

[e]Estimate of the Special Studies Unit based on data corresponding to fiscal years.

Source: Data obtained from operating statements of the agencies.

Table I-10. Latin America: Gross Disbursements from Official Sources, 1961–68 (in Millions of $)

Source	1961	1962	1963	1964	1965	1966	1967	1968
Total Development Credits and Grants	*653.7*	*787.9*	*1,007.8*	*1,106.7*	*1,139.2*	*1,305.2*	*1,259.0*	*1,450.4*
U.S. Government	*545.7*	*571.9*	*594.2*	*658.6*	*764.3*	*833.3*	*762.4*	*914.2*
AID total	201.5	277.9	347.3	360.5	455.7	578.5	426.6	466.2
AID grants	95.9	86.8	124.1	118.3	158.3	126.5	77.6	85.0[e]
AID projects	{ 105.6[a]	{ 191.1[a]	105.2	95.3	128.8	184.5	179.0	180.1
AID programs			118.0	146.9	168.6	267.5	170.0	201.1
EXIMBANK projects	193.6	163.9	98.3	74.1	146.1	162.5	199.8	318.0
P.L. 480, Tit. I, IV	128.5	72.8	79.1	145.2	75.5	49.6	90.0[e]	80.0[e]
P.L. 480, Tit. I, III[b]	22.1	57.3	69.5	78.8	87.0	42.7	46.0	50.0[e]
World Bank	*101.2*	*157.3*	*272.3*	*250.5*	*192.9*	*258.5*	*255.7*	*243.7*
IBRD	96.1	138.5	261.3	233.1	162.8	228.2	223.2	218.8
IDA	—	6.4	7.8	9.5	15.9	20.9	23.0	14.0
IFC	5.1	12.4	3.2	7.9	14.2	9.4	9.5	10.9
IDB	*6.8*	*58.7*	*141.3*	*197.6*	*182.0*	*213.4*	*240.9*	*292.5*
Ordinary Capital Resources	3.3	28.0	60.0	106.3	83.1	98.4	111.6	114.6
Special Fund	2.6	8.6	15.5	24.5	28.5	44.8	69.3	120.4
	0.0	33.1	65.8	66.8	70.4	70.2	60.0	57.5

U.S. Treasury	65.0	34.5	90.5	18.3	13.4	13.5		–
IMF	347.4	95.7	231.5	62.5	147.2	174.0	122.7	270.5
EXIMBANK[d]	476.5	146.4	133.5	58.6	60.0	37.4	37.2	–
Total	1,542.6	1,064.5	1,463.3	1,246.1	1,359.8	1,530.1	1,418.9	1,720.9

[a]Figures for 1961 and 1962 include disbursements for projects and programs.
[b]Due to lack of complete information on actual disbursements, the amounts used have been those authorized for Titles II and III of P.L. 480.
[c]Includes other funds.
[d]EXIMBANK compensatory financing includes refinancing of debts, as follows:
  1961: $221 million
  1962: $38.6 million
  1963: $85.0 million
  1964: $58.5 million
  1965: $59.9 million
  1966: $37.3 million
  1967: $37.3 million
[e]Estimate of the Special Studies Unit of the OAS.

Source: Based on data from the operating statements of the agencies.

21

Considering total disbursements, including development credits and grants and compensatory financing, it may be noted that during the Alliance period gross disbursements fluctuated appreciably from year to year, from a minimum of $1,064.5 billion in 1962 to a high of $1,720.9 billion in 1968. Excluding compensatory credit disbursements, it may be further noted that loans and grants for development maintained a rising trend during the period, increasing from $653.7 million in 1961 to $1,450.4 billion in 1968.

CONDITIONS GOVERNING EXTERNAL FINANCING

The conditions for external financing, including the determination of the aid component for the various countries, is the subject of more detailed analysis in a later section. However, at this point it is worth examining some general characteristics of the conditions for loans authorized in the period 1961–67.

Table I-11 shows the weighted terms of the loans authorized by international institutions. The disparity in terms for loans made by various agencies is obvious. The grace periods granted vary from one year, in the case of the Social Progress Trust Fund of the IDB, up to ten years, in the case of IDA. The weighted average for the region is five years. The amortization periods also vary from agency to agency, the shortest being ten years—the average for EXIMBANK—up to forty years in the case of IDA. For Latin America the weighted average term in that period was eighteen years. Interest rates, plus commissions, also vary considerably. In the case of IDA it amounts to 0.75 percent for commission, since its loans are free of interest. In the case of AID the weighted average is 2.09 percent, and for the IDB Special Operations Fund it is 3.5 percent, while on the operations of EXIMBANK, IBRD, and the Ordinary Capital Resources of IDB the rates were 5.59, 5.70, and 6.15 percent, respectively.

The year-by-year evolution in the conditions of the loans authorized by IDB, AID, and IBRD in the period 1961–67, which is shown in table I-12, discloses that generally speaking there has been a hardening in the conditions for loans authorized by all agencies—with the exception of the IDA—in respect of the rates of interest charged, mainly because of the unfavorable evolution of international capital markets in recent years. It must be emphasized that—because all the necessary information relating to 1968 has not yet been processed—table I-12 only covers the period up to 1967 and does not show the even greater increase in interest rates prevailing since 1968.

Table I-13 shows the weighted terms for the period 1961–67 for each country, again classifying countries according to their per capita product. It is to be noted that, generally speaking, financing terms make allowance for the

Table I-11. Latin America: Weighted Average Terms of Loans Authorized by International Institutions, 1961–67

Institution	No. of Loans	Total Amount Authorized	Average Amount Authorized	Grace Period	Amortization Period	Interest and Commission
	(1)	(2)	(3)	(4)	(5)	(6)
IDB	460	2,443.3	5.31	3	17	4.33
IDB-I	162	946.2	5.84	3	12	6.15
IDB-II	170	971.9	5.72	4	18	3.56
IDB-III	128	525.2	4.10	1	23	2.45
AID	279	2,734.0	9.80	9	27	2.09
IBRD	80	1,792.3	22.40	4	17	5.70
EXIMBANK	678	2,796.8	4.13	3	10	5.59
IDA	15	109.9	7.33	10	40	.75
TOTAL	1,512	9,876.4	6.53	5	18	4.23

Note: IDB-I   = Ordinary Capital Resources.
        IDB-II = Special Operations Fund.
        IDB-III = Social Program Trust Fund.

Source: Information from the operating statements of agencies, as of Dec. 31, 1967.

Table I-12. Latin America: Weighted Average of Conditions of External Loans Authorized by International Institutions, 1961–67 (Years and Percentages)

Condition of Loan	1961	1962	1963	1964	1965	1966	1967
IDB-Total							
Grace period	2	2	3	3	3	3	4
Amortization period	15	20	16	15	16	18	17
Average interest	4.24	3.52	4.94	4.68	4.28	4.15	4.56
IDB-Ordinary Capital							
Grace period	3	3	3	3	3	3	4
Amortization period	11	12	13	12	12	12	12
Average interest	5.75	5.90	5.81	6.04	6.26	6.47	6.81
IDB-Special Fund							
Grace period	3	4	5	4	4	4	3
Amortization period	12	16	16	16	17	19	20
Average interest	4.40	4.00	4.00	3.91	3.57	3.39	3.43
IDB-Trust Fund[a]							
Grace period	1	1	1	1	1	8	8
Amortization period	21	24	26	22	23	33	32
Average interest	2.52	2.46	2.33	2.47	2.49	1.24	2.40
AID-Grace period	6	8	9	9	10	9	9
Amortization period	21	21	27	29	28	29	29
Average interest	1.89	1.43	1.11	2.10	2.56	2.52	2.50
IBRD-Grace period	4	2	4	4	4	5	5
Amortization period	14	19	16	22	16	17	16
Average interest	5.75	5.73	5.50	5.50	5.50	6.00	6.00
IDA-Grace period	10	10	10	10	10	10	10
Amortization period	40	40	40	40	40	40	40
Average interest	0.75	0.75	0.75	0.75	0.75	0.75	0.75
EXIMBANK-Grace period	3	4	2	3	2	1	3
Amortization period	14	7	7	9	7	8	10
Average interest	5.46	5.78	5.72	5.52	5.51	5.11	6.00

[a]Data for 1961–65 refer to loans from the Trust Fund; for 1966–67, data refer to loans from the British and Canadian funds.

Source: Data based on operating statements of the agencies.

Table I-13. Latin America: Weighted Average of Terms for External Loans, 1961–67

Country	Grace Period (Years)	Amortization Period (Years)	Average Interest (Percentage)
Haiti	5	17	3.13
Bolivia	6	23	2.51
Paraguay	5	23	3.24
Honduras	6	23	3.39
Brazil	6	20	4.19
Ecuador	5	21	3.31
Colombia	5	20	4.00
El Salvador	5	21	3.36
Dominican Republic	6	21	3.07
Guatemala	4	20	4.15
Peru	4	17	4.37
Nicaragua	5	21	3.44
Chile	6	19	3.94
Costa Rica	5	20	3.88
Mexico	3	14	5.16
Trinidad and Tobago	4	14	5.80
Panama	5	22	3.42
Uruguay	4	15	4.56
Argentina	4	14	4.76
Venezuela	3	14	4.92

Source: Based on data from operating statements of the agencies.

relative level of development of the countries, since conditions are usually more favorable in the case of the less developed countries of the region. The information contained in table I-13 is reproduced in table I-14, rearranged in a more graphic form.

Table I-14. Average Terms and Conditions of External Financing, 1961–67

Country	Grace Period				Amortization Period				Average Interest					
	3	4	5	6	14-16	17-19	20-22	23 or More	2.5-2.9	3.0-3.4	3.5-3.9	4.0-4.4	4.5-4.9	5.0 or More
Haiti			x			x				x				
Bolivia				x				x	x					
Paraguay			x					x		x				
Honduras				x				x		x				
Brazil				x			x					x		
Ecuador			x				x			x				
Colombia			x				x					x		
El Salvador			x				x			x				
Dominican Republic				x			x			x				
Guatemala		x					x					x		
Peru		x				x						x		
Nicaragua			x				x			x				
Chile				x		x					x			
Costa Rica			x				x				x			
Mexico	x				x									x
Trinidad and Tobago		x			x									x
Panama			x				x			x				
Uruguay		x			x								x	
Argentina		x			x								x	
Venezuela	x				x								x	

Source: Table I-13.

Statistical Appendix to Chapter I

Appendix Table I-A-1. Latin America: Authorization of Loans from International Institutions by Sectors (in Thousands of $)[a]

Sector	1961	1962	1963	1964	1965	1966	1967	Total 1961–67
Agriculture	82,899	102,075	195,070	104,260	118,980	184,690	280,190	1,068,164
Mining	16,235	51,625	24,110	42,600	92	12,900	205,631	353,193
Industry	95,139	78,877	119,446	177,486	141,715	130,095	212,309	955,067
Transportation	263,961	93,350	181,925	235,110	291,757	163,540	172,445	1,402,088
Communications	1,298	0	13,500	0	41,000	2,514	32,963	91,275
Electric power	85,576	304,808	192,515	211,550	293,900	281,009	189,257	1,558,615
Multisectoral	148,631	60,763	70,054	51,300	51,342	120,000	63,900	565,990
Water supply and sewerage	82,536	104,452	39,460	43,623	80,474	83,675	58,812	493,032
Housing	99,368	124,050	48,500	55,950	41,035	54,075	20,970	443,948
Education	0	13,265	7,200	19,300	14,890	40,300	53,270	148,225
Public health	168	0	500	6,500	6,200	6,925	2,000	22,293
Government	70	1,168	1,600	0	0	0	2,200	5,038
Unclassified	24,576	53,039	4,813	10,850	10,000	17,150	5,981	126,409
Program credits	82,500	141,567	82,500	312,500	152,500	290,000	215,300	1,276,957
Total by Sector	982,957	1,129,129	981,193	1,271,029	1,243,885	1,386,873	1,515,228	8,510,294

[a]Includes loans from AID, IDB, IBRD, IDA, and EXIMBANK.

Source: Data obtained from operating statements of each agency.

Appendix Table I-A-2. Member Countries of the OAS: Authorization for Sectoral and Program Loans by International Institutions (in Millions of $)

Sector and Institution	1961	1962	1963	1964	1965	1966	1967	1961-67
Agriculture	*82.9*	*102.1*	*195.1*	*104.3*	*119.0*	*184.7*	*280.2*	*1,068.3*
IDB-I	20.6	13.7	83.9	36.9	–	18.5	26.3	199.9
IDB-II	11.8	17.6	1.1	14.3	26.4	61.4	145.6	278.2
IDB-III	13.0	37.8	14.4	14.5	7.0	–	–	86.7
AID	22.3	30.0	49.3	36.9	21.5	58.2	28.0	246.2
IBRD	15.0	–	39.1	–	63.7	35.7	73.3	226.8
EXIMBANK	0.3	3.0	3.8	1.7	0.4	3.4	5.0	17.6
IDA	–	–	3.6	–	–	7.5	2.0	13.1
Mining	*16.2*	*51.6*	*24.1*	*42.6*	*0.1*	*12.9*	*205.6*	*353.1*
IDB-I	–	–	11.0	28.8	–	–	–	39.8
IDB-II	4.5	–	4.9	–	–	2.5	–	11.9
AID	3.5	–	7.0	–	–	5.4	–	15.9
IBRD	–	–	–	–	–	–	–	–
EXIMBANK	8.2	51.6	1.3	13.8	0.1	5.0	205.6	285.6
Industry	*95.1*	*78.9*	*119.4*	*177.5*	*141.7*	*130.1*	*212.3*	*955.0*
IDB-I	37.5	38.0	40.8	63.7	59.8	31.5	58.8	330.1
IDB-II	10.8	–	–	9.2	7.8	7.5	20.7	56.0
IDB-III	–	–	–	–	–	–	0.9	0.9
AID	3.0	8.4	19.1	19.3	3.9	23.8	12.0	89.5
IBRD	3.0	–	30.0	–	–	25.0	–	58.0
EXIMBANK	40.9	32.4	29.5	85.3	70.2	42.3	120.0	420.6
Transportation	*264.0*	*93.4*	*181.9*	*235.1*	*291.8*	*163.5*	*172.4*	*1,402.1*
IDB-I	–	4.1	10.0	6.0	30.0	–	12.9	63.0
IDB-II	2.3	–	0.3	0.5	80.8	27.5	26.4	137.8
IDB-III	–	–	1.6	4.0	3.0	0.7	–	9.3
AID	25.7	9.9	54.9	109.7	21.4	31.7	23.7	277.0
IBRD	134.5	49.0	83.3	44.3	73.8	16.0	20.0	420.9
EXIMBANK	42.5	22.1	31.9	62.6	79.4	87.6	89.5	415.6
IDA	59.0	8.4	–	8.0	3.5	–	–	78.9

(Continued)

29

Appendix Table I-A-2. Continued

Sector and Institution	1961	1962	1963	1964	1965	1966	1967	1961-67
Communications								
IDB-I	1.3	—	13.5	—	41.0	2.5	33.0	91.3
IDB-II	—	—	—	—	—	—	3.3	3.3
IDB-III	—	—	—	—	—	—	4.0	4.0
AID	1.0	—	—	—	—	—	—	1.0
IBRD	—	—	9.5	—	37.0	—	16.0	62.5
EXIMBANK	3.0	—	4.0	—	4.0	2.5	9.7	20.5
Electric power								
IDB-I	85.6	304.8	192.5	211.6	293.9	281.0	189.3	1,558.7
IDB-II	16.7	17.7	19.6	21.2	28.0	20.4	56.7	180.3
IDB-III	0.2	0.4	14.5	3.5	3.3	9.1	12.8	43.8
AID	—	—	24.6	55.7	68.7	18.1	43.5	210.6
IBRD	54.3	279.0	119.8	59.0	193.9	224.6	47.5	978.1
EXIMBANK	14.3	7.7	14.1	57.3	—	8.9	28.8	131.1
IDA	—	—	—	15.0	—	—	—	15.0
Multisectoral								
IDB-I	144.6	60.8	70.1	51.3	51.3	120.0	63.9	566.0
IDB-II	29.0	—	8.8	6.0	—	20.2	10.0	74.0
IDB-III	17.7	9.8	10.8	8.2	8.8	60.3	16.5	132.1
	—	—	—	—	1.2	3.2	3.5	7.9
AID	101.8	51.0	28.5	22.1	41.4	36.3	29.7	310.8
IBRD	—	—	22.0	—	—	—	—	22.0
EXIMBANK	0.1	—	—	15.0	—	—	4.2	19.3
Water supply & sewerage								
IDB-I	82.5	104.5	39.5	43.6	80.5	83.7	58.8	493.1
IDB-II	23.4	10.0	5.1	5.0	2.6	10.0	—	56.1
IDB-III	—	14.0	3.2	11.6	56.1	47.0	45.4	177.3
AID	40.3	63.5	10.4	27.0	20.5	—	—	161.7
IBRD	3.5	—	20.8	—	1.3	5.4	9.7	40.7
	—	—	—	—	—	21.3	—	21.3
EXIMBANK	15.4	14.0	—	—	—	—	3.8	33.2
IDA	—	3.0	—	—	—	—	—	3.0

Housing	99.4	124.1	48.5	56.0	41.0	54.1	21.0	444.1
IDB-II	–	–	–	–	9.0	47.0	13.8	69.8
IDB-III	62.4	91.6	16.0	27.3	20.9	–	–	218.2
AID	37.0	32.5	32.5	28.7	11.1	7.1	7.2	156.1
EXIMBANK	–	–	–	–	–	–	–	–
Education	–	13.2	7.2	19.3	14.9	40.3	53.3	148.2
IDB-II	–	–	–	–	4.5	29.1	31.9	65.5
IDB-III	–	12.1	4.1	13.1	2.7	11.2	4.0	36.0
AID	–	1.1	3.1	2.8	3.7	–	17.4	39.3
IBRD	–	–	–	–	2.8	–	–	2.8
EXIMBANK	–	–	–	3.4	1.2	–	–	4.6
Public health	2.0	–	0.5	6.5	6.2	6.9	2.0	22.3
AID	–	–	0.5	6.5	0.7	6.9	2.0	16.6
EXIMBANK	2.0	–	–	–	5.5	–	–	5.7
Government	1.0	1.2	1.6	–	–	–	2.2	5.1
AID	–	1.2	1.6	–	–	–	2.2	5.0
EXIMBANK	1.0	–	–	–	–	–	–	0.1
Unclassified	24.6	53.0	4.8	10.9	10.0	17.2	6.0	126.5
IDB-III	–	–	0.6	–	–	–	–	0.6
AID	7.5	–	2.2	10.8	10.0	16.2	2.0	48.7
EXIMBANK	17.1	53.0	2.0	0.1	–	1.0	4.0	77.2
Program credits	82.5	141.7	82.5	312.5	152.5	290.0	215.3	1,277.0
AID	82.5	141.7	82.5	312.5	152.5	290.0	215.3	1,277.0

Note: IDB-I = Ordinary Capital Resources.
IDB-II = Special Operations Fund.
IDB-III = Social Progress Trust Fund.

Source: Data obtained from operating statements of the agencies.

Appendix Table I-A-3. Authorizations for Sectoral and Compensatory Loans by International Institutions, 1961–67 (in Millions of $)

Sector	IDB-I	IDB-II	IDB-III	IDB	AID	IBRD	EXIMBANK	IDA	Total
Agriculture	199.9	278.2	86.7	564.8	246.2	226.8	17.6	13.1	1,068.5
Mining	39.8	11.9	—	51.7	15.9	—	285.6	—	353.2
Industry	330.1	56.0	0.9	387.0	89.5	58.0	420.6	—	955.1
Transportation	63.0	137.8	9.3	210.1	277.0	420.9	415.6	78.9	1,402.5
Communications	3.3	—	4.0	7.3	1.0	62.5	20.5	—	91.3
Electric power	180.3	43.8	—	224.1	210.6	978.1	131.1	15.0	1,558.9
Multisectoral	74.0	132.1	7.9	214.0	310.8	22.0	19.3	—	566.1
Water supply and sewerage	56.1	177.3	161.7	395.1	40.7	21.3	33.2	3.0	493.3
Housing	—	69.8	218.2	288.0	156.1	2.8	4.6	—	444.1
Education	—	65.5	36.0	101.5	39.3	—	5.7	—	148.2
Public health	—	—	—	—	16.6	—	0.1	—	22.3
Government	—	—	—	—	5.0	—	—	—	5.1
Unclassified	—	—	0.6	0.6	48.7	—	77.2	—	126.5
Program credits	—	—	—	—	1,277.0	—	—	—	1,277.0
Total by sector	946.5	972.4	525.3	2,444.2	2,734.4	1,792.4	1,431.1	110.0	8,512.1
Compensatory	—	—	—	—	—	—	1,125.6	—	1,125.6
Grand total	946.5	972.4	525.3	2,444.2	2,734.4	1,792.4	2,556.7	110.0	9,637.7

Note: IDB-I = Ordinary Capital Resources.
IDB-II = Special Operations Fund.
IDB-III = Social Progress Trust Fund.

Source: Data obtained from operating statements of the agencies.

Appendix Table I-A-4. Sectoral Allocation of Authorized Project Credits, 1961–67 (in Millions of $)[a]

Country	Productive Sectors	Multisectoral	Economic Infrastructure	Social Sectors	Others	Total
Argentina	231.1	32.0	298.4	96.9	51.6	710.2
Bolivia	50.2	30.4	91.4	27.3	2.2	201.4
Brazil	345.0	29.7	682.6	179.0	–	1,236.3
Chile	476.8	187.9	165.0	109.0	5.9	944.5
Colombia	215.6	8.9	307.2	104.9	2.1	638.7
Costa Rica	46.1	24.2	33.4	21.9	3.1	128.7
Dominican Republic	22.1	14.7	31.3	19.3	16.1	103.5
Ecuador	27.5	15.3	55.6	50.2	1.9	150.4
El Salvador	20.8	2.5	39.3	29.5	5.3	97.4
Guatemala	13.8	17.2	40.3	15.8	3.0	90.0
Haiti	0.3	3.5	3.2	3.7	–	10.6
Honduras	10.9	13.8	56.8	20.8	3.0	105.3
Mexico	512.0	9.3	584.0	55.9	6.7	1,168.0
Nicaragua	46.1	6.7	31.9	22.2	7.3	114.0
Panama	30.3	8.7	26.6	50.3	2.9	118.7
Paraguay	31.6	3.7	60.6	4.9	–	100.8
Peru	125.8	31.3	182.7	90.3	9.7	439.6
Trinidad and Tobago	5.0	–	46.7	9.3	0.2	61.2
Uruguay	42.8	7.6	22.6	32.1	1.3	106.5
Venezuela	122.8	4.0	292.7	161.5	9.0	590.0
Regional	–	114.7	–	2.9	–	117.6
Total	2,376.4	566.0	3,052.0	1,107.4	131.4	7,233.3

[a]Includes loans from AID, IDB, IBRD, IDA and EXIMBANK.

Source: Data obtained from operating statements of each agency.

CHAPTER II

Measurement of External Aid

METHOD FOR MEASURING EXTERNAL AID

In 1961, when the Charter of Punta del Este was approved and the Alliance for Progress launched, it was pointed out that, in order to reach the economic and social development goals set forth in the charter, Latin American countries would have to receive a significant inflow of external resources during the decade—$2 billion on the average each year. The greater part of that amount would come from public funds, and it was emphasized that contributions, especially those from the United States, would have to take the form of "grants or loans on flexible terms and conditions."

On the details of how the external financial assistance should be granted, the charter was unfortunately somewhat vague. Thus, for example, it did not explicitly state whether the annual $2 billion mentioned above should be regarded as gross contributions or contributions net of amortization and/or interest. It appears clear, considering the charter as a whole, that the above-mentioned figure referred to the needed transfer of real resources from abroad, or to their equivalent, the external financial contribution in net terms. In addition, the charter did not explicitly define how much of that external financial assistance should take the form of grants. Nor did it make clear what was meant by "flexible terms and conditions," even though it seems logical to infer that the intentions of the charter were that the average terms and conditions of financing would be sufficiently "flexible" to prevent the occurrence during this decade, or in subsequent years, of balance-of-payments difficulties that would be induced by heavy debt-service payment and could endanger the orderly and sufficiently rapid course of the development process.

Examination of the trends with respect to amounts and conditions described in chapter I indicates that, especially in recent years, the external contribution has been inadequate, in particular in its terms and conditions. However, it is not possible to compare directly that evolution with the forecasts of the charter, firstly, because of the above-mentioned lack of precision in that document. Secondly, the heterogeneous nature of the terms and conditions described in the previous chapter makes it impossible to deal on the same footing with financing received under different arrangements. Yet in order to obtain a proper basis for future programing it is important that a solution be found for the second difficulty, that is, the lack of homogeneity in the external financing received by Latin America. In this regard it should be pointed out that the main aim of this report is to examine certain alternatives with respect to the volume of and arrangements for external financing, so that in the future Latin American countries and the United States will have at their disposal more adequate information for planning hemispheric financial cooperation than they did in 1961.

In order to define more accurately what is needed for the future and to have an adequate basis for comparing alternative courses of action, as well as appreciating more clearly what has happened in recent years in the field of external financing, it is essential to have a procedure for reducing to a comparable basis the external contributions made under such dissimilar conditions as grants, credits provided on favorable terms by IDA, the Trust and Special Operations Funds of the IDB, and AID, and the much "harder" loans such as those of EXIMBANK and those through which international and inter-American banking institutions channel to Latin America funds obtained in the capital markets of the industrialized countries.

The mere sum of the financing coming from such varied sources as these may be relevant to the analysis of the situation in a given year or of the short-term balance-of-payments prospects. But this sum, or a more complete calculation of the net inflow of funds—that is, the result of subtracting amortizations and interests from gross flows in the same year—does not make it possible to carry out an overall evaluation of the real significance of those financial contributions, nor does it constitute sufficient basis for defining alternative courses of action for the future.

The method adopted in this study for reducing external financing operations to the required comparable basis is to determine the component of that external financing which, according to the definition of Professor Rosenstein-Rodan, cannot be contributed by normal market incentives.[1] Thus that component—the "aid component"—is an attempt to measure, on the one hand, the cost to the donor country of its contributions to the development of other countries and, on the other hand, the benefit to the recipient countries of obtaining those resources on concessionary terms in comparison with what it would have cost to obtain them on commercial conditions. It should be

---

[1] P. Rosenstein-Rodan, "International Aid for Underdeveloped Countries," *Review of Economics and Statistics*, May 1961, No. 2, p. 109, and "Determining the Need for and Planning the Use of External Resources," in *Organization, Planning and Programming for Economic Development, Science, Technology and Development*, Washington, D.C., 1962, p. 71.

pointed out here that, as will be seen later, the cost to the donor country is not equal to the benefit that the receipt of those resources represents for the recipient country—usually it is less.

This method of determining the aid component—which has been developed in recent years and has recently been used by UNCTAD, OECD, and the World Bank—makes it possible to obtain the required comparable basis much more accurately than the procedure used in the past, that is, the sums of the gross or net flows. It must be recognized, however, that, in order to do so, it is necessary on occasion to make assumptions that are to some extent arbitrary and neglect certain qualitative aspects which may be of importance in making a proper evaluation of the effects and characteristics of external financing.

Among the necessary simplifications of reality, mention must be made, for example, of the fact that no quantitative method such as that being used can measure the additional benefit accruing to Latin America from an institution such as the IDB, which has stressed activities of great importance for the development of the region, such as education and health, hitherto neglected by other sources of concessionary financing. Nor is it possible to measure accurately the usefulness, for the recipient country, of technical assistance and other services that usually go hand in hand with the award of development credits.[2]

With these necessary reservations, therefore, an attempt is made in this chapter, first, to analyze the amounts of external financing channeled by the United States to Latin America, whether in the form of bilateral aid or through multilateral agencies, and to calculate the aid component from the standpoint of the United States by estimating what part of that external financing represents a cost to the United States, taking into account the alternative use that might have been made of those funds. Secondly, the analysis will focus on the countries receiving external financing from the United States directly and from international agencies whose headquarters are in Washington, and an attempt will be made to determine the benefit which Latin American countries receive when they obtain financing on favorable terms, that is, the aid component in contrast to the commercial norm. Finally, an effort, albeit a very tentative one, is made to estimate the impact which the tying of these loans to United States imports has on the interest rate and the aid component. The general method used is described in detail in the following section in analyzing the aid component from the standpoint of

---

[2] There are circumstances that do not lend themselves to being incorporated into the measurement of the aid component, but which may increase (or decrease) the sacrifice which the donor country makes; also circumstances may arise which increase—or decrease—the usefulness of the aid for the recipient country.

the cost to the United States; later sections deal with the modifications that must be introduced within that method in order to figure the benefits and effects of tied aid.

Because of the difficulties and delays in obtaining the necessary information the anaylsis presented in this chapter does not cover bilateral financing granted by other industrialized countries nor does it include the year 1968. For the same reason, and also in order to simplify the calculations, this analysis is limited to authorizations of credits and donations and does not take into account the actual date of the disbursements.

UNITED STATES EXTERNAL FINANCING

Main Features of U. S. Financing 1961-67

The external financing authorized by the United States for Latin America as a whole in the period 1961-67 amounted to $8.516 billion. That contribution was made primarily in the form of loans through AID, EXIMBANK, Title IV of P.L. 480, and the Social Progress Trust Fund administered by the IDB. About 66 percent of the total was channeled through those institutions, while donations made through P.L. 480, AID, Peace Corps, and Inter-American Highway programs, accounted for 22 percent of the authorized funds. The remaining 22 percent consisted of contributions to the IDB, primarily to the Special Operations Fund.[3] Most of the aid in the form of loans was made through AID and EXIMBANK and, to a lesser extent, under the Social Progress Trust Fund and Title IV of P.L. 480.[4]

The largest authorizations for United States financing during the period were made in 1961 and 1964—more than $1.4 billion a year.[5] After 1965 there was a continual downward trend. Between 1965 and 1967 total grants and contributions to the IDB shrank significantly while directly authorized loans or loans authorized through the Social Progress Trust Fund increased from $600 to $900 million in that period, although they did not again reach the 1964 level. In other words, the contraction in the total authorized financing between 1964 and 1967 was accompanied by an increase in the proportion of loans over grants.[6]

---

[3] During the period under review the United States did not make any contributions to the World Bank or to IDA.

[4] See hereafter table II-1.

[5] The 1961 figure includes a renegotiation of Brazil's debt which amounted to $298.8 million.

[6] See below table II-2.

The Opportunity Cost for the United States

The method used. In order to reduce the various categories of financing mentioned in the paragraph above to a comparable base, that is, in order to figure its aid component, the following procedures have been used.[7]

1. Loans have been valued on the basis of the difference between the authorized worth and the present worth of the repayment streams,[8] discounted at the prevailing market interest rate.[9] The market interest rate will differ, depending on whether the purpose of the calculation is to determine the cost to the donor country or the benefit to the recipient country. To figure the cost, the interest rate to be selected should reflect the alternative return which the financing country forgoes as a consequence of the outflow of capital, while to figure the benefit, this rate should reflect the price that the recipient country would have to pay to obtain funds on current commercial conditions. In this section, in attempting to quantify the cost of United States external financing to Latin America, the discount rate has been assumed to be equal to the yield of federal government bonds plus 1 percent for administrative costs. In this regard the procedure used has been to determine the financial cost for the United States government of the resources it contributes to the Latin American countries, by comparing the conditions of those contributions with the cost to the government of placing on the market federal debt securities for the same amount. There are, of course, other methods for measuring the opportunity cost of the external financing; the determination of the opportunity cost presents many problems because there is no single rate of interest and it is difficult to determine whether the transfer of funds from the private to the public sector implies a sacrifice of consumption or of investment.[10]

---

[7]The method used in this chapter, with slight modifications, is basically that developed by J. Pincus and G. Ohlen. See J. Pincus, *Costs and Benefits of Aid: a Quantitative Approach*. UNCTAD, TB/B/C.3/38, New York, April 1967; also by the same author "The Cost of Foreign Aid," *The Review of Economics and Statistics*, Vol. XLV, No. 4, November 1963 and *Trade, Aid and Development*, New York: Council on Foreign Relations, 1967, chaps. 8 and 9 and *Economic Aid and International Cost Sharing*, Baltimore: Johns Hopkins, 1965, chap. 5. G. Ohlin, *Foreign Aid Policies Reconsidered*, Paris: OCDE, 1966, chap. 4. This secretariat has already made a similar study relating to Chile, see *El Esfuerzo Interno y las Necesidades de Financiamiento Externo para el Desarrollo de Chile*, CIAP/302, Washington, D.C., November 1968, chap. 3, section D2.

[8]In order to simplify the calculations, it has been assumed that the loans would be completely disbursed at the time of authorization. This assumption obviously tends to overestimate the aid component since theoretically the calculations should be based on the present worth of the disbursements at the time of authorization and not on the total authorized amount.

[9]See appendixes II-A and II-B on methodology for determining the aid component.

[10]This question has been and still is the subject of discussions between U.S. scholars; however, the predominant view is that the social cost of public financing varies between

2. Cash grants have been included *in toto*.

3. Grants made under Titles II and III of P.L. 480 have been valued at the price of the products on the world market, since the price fixed by the Commodity Corporation includes a subsidy to the United States farmer. An alternative that has not been considered in this study is to take the liquidation price of United States agricultural surpluses instead of the present world market price. The first would be lower than the second, since faced with the impossibility of consuming these surpluses domestically the United States would have to place them on the world market, thereby putting a downward pressure on prices, according to the elasticity of each product.[11]

4. In the case of grants and loans made under Title I of P.L. 480, with funds obtained from the sale of agricultural surpluses, the authorized total, valued at the world market price, has been considered a grant, and current expenses in the recipient country which the United States usually pays have been subtracted. This approach was adopted because the loans made under this title are repayable in the currencies of the recipient countries and are not subject to monetary adjustments and, although the United States does not lose control of those loans, their real value decreases in the course of time, especially in countries suffering from inflation. It should be noted, however, that up to 25 percent of the counterpart funds must be used, pursuant to the 1957 Cooley Amendment, for loans to United States enterprises abroad or for foreign enterprises which help to expand the market for United States agricultural products. In both cases, it is debatable whether the total can be considered aid to the recipient country, since in the first case the benefit is directly aimed at United States interests and, in the second, it helps to generate an outflow of foreign exchange for imports. To sum up, the procedure followed in this case generally tends to overestimate the aid component, although it is difficult to estimate the order of magnitude of that overestimation.

5. Loans under P.L. 480, Title IV, are made from funds derived from the sale of agricultural surpluses and are repayable in dollars. In this case the method used is similar to that outlined in par. 1 for loans in general; it was applied to the authorized amount valued at world market prices.

6. Dollar loans payable in the currency of the recipient country, and which are subject to monetary correction involve more aid than current loans

---

5 and 6 percent. See J. V. Krutilla and D. Eckstein, *Multiple Purpose River Development*, Baltimore: Johns Hopkins, 1958, chap. 4.

[11] According to the calculation made by Pincus, "The Cost of Foreign Aid," pp. 365–67, the liquidation value of agricultural surpluses would be 20 percent lower than the world market price. As operations under these two titles represented about 10 percent of U.S. aid to Latin America in the period 1961–67, the overestimate in the total aid component would be in the order of 2 percent.

since although the debits receivable are accumulated in favor of the United States, there is no immediate outflow of capital. The methodology applied to these loans is similar to that described in detail below in discussing the real benefit of external financing to the recipient countries.

7. Finally, the contributions made by the United States to multilateral financing agencies have been considered as grants and are therefore included in their entirety in the calculation of aid. Alternatively, these funds could have been treated as assets whose profitability is shown by the earnings of the institutions, since the United States does not lose ownership of those funds but acquires shares in the multilateral institution. However, in view of the immobility of those assets, and the fact that their profitability is low or zero for the country contributing them, it was decided to make them equivalent to grants.

With the methodology explained above, it was determined that the opportunity cost for the United States of the resources which it contributed to Latin America in the period 1961–67 amounted to somewhat more than 50 percent of the total authorized financing (see table II-1). The cost was greater in cash grants and contributions to the IDB whose coefficients are 100 percent, while the funds channeled through loans only represented a cost equivalent to 28 percent of the authorized value. There are also great differences in the cost of the loans according to the conditions on which they were made. Thus the loans made by AID and through the Social Progress Trust Fund, which are characterized by low interest rates and long grace and amortization periods, represented costs to the United States of 48 and 43 percent, respectively. On the other hand the operations made through EXIMBANK not only did not involve any cost, but represented an additional financial benefit to the United States on the order of 2 percent. External financing authorized by P.L. 480, which is usually regarded as a grant, represents a cost for the United States of about 72 percent for the total value, since although the operations under Title I may be considered to involve a cost of 100 percent, the adjustment of prices in Titles II and III reduces that cost to 70 percent and the loans made under Title IV result in a real cost below 30 percent.

The average cost shows substantial variation during the period under review. The two years in which the highest amounts of external financing were authorized, that is to say, 1961 and 1964, represented costs for the United States of 37 and 48 percent respectively. That was largely due to the fact that a substantial part of the financing authorized, especially in 1961, was channeled through EXIMBANK. On the other hand, the recent hardening of United States financing is reflected in the decrease in cost from average levels of about 57 percent between 1962 and 1966 to 34 percent in 1967. In absolute values the annual cost incurred in the latter year was practically half the annual average for the period (see table II-2).

Table II-1. Estimate of the Cost to the United States of External Financing Granted to
Latin America, 1961–67 (in Thousands of $)

Cost	Gross External Financing Authorized	Cost of Financing	
		Value	Percentages
Loans	*5,574,511*	*1,561,660*	*28.0*
AID	2,729,931	1,324,048	48.5
Trust Fund	504,734	218,168	43.2
P.L. 480, Title IV	231,399	67,776	29.3
EXIMBANK	2,108,447	–48,332	–2.3
Contributions to international			
agencies	*1,050,000*	*1,050,000*	*100.0*
IDB – Ordinary Capital			
Resources	150,000	150,000	100.0
IDB – Special Operations Fund	900,000	900,000	100.0
P.L. 480	*942,031*	*777,459*	*82.5*
Title I	373,990	373,990	100.0
Title II	168,827	122,134	72.3
Title III	399,214	281,335	70.5
Other donations	*949,800*	*949,800*	*100.0*
AID programs	795,000	795,000	100.0
Peace Corps and Inter-American			
Highway	154,800	154,800	100.0
Total	8,516,342	4,338,919	50.9

Note: For the methodology used, see the text.

Sources: Loans: AID, EXIMBANK and IDB statements of loans. *Contributions and Grants:* House Foreign Affairs Committee, *U.S. Overseas Loans and Grants*, Washington, D.C., 29 March 1968. *P.L. 480:* Office of the White House Press Secretary, *Food for Peace; The Annual Report on Activities Carred Out under P.L. 480*, various issues; U.S. Department of Agriculture, *12 Years of Achievement under P.L. 480*, Washington, D.C., March 1968, and *Foreign Agricultural Trade of the U.S.*, Washington, D.C., June 1968.

Although the year-by-year evolution of funds channeled as loans—that is, excluding donations, contributions to the IDB, and operations under P.L. 480—shows no very definite trend, some aspects are of interest. The financing granted in 1961 which, as stated earlier, consisted largely of EXIM-BANK loans, only represented a cost to the United States of 13.3 percent of the authorized value. In the remainder of the period the cost component was about 33 percent; there was a fall and subsequent recovery in 1965 and 1966 respectively, until finally in 1967 it reached a level of 23 percent, substantially lower than the average for the period under review.

Finally, it is interesting to compare the cost of the United States financing to Latin America with the total cost of United States financing to the rest of

Table II-2. Evolution of the Cost to the Government of the United States of the External Financing Granted to Latin America, 1961–67 (in Thousands of $)

Cost	1961	1962	1963	1964	1965	1966	1967	Total
1. *Loans*								
i. Amounts authorized	1,021,929	625,400	595,830	1,025,746	612,489	778,264	914,853	5,574,511
ii. Cost	135,870	208,324	200,738	341,025	174,509	290,810	210,384	1,561,660
iii. Percentage (ii/i)	13.3	33.3	33.7	33.2	28.5	37.4	23.0	28.0
2. *Contributions to IDB*	190,000	60,000	–	50,000	500,000	250,000	–	1,050,000
3. *P.L. 480*								
i. Title I	69,812	103,323	76,625	103,630	15,710	4,890	–	373,990
ii. Titles I and III								
a. Amounts authorized	27,117	68,457	95,292	139,694	115,197	62,246	60,038	568,041
b. Cost	22,074	57,333	69,517	78,774	87,022	42,742	46,007	403,469
4. *Donations*	109,600	126,500	164,300	123,700	149,200	165,200	111,300	949,800
5. *Total*								
i. Amounts authorized $(1_i + 2 + 3_i + 3_{iia} + 4)$	1,418,458	983,680	932,047	1,442,770	1,392,596	1,260,600	1,086,191	8,516,342
ii. Cost $(1_{ii} + 2 + 3_i + 3_{iib} + 4)$	527,356	555,480	511,180	697,129	926,441	753,642	367,691	4,338,919
iii. Percentage (ii/i)	37.1	56.5	54.8	48.3	66.5	59.8	33.9	50.9

Note: For the methodology used, see the text.

Source: See table II-1.

the world. According to the calculations made in Pincus[12] for the period 1963-66, using the same discount rates and almost the same methodology as in this report, the cost component of the total external financing to the United States was about 69 percent of the authorized value. As may be seen, the financing to Latin America represented a lower cost—50.9 percent—and even excluding 1961 and 1967, the years in which lower cost levels were recorded, the cost still averaged about 57 percent.

ESTIMATE OF AID RECEIVED BY LATIN AMERICA

Main Features of External Financing Received by Latin America

Although the flows of external financing authorized for Latin America in the period 1961-67 have been discussed in detail, it is advisable to recapitulate very briefly their main features.[13]

External financing authorized during the period amounted to $11.3 billion, of which more than 83 percent was channeled in the form of loans and the remainder in grants. As to the origin of the loan funds, the shares of the main official sources of Latin American financing—that is, AID, EXIMBANK, IDB, and the World Bank-IDA—were similar and ranged from 20 to 30 percent of the total loans authorized. AID approaches the upper limit (29 percent) having contributed the largest amount of funds; IDB and EXIMBANK come next, each having authorized about 25 percent of the total, while the World Bank-IDA contributed 20 percent of the total funds authorized.

The economic infrastructure sectors (transportation, communications, and electric power) were those which absorbed the highest share of the financing authorized as loans, 33 percent of the total was earmarked for those pur-

[12] Pincus, *Cost and Benefits of Aid*, pp. 16-23. The methodological difference between the calculation made by Mr. Pincus and that made in this report is that here the increase in the cost due to the fact that part of the financing is repayable in local currency—nonconvertible—of the recipient countries is explicitly taken into account, in accordance with the procedure described below in estimating the benefit for Latin America. In any event, the modification adopted here tends slightly to increase the estimate of the cost for the United States of the financing supplied to Latin America. That methodological difference does not invalidate but rather strengthens the conclusions reached in this report.

[13] In this section funds from loans made by AID, EXIMBANK—including compensatory financing—IDB, and World Bank-IDA, operations under P.L. 480 and U.S. grants to Latin America, are included as external financing. The authorizations of the IMF and the U.S. Treasury are excluded from those summarized in table II-1. In addition, within the operations of the institutions included in this analysis there are some credits—of relatively small size—that have not been taken into account in this chapter because the necessary information for determining the aid component was not available. For this reason there are some discrepancies between the figures used in this chapter and those used in chapter I.

poses. The productive sectors (agriculture, industry, and mining) received 25 percent of the total, of which about half was earmarked for the agricultural sector. The social sectors (education, housing, and health) received 7 percent of the total, but their share rises to 12 percent if funds for water supply and sewerage systems are included.[14] The remaining funds were channeled globally either as program loans (13.9 percent), multisectoral loans (6.2 percent), or compensatory loans (8.7 percent).[15]

Estimate of the Aid Component in the External Financing Received by Latin America

The method used. 1. *General characteristics.* Since we are attempting to determine the aid component of the external financing for the recipient country, that rate must reflect the alternative cost that Latin American countries would have to pay if they did not have access to financing on concessional terms. The difficulties encountered in attempting to determine the "normal" interest rate arise from the fact that the countries in the region have little recent experience in placing bonds in the capital markets. In this report it is assumed that the rate was 9 percent in 1967. This is based on recent placements of government bonds of three Latin American countries on external capital markets at rates ranging between 7 and 8 percent.[16] The countries that have used these markets are among those with the highest level of internal and external financial solvency in the region so that an average rate, somewhat higher than that obtained by them, appears indicated.[17] It was thought inappropriate to use an interest rate of more than 9 percent in view of the many suppliers' credits that the Latin American countries have received at lower rates. Starting from a rate of 9 percent in 1967, it is assumed that in the other years in the period that level kept pace with the yields of United States federal government bonds.

2. *Loans repayable in local currency.* That a substantial proportion of the credits granted by IDB and AID are repayable in local currency undoubtedly entails an increase in the aid component of that financing. Where amortizations and interests are repayable in the amounts originally provided for in

---

[14] It must be again pointed out that most of the funds earmarked for the social sectors were supplied by the IDB.

[15] In the sectoral distribution only loans from agencies headquartered in Washington are included; but excluding operations under Title IV of P.L. 480.

[16] Placements by Argentina, Mexico, and Venezuela.

[17] An alternative possibility would be to utilize different discount rates for each country. Although that method would allow countries or groups of countries to be distinguished from each other, the information available is insufficient to draw up accurate criteria for making assumptions.

local currency without monetary correction for variations in those currencies relative to the dollar, the total credit has been considered a grant, i.e., its aid component is rated at 100 percent.[18]

A different problem arises where the amortizations and interests to be paid in local currency must be adjusted according to variations in the value of those currencies relative to the dollar, especially—as occurs with the Special Operations Fund of the IDB—when the balances which the loan agencies maintain in the currencies of the recipient countries are also adjusted. In these cases, loans in local currency cannot be classified as grants, since that would presuppose that the currencies would continue to be nonconvertible indefinitely, and of no value to the lending agency.

Consequently, in order to indicate that in these cases there is actually a large aid component, but one smaller than in the case of grants, it has been arbitrarily assumed in this calculation that, on the average, the respective currencies will be freely convertible by 1985.[19] This would mean a special grace period up to that year when, generally speaking, the outstanding amounts would be paid in dollars.[20]

3. *Contributions of Latin American countries to international financing institutions.* This report will not attempt to evaluate the operations of the financial institutions as such but to measure the financial benefit to the region resulting from the transfer of resources from the United States and other industrialized countries—either directly or through multilateral agencies—in order to provide a suitable basis for future courses of action. Thus, to determine that benefit, the contributions which Latin America has made to multilateral institutions, albeit diminishing, must also be taken into account, since they reduce the net amount of that benefit. For that purpose the dollar contributions of the aid component have been deducted.[21]

---

[18] As usual, those debt-service payments will represent some value—even in countries with acute inflation. This tends to overestimate the aid component, but in the absence of a more adequate basis, it has been thought preferable to use the procedure indicated rather than to make any other distinction which would necessarily be even more arbitrary.

[19] This means that, generally speaking, dollars would begin to be exchanged before this date but that the average effect of this exchange would make itself felt in 1985. This assumption does not imply that all the local currency will be exchanged in that year. The assumption also covers the case of the local currencies being used for a shift in trade and therefore an opportunity cost in dollars. That would not be the case if the local currencies were used to create trade, but to accept an intermediate situation would not introduce any significant changes in the calculations in view of the long amortization period that has been assumed.

[20] See appendix II-A.

[21] For the case of contributions in local currency by Latin American countries, see appendix II-A, describing the method used for local currency operations.

The aid component in the period 1961–67. The aid component of the external financing received by Latin America in the period 1961–67 was determined according to the method described above. Thus, only 46.8 percent of the $11.3 billion authorized, that is $5.3 billion, can properly be considered to be aid, since the remainder was financing on conditions similar to those prevailing on the market. Obviously, the largest aid component is to be found in cash grants and in operations under Title I of P.L. 480; while the aid component of authorized loans was 37.8 percent of the total. The grants in kind made under Title II and III of P.L. 480 present an intermediate situation representing aid in the amount of 70.0 percent, due to differences in the prices used for valuing agricultural surpluses (see table II-3).

Table II-3. Determination of Aid Component for Latin America, 1961–67
(in Thousands of $)

Type of Aid	Gross External Financing Authorized	Aid Component	
		Value	Percentages
Loans	*9,395,162*	*3,553,449*	*37.8*
AID	2,729,931	1,857,670	68.0
P.L. 480, Title IV	231,399	105,729	46.0
IDB	2,423,185	802,976[a]	33.1[a]
IBRD and IDA	1,902,200	448,595[b]	23.6[b]
EXIMBANK	2,108,447	338,479	16.1
P.L. 480	*942,031*	*777,459*	*82.5*
Title I	373,990	373,990	100.0
Titles II and III	568,041	403,469	71.0
Other grants	*949,800*	*949,800*	*100.0*
AID Programs	795,000	795,000	100.0
Peace Corps and			
Inter-American Highway	154,800	154,800	100.0
Total	*11,286,993*	*5,280,708*	*46.8*

[a]As stated in the text, $150,527,000 have been subtracted for the dollar contributions of Latin American countries. Before this subtraction, the aid component amounted to $935,503,000 or 34 percent of the total financing authorized. Of that total the aid components were as follows: IDB-Ordinary Capital Resources: $105.3 million (11.4 percent); Social Progress Trust Fund: $363.7 (72.1 percent); British and Canadian Resources: $13.4 million (65.7 percent).

[b]Of this aid component IBRD accounted for $360.5 million (20.1 percent); and AID, $88.1 million (80.1 percent).

Note: For the methodology used, see the text and appendix II-A.

Sources: Same as table II-1 and IBRD–IDA statements of loans.

In the area of external financing channeled as loans, the largest aid component was that from AID, which amounted to 68 percent of the total lent by that institution. At the other extreme, the table shows that the aid component from EXIMBANK was 16 percent of the authorized amount, while the World Bank's—including IDA—was 23.6 percent. A similar favorable situation is that presented by the IDB—considering its operations as a whole—which granted aid in the amount of 39 percent of the funds loaned—33 percent if we bear in mind the dollar contributions made by Latin American countries, as explained earlier.

It should also be kept in mind that the aid components shown in table II-3 are the result of two distinct types of financial operations. On the one hand, there are grants and credits on concessional terms channeled either bilaterally or multilaterally, by means of which the United States—and to a much smaller extent other industrialized countries—help to reduce the cost of financing for Latin American countries. This group comprises the grants and credits of the Social Progress Trust Fund, the Special Operations Fund, and the British and Canadian resources of the IDB; those of AID and IDA, and operations under P.L. 480. On the other hand, there are credits granted by EXIMBANK, the World Bank and by the IDB from its ordinary capital resources. In these cases the aid component is necessarily smaller because these institutions must charge enough for their loans to cover the cost of the capital obtained plus their operating costs. The aid component granted by these agencies, therefore, tends only to measure—theoretically at least—the difference between the agencies' cost of capital plus operating costs and what that cost would be for the recipient countries if they raised the money directly on the international capital markets. The data in footnote *a* to table II-3 could be aggregated to show that the aid component of the first group amount to a total of $4.627 billion, the equivalent of 71.6 percent of authorized financing, whereas the component in the second group is only $804 million or 16.7 percent of the total loans.[22]

Table II-4 shows that there was a downward trend in the aid component in total financing in 1965 but that the increase in 1966 partly offset the decline which had occurred in the previous year. Thus, from an average of about 50 percent in 1962 and 1963, and a peak of 53 percent in 1964, the aid component in 1967 dropped to 42.5 percent, the lowest level since 1961.

It is also interesting to try to compare the aid component contained in the external financing received by Latin America with that of other regions of the world. For this purpose we can use a calculation made by the World Bank for

---

[22]Without subtracting, in both cases, the dollar contributions of the Latin American countries to the IDB.

Table II-4. Evolution of the Aid Component, 1961–67 (in Thousands of $ and Percentages)

Type of Aid	1961	1962	1963	1964	1965	1966	1967	Total
1. *Loans*								
i. Amounts authorized	1,462,127	1,090,008	1,116,924	1,362,195	1,308,246	1,490,720	1,564,942	9,395,162
ii. Aid	403,151	393,894	408,376	614,778	487,950	664,093	581,206	3,553,449
iii. Aid component (ii/i)	27.6	36.0	36.6	45.1	37.3	44.5	37.1	37.8
2. *P.L. 480*								
i. Title I	69,812	103,323	76,625	103,630	15,710	4,890	–	373,990
ii. Titles II and III								
a. Amounts authorized	27,117	68,457	95,292	139,694	115,197	62,246	60,038	568,041
b. Aid	22,074	57,333	69,517	78,774	87,022	42,742	46,007	403,469
3. *Donations*	109,600	126,500	164,300	123,700	149,200	165,200	111,300	949,800
4. *Total*								
i. Amounts authorized $(1_i + 2_i + 2_{iia} + 3)$	1,668,656	1,388,288	1,453,141	1,727,219	1,588,353	1,723,056	1,736,280	11,286,993
ii. Aid $(1_{ii} + 2_i + 2_{iib} + 3)$	604,637	681,050	718,818	920,882	739,882	876,925	738,513	5,280,708
iii. Aid component $(4_{ii} / 4_i)$	36.2	49.0	49.4	53.2	46.5	50.8	42.5	46.8

Note: For the methodology used, see the text.

Source: See table II-3.

1965 and 1966,[23] which, although differing somewhat from the method used in this study, indicates an aid component for the region similar to that figured here.[24] The methodological differences mainly relate to what in this study is called the loan level; to the special treatment given to loans repayable in dollars and to the discount rate, since 8.81 percent was used for this calculation for 1966, while the World Bank presents two alternative discount rates of 8 and 10 percent.

Taking the alternative discount rate of 10 percent in accordance with the calculations made by the World Bank, Latin America received an aid component only slightly greater than that of the less developed countries of Europe (Cyprus, Greece, Malta, and Spain), while the other regions received a percentage of aid 1.6 times greater than that received by Latin America.[25]

Distribution of aid by country. As shown in table II-5, the percentage aid component received by Latin American countries generally maintained an inverse relationship to the degree of development of each country. Thus, it is possible to distinguish at least five different groups of countries. The first of these is composed of two countries in a very early stage of development: Haiti and Bolivia. They shared the highest aid components, 85 and 75 percent respectively, although in the case of Haiti the absolute amount of that aid has been very small—less than $40 million in the period 1961–67 (see table II-5). There is a second group of countries whose aid component ranged between 60 and 70 percent and whose economic structures can be considered as less developed. This group comprises the Dominican Republic, Nicaragua, Paraguay, Panama, Guatemala, and Ecuador. On the other hand, Costa Rica, El Salvador, and Trinidad and Tobago, whose degree of development may be described as intermediate, received an aid component in the order of 50 percent. A fourth group, composed of Peru and three of the four countries which received the highest amounts of financing—Brazil, Chile, and Colombia[26] — and which, because of their level of development, may be grouped as intermediate-high, received an aid component ranging from 45 to 50 percent.

[23]World Bank-International Development Association, *Annual Report 1968*, Washington, D.C., September 1968, pp. 56–59.

[24]Using the 10 percent discount rate, Latin America, according to the World Bank calculation, received an average aid component of 47.3 percent in 1965–66; in our calculation the average was 48.6 percent.

[25]In 1966, Africa received an aid component of 73.2 percent; the Middle East (Iraq, Israel, Jordan), 75.1 percent; and South Asia (Ceylon, India, Pakistan), 78.7 percent; whereas Latin America received 46.1 percent. East Asian countries are in an intermediate position since they received 62.2 percent. World Bank-International Development Association, *Annual Report 1968*, p. 59.

[26]The four countries that received the highest amounts from the institutions cited are Brazil, Chile, México, and Colombia.

Table II-5. Evolution of the Composition of Aid by Country (in Percentages)

Country	1961	1962	1963	1964	1965	1966	1967	Total Financing	Aid Component, 1961–67
Argentina	-6.1	26.6	37.1	8.2	20.2	50.5	27.6	783,074	24.7
Bolivia	76.1	91.1	79.7	78.1	87.1	58.8	66.8	396,961	75.2
Brazil	30.3	71.1	74.2	59.7	50.9	50.9	49.9	3,015,509	52.0
Chile	61.7	40.0	43.7	52.5	54.8	54.2	29.8	1,459,793	46.2
Colombia	29.0	48.1	37.5	53.1	60.0	42.7	46.2	1,138,049	44.8
Costa Rica	41.9	25.0	48.9	77.8	57.5	55.0	76.9	157,028	50.8
Ecuador	54.9	67.5	71.6	55.7	54.5	62.8	50.2	242,716	60.1
El Salvador	26.6	84.2	52.5	64.3	64.9	82.1	60.4	141,049	56.5
Guatemala	65.5	79.6	70.5	51.9	84.7	64.3	47.3	138,221	61.8
Haiti	85.5	92.9	39.6	68.9	100.0	85.8	93.0	39,595	84.7
Honduras	68.4	72.0	73.0	76.7	61.1	55.7	55.3	131,088	63.2
Mexico	-5.5	24.8	25.2	26.7	22.2	17.4	27.4	1,202,476	22.3
Nicaragua	46.7	81.3	64.7	55.3	54.9	57.8	76.5	87,226	68.5
Panama	71.7	62.4	51.8	53.1	70.7	61.4	74.0	172,755	63.4
Paraguay	68.8	76.9	67.8	64.6	60.1	63.7	57.2	139,474	64.8
Peru	44.3	46.1	36.3	50.6	36.2	53.5	57.9	247,391	45.9
Dominican Republic	-117.0	53.4	73.0	42.0	79.6	79.9	64.8	375,068	71.4
Trinidad and Tobago	24.6	100.0	76.4	100.0	52.9	98.8	37.6	96,353	48.1
Uruguay	7.8	28.2	58.3	61.4	28.2	72.0	46.6	119,597	37.8
Venezuela	22.5	50.0	26.7	25.0	30.5	22.2	19.6	620,100	28.0
Total	36.2	49.8	49.4	53.2	46.5	50.8	42.5	11,286,993	46.2

Note: For the methodology used, see the text.

Source: See table II-3.

Finally, the countries with the highest income level in the region (Argentina, Mexico, Venezuela and, with a somewhat higher component, Uruguay) show lower levels of aid.

The year-by-year evolution of the aid component by country coincides with the trend noted above for the total, namely, that in the year 1967 there was a hardening of external financing. Exceptions to this phenomenon are Argentina and Mexico, which have received very little concessionary financing, and Haiti, which stands at the other extreme because financing in this case has basically been in the form of cash grants and agricultural surpluses. In the case of Costa Rica, Panama, Nicaragua, and Peru the above-mentioned trend is not clear-cut.

Distribution of aid by sectors. Table II-6 shows the aid component of external financing channeled in the form of loans in the period 1961–67, by country and by sector.[27]

Apparently there is a close relationship between the aid component and the sector to which it was directed. Thus, if we exclude global loans for programs and to the government sector, the loans intended for social sectors (housing, education, and health) were those which had the highest aid component, averaging more than 60 percent for the three sectors. The aid component of the agricultural sector was close to the average, while that of the transportation and electric power sectors was about 30 percent of the external financing directed at those sectors. Finally, the aid component in the loans made to the industrial, mining, and communications sectors and compensatory loans[28] was less than 20 percent of the total authorized.

For each sector the percentage aid component is relatively uniform in almost all countries; most of the exceptions—and therefore the differences between the countries—are to be found in the allocation of aid from loans made in the agricultural, industrial, and transportation sectors.

Allocation of aid by source and destination. In the foregoing pages it was noted that there was a close relationship between the percentage aid component of external financing in the various Latin American countries and the relative degree of development, and that the differences in the level of the percentage component of each country originated in the agricultural, industrial, and transport sectors. It should be added that this distribution of the aid component reflects, as far as sources of financing are concerned, the operations of the IDB and IDA. Virtually all the IDA operations were intended for highway construction and hence the transportation sector shows different total aid coefficients for country, while differences in the IDB operations were concentrated in the agricultural and industrial sectors (see table II-7).

[27] Does not include loans under Title IV of P.L. 480.
[28] Does not include operations of the IMF and the U.S. Treasury.

Table II-6. Aid Component by Sector (in Percentages)

Country	Agriculture	Mining	Industry	Transportation	Communications	Electric Power	Multisectoral	Water Supply and Sewerage	Housing	Education	Public Health	Government	Unclassified	Program Credits	EXIMBANK Compensatory	Total
Argentina	31.7	—	12.3	32.3	—	15.7	27.7	46.0	72.1	73.0	—	—	—	31.0	8.8	27.9
Bolivia	73.2	63.6	51.0	73.4	—	71.8	59.5	61.0	57.2	56.9	—	—	78.1	—	38.4	63.2
Brazil	46.1	10.9	26.2	56.4	—	38.0	66.9	53.2	55.8	55.6	73.4	—	—	71.6	18.5	40.7
Chile	49.8	19.2	13.9	41.7	20.8	27.2	62.7	53.7	63.8	60.8	—	—	72.0	71.4	10.5	43.1
Colombia	40.4	76.6	20.8	25.0	21.0	21.6	47.5	43.9	62.4	42.2	—	—	—	64.8	8.5	40.4
Costa Rica	59.8	—	33.1	63.5	—	33.5	24.6	47.4	75.7	56.9	72.4	—	72.0	—	10.7	44.9
Ecuador	46.6	—	53.9	53.3	20.0	24.8	64.3	62.6	61.8	71.7	26.9	67.0	—	46.7	—	51.7
El Salvador	67.4	—	50.4	50.8	—	19.7	9.8	59.2	74.7	72.5	72.2	—	54.5	—	10.1	48.7
Guatemala	62.5	—	70.4	51.4	—	22.9	22.8	64.1	76.4	61.6	72.4	72.0	73.7	—	—	46.0
Haiti	59.2	—	—	78.9	—	—	64.8	68.6	—	69.1	—	—	—	—	—	67.1
Honduras	64.0	—	13.0	52.8	—	—	60.4	65.4	66.2	71.6	71.2	—	72.4	35.2	—	57.2
Mexico	30.6	13.1	14.7	16.6	14.0	18.8	12.3	54.8	60.1	46.4	19.2	—	14.3	—	—	22.2
Nicaragua	40.5	—	50.2	55.2	—	21.9	72.6	78.9	74.1	67.5	71.2	—	71.4	—	—	54.9
Panama	40.5	—	56.1	45.4	—	18.7	56.0	70.9	65.7	69.5	—	—	52.1	19.9	—	51.4
Paraguay	69.8	—	36.4	56.5	50.7	52.1	54.4	—	75.1	72.2	—	—	—	—	—	57.8
Peru	43.5	10.7	12.1	25.2	—	26.9	61.8	56.2	76.1	71.8	—	70.6	45.4	—	—	38.4
Dominican Republic	38.3	—	32.1	8.7	—	18.5	71.9	52.4	71.1	73.6	—	—	70.9	63.3	—	53.6
Trinidad and Tobago	22.8	—	—	23.5	16.7	17.6	—	14.7	—	—	—	—	—	—	—	18.3
Uruguay	34.9	—	28.9	16.8	—	—	28.5	31.5	75.2	—	—	—	8.3	—	—	33.9
Venezuela	40.8	—	10.7	16.9	18.8	21.0	29.6	31.5	62.1	34.5	—	—	10.3	—	—	26.7
Total	40.7	21.3	20.3	34.0	19.4	28.0	54.8	49.1	66.3	59.8	55.9	70.0	60.0	67.3	17.3	38.6

Source: See table II-3.

Table II-7. Aid Component by Sources of Financing (in Percentages)

Country	IDB	IBRD	IDA	AID	EXIMBANK
Argentina	1	1	–	3	1
Bolivia	3	–	4	3	2
Brazil	2	1	–	3	1
Chile	2	1	4	3	1
Colombia	2	1	4	3	1
Costa Rica	2	1	–	3	1
Ecuador	3	1	4	3	1
El Salvador	3	1	4	3	1
Guatemala	2	1	–	3	1
Haiti	2	–	4	3	–
Honduras	3	1	4	3	1
Mexico	1	1	–	3	1
Nicaragua	2	1	4	3	1
Panama	3	1	–	3	1
Paraguay	3	1	4	3	–
Peru	3	1	–	3	1
Dominican Republic	2	–	–	3	1
Trinidad y Tobago	3	1	–	–	1
Uruguay	2	1	–	3	1
Venezuela	2	1	–	3	1
Total	2	1	4	3	1

Note: The numbers in the table stand for the following:
   1: Aid component less than 25 percent of the financing authorized.
   2: Aid component between 25 and 50 percent of the financing authorized.
   3: Aid component between 25 and 75 percent of the financing authorized.
   4: Aid component more than 75 percent of the financing authorized.

Effects of tying on the aid component.[29] So far, in calculating the aid component, only the financing conditions of the loans have been taken into account. However, this assumption results in an overestimation of the aid received by Latin America as well as a distortion in the comparison of the aid according to the source of financing. Thus, whereas financing from the World Bank and IDB (ordinary capital resources) does not impose any limitation on the source of the imports purchased with such financing, the loans made by AID, EXIMBANK, and the IDB under its Special Operations Fund and Social Progress Trust Fund establish conditions with respect to the source of the imports and their transportation.[30]

[29] See the analysis in chap. V of other aspects of tied aid procedures.

[30] Also, there are conditions requiring projects to be prepared by specific consulting firms. However, the World Bank also has this requirement; in view of this and of the difficulty in calculating its additional cost, it has not been taken into account for the purpose of this calculation.

Apart from the effect of tying in terms of technology and technical assistance, financially it means increasing the cost of imports relative to what would have been paid in alternative sources. This increased cost implies, in turn, a reduction in the nominal amounts of financing, i.e., a hardening in the financial conditions through a higher effective interest rate. On the other hand, an increase in the effective interest rate reduces the aid component of the financing.

It is difficult to calculate the additional cost, since because of the disparate nature of the products, identification problems arise in determining alternative prices.

On the other hand, no complete studies relating to Latin America have attempted to estimate that additional cost. Nevertheless, it is worth making the calculation if only to illustrate the situation rather than to achieve a quantitative result. For the purpose of calculation two alternative additional cost coefficients have been adopted. The first of these, 12.5 percent, was calculated by the Chilean Development Corporation (CORFO) for UNCTAD and resulted from comparing the prices paid by or quoted to importers by suppliers of equipment purchased with tied loans, with the lowest prices available from other closely equivalent sources.[31] The order of magnitude of the above-mentioned coefficient appears to be in agreement with the lowest estimates made by other countries. Thus, for example, Mul Haq finds a coefficient of 12 percent for Pakistan.[32] However, since the additional cost calculated for Chile refers to the comparison of the f.o.b. quotations for imports, it is possible that the coefficient is being underestimated, since the United States usually requires that at least 50 percent of the cargoes be carried in United States vessels at costs which frequently exceed the current freight rates in the world market. Thus, for example, in the Haq study mentioned above, it was estimated that freight charged by American bottoms for goods under tied loans ranged from 43 to 113 percent above the lowest international quotation.[33] Hence, as a second alternative, a coefficient of 24 percent was used, by way of illustrating the higher cost which could result from additional costs for freight, insurance, and other charges.

For the calculation of the effective interest rate, the operations of AID, EXIMBANK, IDB's Special Operations Fund and Social Progress Trust Fund were included. Although in the case of loans made under the Special Operations Fund, goods can be imported alternatively from any member country of

[31] UNCTAD, *Informe sobre los Créditos Condicionados*, Chile ID/7/s, pp. 8/add. 1, New Delhi, 1 February 1968.

[32] Mul Haq, *Tied Credits—a Quantitative Analysis*, document submitted to the Round Table on Capital Movements, organized by the International Economic Association, Washington, D.C., 1965, pp. 1–11.

[33] Haq, *Tied Credits*.

the bank, the relative competitive position of Latin American industries vis-à-vis United States industries has resulted in most cases in the United States being the country in which purchases are made. In that respect it is advisable for the IDB—as in the case of the IBRD—to consider a margin of preference for the industries of the recipient countries and to extend this margin in all cases to the industries of all Latin American countries.

The effective interest rate paid by Latin America varied between 4.3 and 4.7 percent, depending on which additional cost formula was used. Taking the group for which the effective interest rate was calculated, the percentage difference with respect to the nominal rate fluctuates between 0.7 and 1.3 percentage points in the case of AID and 2.0 to 3.8 in that of EXIMBANK. The effective interest rate charged in the operations of the Social Progress Trust Fund and the Special Operations Fund of the IDB exceed the nominal rates by 1.1 to 2.1 percentage points. On the average, the effective interest rate for institutions included in the calculation was 0.6 to 1.25 percentage points greater than the nominal interest rate. The additional cost resulting from tying affected the EXIMBANK interest rate more than that of AID's, while the IDB was in an intermediate situation. These differences are basically due to loan conditions granted by each institution, since harder loans in terms of higher nominal interest rates and shorter grace and amortization periods result in higher additional costs (see table II-8).[34]

---

[34] For the method used in the calculation see appendix II-A.

Table II-8. Effect of Tying on Interest Rate

Institution	Nominal Interest Rate	Effective Interest Rate	
		Formula A[a]	Formula B[b]
AID	1.86	2.58	3.14
EXIMBANK	5.62	7.68	9.39
IDB			
Special Operations Fund	3.56	4.73	5.70
Social Progress Trust Fund	2.48	3.58	4.53
Subtotal[c]	3.39	4.02	4.54
Total[d]	3.76	4.27	4.68

[a] Additional cost coefficient of 12.5 percent.
[b] Additional cost coefficient of 24 percent.
[c] Includes AID, EXIMBANK, and IDB Special Operations Fund and Social Progress Trust Fund.
[d] Includes, in addition, IBRD, IDA, P.L. 480, Title IV, and IDB Ordinary Capital Resources and British and Canadian Resources.

Finally, table II-9 shows the aid component calculated by using the effective interest rate instead of the nominal interest rates for the loans included in the previous table. The aid component of external financing which had been estimated at 46.8 percent falls to 42.2 percent when considering an additional cost of 12.5 percent resulting from the tying of the loans, and declines to 38.3 percent if the additional cost is 24 percent. On breaking down the loan funds by origin, EXIMBANK, which showed the lowest aid component—about 16 percent for authorized loans—only granted 5.3 percent in aid under the first formula for the additional costs of tying of the loan; under the second formula, the calculation made shows that financing granted by EXIM-BANK, instead of representing aid to the region, would entail a cost of 3.5 percent.

Table II-9. Aid Component Adjusted for Tying of External Financing
(in Thousands of $)

Institutions	Gross External Financing	Aid Component			
		Formula A[a]		Formula B[b]	
		Value	Percentages	Value	Percentages
Loans	*9,395,162*	*3,034,587*	*32.3*	*2,594,344*	*27.6*
AID	2,729,931	1,680,892	61.6	1,542,463	56.5
P.L. 480, Title IV	231,399	105,729	46.0	105,729	46.0
IDB	2,423,185	688,299	28.4	570,847	23.6
IBRD and IDA	1,902,200	448,595	23.6	448,595	23.6
EXIMBANK	2,108,447	111,072	5.3	−73,290	−3.5
Grants[c]	*1,891,831*	*1,727,259*	*91.3*	*1,727,259*	*91.3*
Total	*11,286,993*	*4,761,846*	*42.2*	*4,321,603*	*38.3*

[a]Additional cost coefficient of 12.5 percent.
[b]Additional cost coefficient of 24 percent.
[c]Includes P.L. 480, Titles I, II, III, and grants made under AID, Peace Corps, and Inter-American Highway programs. See table II-3.

Appendixes to Chapter II

APPENDIX II-A: OPERATIONS IN LOCAL CURRENCY

Since certain operations carried out by AID and IDB involve situations which are difficult to solve with respect to the combination of local currencies of the borrowing countries and foreign currencies—in disbursements, in amortization and interest payments, and in contributions made by Latin American countries—it is appropriate to clarify how these are dealt with in this study.

1. *Loans granted through the Regular Operations Fund.* In this Fund, loans are granted in dollars and in the currency of the borrower country and should be serviced in the same currency in which disbursement was made. In order to determine the aid component for each operation, the methodology described for estimating the cost of loans was applied to the portion authorized in dollars. It was felt, however, that the portion authorized in the currency of the borrowing country did not have an aid component in this case, according to the definition set forth in chapter II.

2. *Loans granted through the Special Operations Fund of the IDB, and loans from AID payable in revalued local currency.* Loans authorized in the case of the Special Operations Fund of the IDB are disbursed in the currency of the borrowing country and in dollars. Amortization and interest payments for such loans may be made in the currency of the borrowing country at the country's option, except in the case of Mexico and Venezuela, which should make reimbursements in the currency received, i.e., in reimbursement terms similar to those established for loans made by the Regular Operations Fund. In determining the aid component, it was felt that the portion authorized in the currency of the country did not constitute aid as such. On the other hand, in estimating the aid component of that portion of the loan authorized in dollars, but which will be repaid in local currency,[1] a basic assumption was introduced according to which the local currency will be freely convertible until 1985, which is tantamount to paying an average amount of dollars callable in that year.[2]

---

[1] For the purposes of computation, it was assumed that all of the authorized countries would prefer making payments in local currency, since very few exceptions have been noted in this regard.

[2] "Average" means that the dollars would begin to be exchanged previously and that their median effect would occur in 1985. This assumption does not imply that the total amount of local currency would be convertible during that year. The assumption also covers the use of national currencies involving a commercial deviation and thus an opportunity cost in dollars. This would not be the case to the extent that such a use generates trade; however, acceptance of an intermediate situation would not entail significant changes in the computations, owing to the long amortization period assumed.

This assumption was based on the following considerations:

a. First of all, local currency held by the IDB is automatically revaluable, in order to maintain the equivalent amount in dollars (Article V, Section 3, of the Articles of Agreement).

b. Moreover, the IDB is authorized to grant loans in the currencies of other Latin American countries (Article V, Section 1, of the Articles of Agreement). At present, the Inter-American Development Bank is already using the currencies of Mexico and Venezuela for loans to other countries in the region, and it seems that it is its policy to broaden this procedure substantially by trying to include the currencies of all of the member countries.

c. Since the Declaration of the Presidents of America sets 1985 as the year in which the integration process is to culminate, the same year has been adopted for the purposes of computation, although obviously the choice of any other year would not alter the methodology used.

As indicated in the text, the effect of the basic assumption mentioned above with respect to computing the aid component may be considered as tantamount to an extension of the grace period to the "convertibility year." Nevertheless, such a grace period presents special features making it different from the usual one stipulated in loans, because of the fact that although the IDB recovers nonconvertible currency in the form of amortization and interest, according to this assumption it would re-lend such funds to the same country, until it is able to use them freely. In this manner, the funds accumulated to the credit of the IDB during the "convertibility year" would be equal to the amounts amortized, plus compound interest added since the amortization date, minus the balance of loans maturing.[3] With respect to the remainder maturing after the "convertibility year," these have been handled in a manner similar to the procedures followed in the case of loans repayable in United States dollars.

In the case of AID loans repayable in local currency, the amounts of which are revaluated in a manner similar to the procedure established for the Special Operations Fund of the IDB, the same procedure used by the latter was followed in accordance with the principles set forth in the preceding paragraphs.

3. *Loans granted by the Social Progress Trust Fund.* The procedure followed for the loans granted by this Fund was similar to the one indicated for the Special Operations Fund. As happens in the latter case, loans are disbursed in the currency of the country and in United States dollars, while

---

[3]The implicit assumption in this procedure is that payments for amortization and interest will be reinvested immediately at the same interest rate as in the original case.

the servicing of these loans (amortization plus interest) is made in the currency of the country. The only difference from the Special Operations Fund's procedure is that there is no maintenance of value clause covering balances in local currency held by the IDB. Nevertheless, this is not the equivalent of the nonreadjustable loans made in accordance with P.L. 480—according to statements made in chapter II—however, the exchange rate is determined at the time of payment. Thus, if as actually happens, the IDB makes another loan within a short period of time, losses incurred because of exchange-rate differences are minimized. Furthermore, pursuant to special authorization granted by the Board of Executive Directors in April 1967, local currencies received by this fund may be transferred to the Special Operations Fund as part of the loans granted by the latter; for hence the IDB has an additional instrument to protect itself against devaluation of balances in local currencies.

It should also be pointed out that in the three aforementioned Funds of the IDB, current expenditures of the IDB paid in local currencies of the borrowing countries are recorded. For the purposes of the computations set forth herein, this utilization of local currencies should be indicated in United States dollar equivalents, since if the IDB does not have these funds available, it must resort to the foreign exchange market. Nevertheless, since the necessary data were not available, and because of the additional problem caused when these expenditures finance technical assistance, these expenditures were not taken into account in this study.

APPENDIX II-B: MATHEMATICAL FORMULATION

DETERMINATION OF THE AID COMPONENT

The following equation[1] was used in order to determine the current values of the reimbursements:

$$VA = \frac{i}{q} L (1 - e^{-qG}) + \frac{i}{q} L_e^{-qG} + (1 - \frac{i}{q}) L \frac{e^{-qG} - e^{-qT}}{q (T - G)}$$

[1] For the basic equations, see J. Pincus, *Costos y beneficios de la ayuda: Análisis cuantitativo*, UNCTAD ID/B/C.3/38, New York, April 1967, annex, p. 4, and G. Ohlin, *Foreign AID Reconsidered*, Paris: OECD, 1966, pp. 101–3.

in which

i = rate of interest on the loan
q = discount rate
L = amount authorized for the loan
G = grace period, and
T = maturity date = G + amortization period,
VA = current value

The following equation was used for loans granted by AID, the interest rate for which is lower during the grace period:

$$VA = \frac{i_1}{q} L (1 - e^{-qG}) + \frac{i_2}{q} L\, e^{-qG} + (1 - \frac{i_2}{q}) L \frac{e^{-qG} - e^{-qT}}{q (T - G)}$$

in which

i_1 = interest rate during the grace period;
i_2 = interest rate during the amortization period.

In order to simplify the computations, it was assumed that the loans would be disbursed in their entirety as soon as authorized. Theoretically, it would be necessary to use the capitalized disbursement instead of the authorized amount.

The following equations were used for loans granted by the IDB:

i. Regular Operations Fund:

$$C_A = \frac{\Sigma (L_1 - VA_1) - A}{\Sigma L_T}$$

in which

C_A = aid component
L_1 = portion authorized in $
VA_1 = current amount of the portion authorized in $
L_T = total amount authorized ($ + local currency)
A = contribution in $ made by the country

ii. Special Operations and Social Progress Trust Funds

$$C_A = \frac{\Sigma\,(L_T - VA) - A}{\Sigma\,L_T}$$

in which

$$VA = [\,L\,(1 + i)^H - \frac{L\,(T - H)}{(T - G)}\,]\,e^{-qH} + {}_H\!\int^T [\,\frac{L}{T - G}$$

$$+ L_i\,(1 - \frac{t - G}{T - G})\,]\,e^{-qt}\,d_t$$

resulting in

$$VA = [\,L\,(1 + i)^H - \frac{L\,(T - H)}{T - G}\,(1 - \frac{i}{q})\,]\,e^{-qH}$$

$$+\,(1 - \frac{i}{q})\,L\,\frac{e^{-qH} - e^{-qT}}{q\,(T - G)}$$

in which the terms have been defined above, and H is equal to the number of the years elapsing between the loan authorization date and the convertibility year.

EFFECT OF TIED AID ON THE INTEREST RATE

The following equation[2] was used in order to determine the actual rate of interest, including the surcharge caused by the tying provision:

$$\frac{A_g}{1} = \frac{A + e^{-i'G}\,(1 - A) - e^{-i'T}}{i'}$$

in which

A = $(1 - e^{-i\,(T-G)})$
g = the relationship between the lowest prices quoted and the prices paid for tied aid. Both prices are based on f.o.b.
i' = actual rate of interest.

The other components have already been defined in item 1.

[2] For the original equation see Pincus, *Costos y beneficios de la ayuda*, annex p. 7.

CHAPTER III

Direct Foreign Investment

Taking into account the past and present importance of foreign private investment in the economic development of Latin America and in regional external transactions, this chapter endeavors to supplement, through its analysis, the examination of external public financing made in preceding pages. It should be noted, however, that available information on private investment is much less complete and reliable than data on the flow of public resources and, consequently, this study must be less conclusive.

SIZE OF FOREIGN INVESTMENT

It is very difficult to specify with any precision the total amount of foreign investments in Latin America, due to the lack of comparable information available in either the Latin American or the capital-exporting countries. Any estimate is still further complicated by the fact that the accounting value generally underestimates the market or replacement value of the investment.

Despite these reservations, mention should be made here of available estimates of this total value, in order to give an idea of its size. The IDB, in 1964,[1] estimated the accounting value of direct foreign investment in Latin America at approximately $12 billion to $13 billion. This figure can be compared with the $8.5 billion which, according to calculations by the United Nations, was the accounting value of foreign investment in Latin America at the beginning of World War I.[2] It should be remembered that between these periods a sizable share of European investment, especially from the United Kingdom, recorded a sharp drop in the level of assets because of the repatriation of capital in public services and railroads. Direct private investments by the United States, on the other hand, rose substantially between these two periods and significantly increased their share of the whole. At the beginning of World War I, this share is estimated at 20 percent of total foreign private investment in Latin America, while it currently represents approximately 70 percent.

[1] Inter-American Development Bank, *European Participation in Latin American Development Financing*, Washington, D. C., 1964.

[2] See United Nations, *Las Inversiones Extranjeras en América Latina*, 1955.

Given this unquestionable importance of United States investment in recent periods and considering the scant information available on investment by other countries, the analysis in the rest of this chapter will be confined almost exclusively to direct private investment originating in the United States, which, for the effects of the analysis presented here, is defined as United States participation in all companies of which at least 25 percent is owned by a United States resident, either a juridical or natural person.[3]

TRENDS BY COUNTRY AND SECTOR

The book value of United States investment has been increasing at an average rate of 4.6 percent during the present decade, that is, similar to that of the regional GDP (gross domestic product). This growth is less than that recorded for the 1950's, which was 7.3 percent, mainly because the book value of investments in petroleum showed virtually no increase between 1960 and 1967, in contrast to an average rise of almost 11 percent during the previous decade. United States investment during the present decade has been concentrated primarily in the manufacturing sector. For this sector, the average increase in book value was 9.4 percent during the period 1960–67, as compared to 6.6 percent a year between 1950–59.

Table III-1 shows the value of direct United States investment in the Latin American countries. It will be observed that in 1967 more than 60 percent of United States investment was concentrated in four countries: Argentina (10.6 percent), Brazil (13 percent), Mexico (13.1 percent), and Venezuela (25 percent). Chile, Colombia, and Peru accounted for approximately one-half of the remaining investment. This table also shows certain significant trends in the distribution of this investment by country during the past fifteen years.

First of all, it is evident that investment in "other countries"—countries where the size of direct investment is not large as compared to the total, although it may have a comparatively significant weight within the various economies—is expanding (from 13.6 percent in 1950 to 17.8 percent in 1967). Secondly, the value of investments in relation to the whole has also risen in Colombia, Peru, and Mexico. And finally, an opposite trend is apparent with regard to United States investment in Venezuela, Brazil, and Chile. In the case of Venezuela, the comparative decline is highly significant during

---

[3]In 1957, 85.4 percent of the book value of direct United States investment was derived from 2,313 companies at least 95 percent of which belonged to United States investors (U.S. Department of Commerce, *U.S. Business Investment in Foreign Countries*, Washington, 1960, p. 101, table 13). No later information is available. Under this classification, loans to a subsidiary by a parent company controlling more than 25 percent of its shares are computed as direct investment.

Table III-1. Book Value of United States Direct Private Investment in Latin America, by Country (in Millions of $)

Country	1950		1960		1965		1967[a]	
	Absolute	Relative	Absolute	Relative	Absolute	Relative	Absolute	Relative
Argentina	356	9.4	472	6.4	992	10.6	1,080	10.6
Brazil	644	16.9	953	12.8	1,074	11.4	1,326	13.0
Chile	540	14.2	738	9.9	829	8.8	878	8.6
Colombia	193	5.1	424	5.7	526	5.6	610	6.0
Mexico	415	10.9	795	10.6	1,182	12.6	1,342	13.1
Peru	145	3.8	446	6.0	515	5.5	605	5.9
Venezuela	993	26.1	2,569	34.6	2,705	28.8	2,553	25.0
Other countries	517	13.6	1,035	13.9	1,568	16.7	1,817	17.8
Total[b]	3,803	100.0	7,431	100.0	9,391	100.0	10,213	100.0

[a]Preliminary.
[b]Does not include Cuba.

Source: U.S. Department of Commerce, Survey of Current Business, various issues.

the present decade, due to amortization of the heavy investments made during the second half of the preceding decade, although with 25 percent of the United States investment in the region, it still accounted for the largest share in 1967.

Sectoral distribution of the total value of the United States investment is shown in table III-2 for the period 1929-67, indicating important changes in this distribution. In 1929, United States investment was located primarily in the sectors of mining, public services, and "other," which includes investments in the agricultural sector. This distribution varied considerably in subsequent years, when there was a marked trend in favor of the manufacturing sector, which in 1929 represented only 6.6 percent of the total value, increasing its share of the whole sharply to about 20 percent during the 1950's, probably as a result of the process of import replacement carried out in the larger countries of the region. The manufacturing sector has expanded still more rapidly in this decade, topping all other sectors, with about one-third of the total book value, in 1967. This recent increase is also partly the result of a continuation of import replacement in the region, and partly of the process of acquisition of existing national companies during the past few years, although the Secretariat has no figures to document this trend.

Participation by the commercial sector follows a course parallel to investments in manufacturing because of its close complementation with that sector. Accordingly, the relative share of the value of United States investment in commerce rose steadily, from 3.4 percent in 1929 to 11.8 percent in 1967. In contrast, investment in mining and refineries, especially during the present decade, reduced the comparative importance it held in 1929, although the decline is less abrupt than in the case of public services.

In examining the flow of new investment net of amortizations to Latin America and the reinvestment of profits, the new sectoral orientation of United States investment in the region is more clearly perceived. To this end, the respective comparison is presented in table III-3, which also illustrates more graphically the variation noted in sectoral distribution of United States investment in favor of manufacturing.

Finally, for an overall view of the major financing flows of the balance of payments relating to United States investment in the various sectors, table III-4 shows that, during the period 1950-67, net United States investment, including reinvested profits, amounted to $7.473 billion, while total profits generated, also including reinvested profits, aggregated $16.079.[4] In terms of

---

[4]These figures are for Latin America excluding Cuba. The table does not include the flow of funds from subsidiaries to the United States for royalties and other rights. This flow amounted to $1.033 billion (excluding Cuba but including other states not belonging to the OAS) for the period 1961-67.

Table III-2. Book Value of United States Direct Private Investment in Latin America, by Sector (in Millions of $)

Sector	1929 Absolute	1929 Relative	1950 Absolute	1950 Relative	1960 Absolute	1960 Relative	1965 Absolute	1965 Relative	1967[a] Absolute	1967[a] Relative
Mining and refineries	732	20.8	628	16.5	1,153	15.5	1,114	11.9	1,218	11.9
Petroleum	617	17.5	1,213	31.9	2,740	36.9	3,034	32.3	2,917	28.6
Manufacturing	231	6.6	726	19.1	1,499	20.2	2,745	29.2	3,301	32.3
Public services	887	25.2	656	17.2	820	11.0	596	6.3	614	6.0
Commerce	119	3.4	221	5.8	674	9.1	1,041	11.1	1,207	11.8
Others	933	26.5	367	9.7	546	7.3	861	9.2	956	9.4
Total[b]	3,519	100.0	3,803	100.0	7,431	100.0	9,391	100.0	10,213	100.0

[a]Preliminary.
[b]Excludes Cuba and other OAS nonmember states.

Source: U.S. Department of Commerce, Survey of Current Business, various issues.

Table III-3. Net Inflow of United States Direct Private Investment to Latin America[a] (in Millions of $)

Sector	1957[a]		1960		1965		1967	
	Absolute	Relative	Absolute	Relative	Absolute	Relative	Absolute	Relative
Mining and refineries	150	9.7	-70	-17.5	67	11.2	93	21.7
Petroleum	965	62.3	63	15.8	-37	-6.2	6	1.4
Manufacturing	166	10.7	208	52.0	411	69.0	259	60.4
Others	268	17.3	199	49.8	155	26.0	69	16.1
Total[b]	1,550	100.0	400	100.0	596	100.0	429	100.0

[a]Includes Cuba.
[b]Includes other agencies. Investment is given net of amortization.

Source: U.S. Department of Commerce, Survey of Current Business, various issues.

Table III-4. Direct Private United States Investment in Latin America,[a] 1950–67
(in Millions of $)

Sector	Direct Investments Receipts			Profits and Dividends		
	New Invest-ments	Rein-vested Profits	Total	Remitted[b]	Rein-vested	Total[c]
	(1)	(2)	(3)	(4)	(5)	(6)
Manufacturing						
1950–54	210	355	565	287	355	·641
1955–59	353	328	681	245	328	559
1960–64	516	505	1,021	370	505	865
1965–67[d]	495	435	930	410	435	832
1950–67[d]	1,574	1,623	3,197	1,312	1,623	2,897
Petroleum						
1950–54	–11	200	189	1,496	200	1,656
1955–59	1,370	161	1,531	2,173	161	2,326
1960–64	–169	128	–41	2,139	128	2,274
1965–67[d]	–156	40	–116	1,384	40	1,450
1950–67[d]	1,034	529	1,563	7,192	529	7,706
Commerce						
1950–54	104	92	196	107	92	198
1955–59	96	211	307	136	211	339
1960–64[e]	37	74	111	31	74	103
1965–67[e]	–	–	–	–	–	–
1950–67[e]	237	377	614	274	377	640
Other Industries						
1950–54	386	125	511	764	125	841
1955–59	429	179	608	907	179	1,008
1960–64	77	422	499	1,293	422	1,629
1965–67[d]	183	284	467	1,080	284	1,351
1950–67[d]	1,075	1,010	2,085	4,044	1,010	4,829
Total						
1950–54	690	773	1,463	2,654	773	3,343
1955–59	2,246	880	3,126	3,460	880	4,231
1960–64	461	1,130	1,591	3,833	1,130	4,871
1965–67[d]	524	769	1,293	2,872	769	3,634
1950–67[d]	3,921	3,552	7,473	12,819	3,552	16,079

[a]Excludes Cuba and other OAS nonmember states.

[b]Includes minor interest items.

[c]Does not include small interest remittances which are found in col. 4; because of this the sum of cols. 4 and 5 is slightly higher than col. 6. The U.S. Department of Commerce publishes these profit figures in the same form printed here.

[d]Preliminary.

[e]Beginning in 1961, commerce is included in "Other Industries."

Source: U.S. Department of Commerce, *Survey of Current Business*, various issues, and *Balance of Payments Statistical Supplement*, rev. ed., 1963.

net transfers and resources—that is, new investments net of amortization and actual profit remittances—the figures are $3.921 and $12.819 billion, respectively. Naturally, these figures should not be taken as the net contribution of direct United States private investment to the Latin American balance of payments, since they do not take into account such other factors as export value or the value of imports replaced. Moreover, it should be kept in mind that profits are a function of the value of total existing investments and not of the additional investment incrementing the invested value.

With regard to this last point, table III-5 shows the rate of earnings for United States companies on total investment and in the manufacturing and petroleum sectors. For the period 1951–67, the average profit for total United States investment was 13.4 percent on invested capital. The rate in the manufacturing sector was 10.5 percent, almost equal to that of the other sectors combined excluding petroleum, but that of petroleum amounted to 18.9 percent, the highest for any sector.[5]

INTERNAL EFFECTS OF DIRECT UNITED STATES PRIVATE INVESTMENT IN LATIN AMERICA

The actual importance of United States investment in Latin American economic development is difficult to pinpoint, since a wide range of factors, both positive and negative, is involved in its contribution to economic development that cannot be quantified numerically. Nevertheless, certain general observations on some aspects of its contribution to regional development can be stated.

Increased Production and Domestic Market Competition

As already noted, the structure of United States investment has gradually changed in recent years, gravitating toward the manufacturing sector. This change in the composition of foreign investment results partly from the gradual nationalization of the primary sectors and public services, but also from the entrance of foreign investment into the most dynamic sectors of the economy, which are the very industrial fields that, for reasons of technology,

---

[5]While it is true that the market value of United States investment may, on the average, exceed the book value, real profits are also underestimated because the accelerated depreciation, often authorized as an incentive to investment in Latin America, allows United States companies to repatriate funds as amortization that would otherwise be considered as profits. The Secretariat has no figures available to quantify the extent to which these flows could alter the real profit rate of United States investment in the region.

Table III-5. Direct Private United States Investment: Rate of Earnings[a] in Manufacturing and Petroleum Sectors and Total Investment, 1950-67 (in Millions of $ and Percentages)

Year or Period	Total			Manufacturing			Petroleum		
	Book Value	Profits	Rate of Earnings	Book Value	Profits	Rate of Earnings	Book Value	Profits	Rate of Earnings
1950	3,803			726			1,213		
1951	4,151	743	19.5	919	164	22.6	1,193	323	26.6
1952	4,679	757	18.2	1,088	151	16.4	1,352	355	29.8
1953	4,919	648	13.9	1,073	114	10.5	1,447	361	26.7
1954	5,048	649	13.2	1,163	118	12.1	1,438	355	24.5
1955	5,320	824	16.3	1,293	111	9.5	1,510	461	32.1
1956	6,083	925	17.4	1,450	117	9.8	1,871	525	34.8
1957	6,585	1,023	16.8	1,169	120	8.3	2,584	634	33.9
1958	6,894	714	10.9	1,210	98	8.4	2,709	391	15.1
1959	7,164	745	10.9	1,285	113	9.3	2,715	315	11.6
1960	7,431	829	11.6	1,499	146	11.4	2,740	345	12.7
1961	8,236	964	13.0	1,686	170	11.3	3,250	449	16.4
1962	8,424	1,010	12.3	1,893	167	9.9	3,159	490	15.1
1963	8,662	964	11.4	2,102	153	8.1	3,095	480	15.2
1964	8,894	1,104b	12.7	2,341	229b	10.9	3,102	510b	16.5
1965	9,391	1,170b	13.2	2,745	269b	11.5	3,034	496b	16.0
1966	9,826	1,261b	13.4	3,081	311b	11.3	2,897	479b	15.8
1967	10,213b	1,203b	12.2	3,301b	252b	8.2	2,917b	475b	16.4
1951-59	47,482	7,028	14.8	10,091	1,106	11.0	15,317	3,720	24.3
1960-67	68,028	8,505	12.5	16,632	1,697	10.2	23,992	3,724	15.5
1951-67	115,510	15,533	13.4	26,723	2,803	10.5	39,309	7,444	18.9

[a]Rate of earnings is defined in this table as the ratio between profits for each year and book value at close of the previous year.
[b]Preliminary.

Source: U.S. Department of Commerce, Survey of Current Business, various issues.

managerial capacity, and the amount of capital required, are less accessible to local investment and more attractive to foreign capital.

Table III-6 compares the growth indexes for the industrial product in four of the larger countries of the region during the period 1961–65 with the indexes for increased sales of manufacturing companies owned by the United States operating in those countries. Although these indexes are not fully comparable, their joint presentation strengthens the previous impression regarding the greater dynamism of the Latin American industrial subsector owned by United States companies.

Generally speaking, the comparatively scant information available appears to support the hypothesis that a polarization is taking place in Latin America within the industrial sector whereby Latin American firms are acquiring predominance in less sophisticated, established industries and technologies, while United States private investment—and probably that from other industrialized countries as well—is rapidly increasing its participation in certain dynamic industries that require a fairly high level of technological progress and are more important in determining the course of economic development.

The expansion of sales by United States companies appears to be concentrated in the local market rather than in export operations. It should be noted that, in the recent years for which information is available, the percentage of total sales of manufactures, by United States subsidiaries operating in Latin

Table III-6. Comparison between Industrial Product Index and Sales Index of United States–Owned Manufacturing Companies   *(1961 = 100)*

Country	1961	1962	1963	1964	1965
Argentina					
Industrial product	100.0	93.2	87.3	99.8	112.5
Sales by United States-owned manufacturing companies	100.0	96.0	100.9	131.9	166.3
Brazil					
Industrial product	100.0	108.1	107.8	113.3	109.2
Sales by United States-owned manufacturing companies	100.0	119.7	120.2	111.5	120.0
Mexico					
Industrial product	100.0	106.5	116.3	132.8	142.2
Sales by United States-owned manufacturing companies	100.0	119.8	136.5	175.4	186.8
Venezuela					
Industrial product	100.0	108.9	117.6	134.1	145.6
Sales by United States-owned manufacturing companies	100.0	101.3	121.3	148.0	164.5

Sources: U.S. Department of Commerce, *Survey of Current Business*, November 1966, and CIAP, country reviews.

America, which are earmarked for exportation dropped significantly, from 10 percent of the total in 1962 to 7.5 percent in 1965.[6]

The incomplete information on hand further indicates that the growing share of companies which are United States owned in the Latin American industrial product during the past few years results not only from the greater dynamism of those companies and of the subsectors in which they operate, but also from the acquisition of Latin American industrial companies by United States interests during these years.[7]

Financing of United States Private Enterprise in Latin America

One of the most important factors determining the advantageous competitive position of the foreign company over the national company is the better access enjoyed by the former to both domestic and external credit resources. The national commercial banks of the Latin American countries consider it extremely desirable to grant credit requests from United States subsidiaries, since they operate with broad guarantees from their parent companies or foreign banks and, because of the sizable volume of their banking operations, they are attractive clients. Moreover, the proliferation of branches of United States banks throughout the region during the last few years has enabled United States companies to establish financing ties in Latin American territory parallel to those which exist in their home offices in the United States.

During the period 1960–64, funds obtained from sources located in the Latin American countries through credits, loans, and self-financing represented slightly over 95.7 percent of the funds required by all United States companies in the region, a ratio that is reduced to slightly over 80 percent for industry, while net transfers of funds from the United States came to less than 5 percent and 20 percent, respectively, of total funds (see table III-7).

The increase in net funds obtained in Latin America, excluding those derived from profits and from provisions for depreciation and depletion, rose

---

[6] Based on data published by the U.S. Department of Commerce, *Survey of Current Business*.

[7] In a recent CIAP survey, many of the Latin American businessmen interviewed stated their concern over the recent trend toward entrance of foreign companies into activities already covered by national producers. See also E. Lízano F., "El Problema de las Inversiones Extranjeras en Centro América," *Revista del Banco Central de Costa Rica*, No. 67, Sept. 1966, p. 58: "Well known international firms such as Royal, Colgate-Palmolive, Procter & Gamble, National Biscuit, Grace and Co., Sterling Products, etc., these and many other companies whose names would comprise a lengthy list, have created serious problems for Central American producers of gelatin, toothpaste, detergents, biscuits, textiles, paints, cosmetics, pharmaceutical products, etc., to cite only a few products."

Table III-7. Sources and Uses of Direct Private United States Investment Funds in Latin America (in Millions of $)

Source and Use	Total					Manufacturing				
	1960	1961	1962	1963	1964	1960	1961	1962	1963	1964
Source										
Profits	789	874	1,016	980	1,123	170	178	203	201	286
Depreciation and depletion	522	611	581	577	608	80	105	111	125	180
Funds obtained in Latin America	314	186	225	146	490	277	206	150	175	425
Funds from United States	89	110	−21	206	20	125	86	154	158	155
Total	1,714	1,781	1,801	1,909	2,241	652	575	618	659	1,046
Use										
Plant and equipment	625	643	720	724	855	207	250	246	308	402
Inventories	124	37	75	135	191	126	60	95	115	195
Credits receivable	256	223	96	108	310	120	130	66	88	230
Other assets	25	144	180	92	160	125	49	86	75	124
Distributed profits	684	734	730	850	725	74	86	85	73	95
Total	1,714	1,781	1,801	1,909	2,241	652	575	618	659	1,046

Source: U.S. Department of Commerce, *Survey of Current Business*, November 1965.

during the period 1960–64 to almost equal the increase recorded in the major items of working capital—inventories and accounts receivable—of United States companies operating in the region, which tends to indicate that these United States subsidiaries resort to such local funds basically to finance the following costs.

Source of Funds	Total	Manufacturing
Net funds obtained in the Latin American countries (except profits, depreciation, and depletion)	1,361	1,233
Working capital	1,555	1,225
Inventories	562	591
Credits receivable	993	634

Source: Table III-7.

Most investment in plant and equipment is apparently financed with undistributed profits and the depreciation and depletion reserves generated internally by the United States subsidiaries themselves, with a smaller proportion of such financing corresponding to funds received from the United States (see table III-7).

The competitive advantage of the foreign company with regard to availability of credit resources increases when the recipient countries apply restrictive monetary and credit policies with a view to controlling price rises. Under these circumstances, and in addition to credit resources that may be attracted within the Latin American countries, the affiliates of foreign companies receive direct financial support from their parent companies and from the banks operating with them in their countries of origin.[8] This abundance of financial resources, at a time of very scant liquidity for the local companies, has on occasion favored acquisition of some of these national firms by foreign interests.

The competition between United States and national capital for control of markets, utilization of credit, and other fields does not mean that the net contribution of the United States capital is negative. But it does indicate that in avoiding competition, or in competing unsuccessfully with United States capital in a given activity, the local entrepreneur diverts resources and talent to other, probably less productive fields of activity, where United States capital does not compete. In substance, this represents a loss of productivity for local capital which, though compensated to some extent in terms of overall economic activity by the net contribution of United States capital,

[8] In the case of the great international corporations the transfer of financial resources is multilateral. Consequently, cases of financial transfers between subsidiaries of United States companies operating in Europe and in Latin America are common.

implies a redistributive effect of profits and losses between local and foreign capital.

Operating Expenses of United States
Private Companies in Latin America

For a better appreciation of the impact of United States enterprise, it is useful to observe the composition of its costs. Unfortunately, the most recent data available apply to 1957; nevertheless, it is advisable to analyze these expenditures (see table III-8).

The largest item corresponds to costs of materials and services, which accounts for 51.5 percent of current expenditures (40 percent if imported inputs are excluded). This percentage undoubtedly exerted a significant impact, considering that expenditures on goods and services have a derivative effect, through backward linkages, on the rest of the economy. However, the margin of utilization of expenditures on materials and services by the Latin American economies is probably still ample.

Next in importance (table III-8) is salaries and wages, accounting for 20 percent of the total cost of operations in that year. Finally, taxes paid by the companies represent 15.6 percent of total spending.

A comparison of amounts invested and employment by United States subsidiaries in Latin America with the corresponding figures for Europe reveals a significant fact, namely, according to available data for 1957—there are none for more recent years—the capital intensity of companies established in Latin America was higher than for those in Europe. This results partly from the peculiarities of petroleum investment, but the same was true for the aggregate of other activities, though the difference was less (see table III-9). This apparently indicates that absorption of employment by United States enterprises is lower, or at least was lower in 1957, than what could have been expected within the regional level of development.

CONCLUSIONS

The overall size and sectoral composition of flows of investment and profit resources, the recent trend toward concentration of foreign private investment in dynamic sectors apparently oriented toward the domestic market, competition for the domestic market and for local financing resources, and the other aspects of foreign private investment studied briefly in this chapter, together with others—such as the transfer of technology—not analyzed here because of insufficient information, underline the undoubted importance of this question to economic development of Latin America.

Table III-8. Current Expenditures of Private United States Companies in Latin America in 1967 (in Millions of $)

Expenditure	Total Cost	Materials and Services	Salaries and Wages	Depreciation and Depletion	Interest	Indirect Taxes	Income Taxes	Others and Unaffected Expenditures
Absolute	6,951	3,580	1,374	426	96	508	575	392
Relative	100.0	51.5[a]	19.8	6.1	1.4	7.3	8.3	5.6

[a]Approximately 40 percent of this percentage corresponds to national inputs and 11.5 percent to imported inputs.

Source: U.S. Department of Commerce, U.S. Business Investments in Foreign Countries, Washington, 1960, p. 116, table 29.

Table III-9. Capital Employment Ratios of United States Private Companies Operating in Latin America and Europe, 1957

Location of Company	Invested Value (Millions of $)	Employment (Thousands of Persons)	Invested Value/ Employment (Thousands of $ per Person Employed)
Subsidiaries in Latin America	7,434	939	7,917
Subsidiaries in Latin America (excluding petroleum and mining)	3,620	796	4,548
Subsidiaries in Europe	4,151	1,079	3,847

Source: U.S. Department of Commerce, *U.S. Business Investment in Foreign Countries,* Washington, D.C., 1960.

All indications are that this importance will increase as regional economic integration progresses. It is necessary to stress the need for Latin American countries to consider jointly a search for and implementation of formulas designed to facilitate the transfer of technology with all possible efficiency and the least possible cost to the recipient countries. The Latin American countries should also define a uniform policy which would allow them to take advantage of the prospective contributions of foreign enterprise while preventing such enterprise from absorbing most of the benefits of import replacement at the regional level entailed in the integration process.

CHAPTER IV

External Financing Requirements and Procedures

OBJECTIVES AND PROCEDURES EMPLOYED

This chapter aims to give an idea of the scope of domestic efforts and external financing required over the next few years to enable Latin American countries to attain at least the 2.5 percent growth in per capita product stipulated in the Charter of Punta del Este.[1] Certain aspects of the direction which the domestic effort should take and of the ways in which external assistance should be granted in order to achieve the stated goal are also indicated.

It should be emphasized that the basic assumption of attaining an average growth rate of 2.5 percent over extended periods implies that the projections given in this chapter should be considered as indications of the minimum levels of domestic effort and external cooperation to be programmed for the next decade and the years thereafter. Several countries of the region are in a position to achieve higher growth rates and have done so in recent years, while others will reach that stage during the next decade; for them, external cooperation needs may be greater than those stated here.

As a basis for the projections presented in this chapter, a system involving two gaps—savings and trade—has been used.[2] This method of projection has been utilized since it is already well known in Latin America through the application of similar procedures in recent years by UNCTAD, ILPES, ECLA, AID, the CIAP Panel of Experts, and Professor Hollis B. Chenery, in addition to calculations made in individual countries by national experts or foreign consultants. The two-gap method also makes it possible to set forth explicitly certain important relationships between domestic effort and external evolution. In countries where trade is the predominant gap, little progress can be

---

[1] The assumption of a uniform 2.5 percent growth in the per capita product for all the countries in the region is used in order to simplify the procedure, since different goals should, strictly speaking, be established according to the potential growth capacity of each country.

[2] According to the method employed, the dominant gap in each case will be equivalent to the balance-of-payments result for goods and services transactions, excluding financing services.

made in securing the resources necessary for development through measures aimed at increasing savings unless, at the same time or earlier, external resources are increased to the extent necessary by means of expanded exports or additional financing.

This chapter presents three alternative projections, all based on the same assumption of a 2.5 percent annual growth in the per capita product. The first, alternative A, basically projects the historic trend in terms of both savings and exports. The result, logically, is a gap represented by an increasing and extremely high level of resources that exceed the possibilities for financing through external credits and grants. Alternative B assumes a greater domestic effort designed primarily to expand exports and/or increase savings. This greater effort significantly reduces the resource gap in net terms. This alternative also assumes that average conditions of external financing will be maintained at levels similar to those prevailing in recent years, with the result that gross financing requirements will increase rapidly during the period and debt service will eventually absorb an excessively high share of foreign exchange earnings for most of the countries. Finally, alternative C, utilizing the same projections of the gap in real resources as alternative B, assumes that external financing conditions will be changed to permit maintenance of the debt-service/foreign-exchange-earnings coefficient at acceptable levels.

The chapter also proposes measures that would have to be adopted, at the inter-American and international levels, to ensure that external financing received by Latin America will be adjusted, in both amount and conditions, to the needs of the regional development process. Finally, the projections presented in this chapter do not attempt to predict accurately the external financing requirements of each individual country, since this would involve a much more profound study of various aspects of the strategy necessary to attain the desired objectives, including the sectoral and subsectoral levels. Despite the limitations inherent in any method such as the one used here, in basing projections on the most recent information available for each country and on fairly extensive historical series, the Secretariat expresses its confidence that these projections, for the region as a whole, constitute a reasonable approximation of the minimum external financing needs compatible with attainment of the minimum growth goal stipulated in the Charter of Punta del Este.

Appendix IV-A of this report describes in some detail the model of savings and trade gaps utilized in these projections. In drawing up this model considerable use has been made of background material from the recent study on the same topic by the CIAP Panel of Experts, as well as material from the latest CIAP country reviews. In the following pages, therefore, only very brief references are made to the procedure employed.

PROJECTIONS OF GROSS EXTERNAL FINANCING REQUIREMENTS

Projection of Historical Trends: Alternative A

Resource gap. This first alternative is based primarily on the projection of historical trends, especially with regard to the coefficient of savings and rate of export expansion,[3] as well as on achieving a growth of 2.5 percent in per capita product for all countries of the region. Table IV-1 compares the growth rate of the total product required to meet that goal for 1969–85 with the averages achieved during the period 1950–68 for each country in the

[3]In projecting the growth rate of exports for each country, account is also taken of the prospects for its major export products as indicated in the respective CIAP annual reviews.

Table IV-1. Growth of Gross National Product: Historic Rates and Requirements for Attaining Proposed Goal (in Percentages)

Country	Historic Rates						Required 1969–85a
	1950/52–1960/62		1960/62–1966/68		1950/52–1966/68		
	Total	Per Capita	Total	Per Capita	Total	Per Capita	Total
Argentina	3.4	1.4	2.8	1.2	3.2	1.4	4.0
Bolivia	0.2	-1.9	5.6	3.3	2.2	0.0	5.0
Brazil	5.9	2.9	4.2	1.5	5.3	2.3	5.4
Chile	3.6	1.2	4.5	2.0	4.0	1.6	4.8
Colombia	4.7	1.5	4.6	1.2	4.6	1.3	6.0
Costa Rica	6.9	3.1	6.6	2.8	6.8	3.0	6.5
Ecuador	5.2	2.2	4.9	1.5	5.1	1.9	5.9
El Salvador	4.7	2.0	5.8	2.7	5.1	2.2	5.9
Guatemala	3.9	1.0	6.3	3.3	4.8	1.8	5.5
Honduras	3.7	0.8	4.8	1.4	4.1	1.0	6.1
Mexico	5.9	2.8	6.8	3.3	6.2	3.0	6.0
Nicaragua	4.7	1.8	6.6	3.6	5.4	2.5	5.6
Panama	5.4	2.5	7.7	4.5	6.3	3.2	5.9
Paraguay	3.2	0.5	4.2	0.9	3.6	0.6	5.9
Peru	5.1	2.8	5.6	2.5	5.3	2.6	5.6
Dominican Republic	4.8	1.7	3.0	-0.3	4.1	1.9	6.1
Uruguay	1.8	0.3	0.1	-1.2	1.1	-0.3	3.8
Venezuela	6.9	3.1	4.9	1.6	6.2	2.6	6.1
Total	5.1	2.3	4.7	1.8	4.9	2.0	5.4

aProposed goal: 2.5 percent in per capita growth.

Sources: CIAP Panel of Experts, *La Brecha Externa de la América Latina*, December 1968. CELADE, *Boletín Demográfico*, October 1968. CIAP, country reviews.

region. As may be noted, the regional growth goal is set at 5.4 percent per annum, a level higher than the 4.7 percent average for this decade.

Table IV-2 gives the annual growth rate for exports during the same period. Also shown are the rates used in the projections made by Professor Chenery, and by the CIAP Panel of Experts, together with the rate used in the projection for both alternatives A and B. High and low rates are selected for each country under each of the three projections; those selected for use in this study represent an intermediate level between the ones utilized by Professor Chenery and those of the Panel of Experts. The "low" rate used in this work is almost equal, as an average for the region, to that attained in the years 1960–62/1966–68, although there are significant differences in the individual countries, since greater weight was given in each of them to recent trends and export market prospects observed in the cycle of country reviews.

Table IV-2. Growth of Exports of Goods and Services: Annual Historic and Projected Rates (in Percentages)

Country	Historic Averages			Projections		
	1950/1952–1960/1962	1960/1962–1966/1968	1950/1952–1966/1968	A	B	C
Argentina	4.2	3.1	3.8	2.9–3.7	5.0–7.0	4.0–
Bolivia	–0.9	10.7	3.3	1.0	5.0–6.0	4.0–7.3
Brazil	2.8	6.0	4.0	2.8–3.7	4.0–6.0	4.0–5.7
Chile	2.5	6.0	3.8	1.9–2.5	4.0–4.9	3.5–5.6
Colombia	3.5	1.4	2.7	2.7–3.6	8.0–10.1	3.5–5.3
Costa Rica	6.1	8.1	6.8	3.5–4.6	9.0–10.4	7.0–
Ecuador	7.5	3.2	5.9	3.4–4.4	4.0–5.5	3.0–6.4
El Salvador	7.0	6.5	6.8	3.7–4.9	5.8–6.8	5.5–7.1
Guatemala	5.8	11.5	7.9	3.4–4.5	9.0–11.4	6.5–
Honduras	1.5	9.1	4.3	1.9–2.5	6.0–7.3	5.0–6.7
Mexico	5.5	6.1	5.7	5.4–7.0	4.0–6.0	5.0–5.6
Nicaragua	6.3	11.1	8.1	3.4–4.4	6.0–7.6	6.0–7.3
Panama	3.6	10.4	6.1	1.4–1.9	6.5–7.5	6.5–
Paraguay	4.1	–0.5	2.3	0.5–0.7	7.1–8.0	1.0–7.3
Peru	9.7	4.8	7.8	5.2–6.8	6.0–7.5	5.0–6.2
Dominican Republic	5.3	–2.2	2.4	–	5.0–6.0	5.0–
Uruguay	0.2	3.8	1.5	–	3.0–6.5	3.0–
Venezuela	6.5	0.1	4.1	2.0–2.8	2.0–3.2	2.5–4.6
Total	4.8	4.0	4.5	3.2–4.3	4.7–6.4	4.1–5.4

Notes: Projections: A: Rates projected for 1962–75 by H. Chenery and A. Strout, *Foreign Assistance Economic Development*, AID Discussion Paper No. 7, June 1965.

B: Rates projected for 1969–73 by CIAP Panel of Experts, *La Brecha Externa de la América Latina.*

C: Rates projected in this study for 1970–85 are based on historic experience and long-range prospects.

Table IV-3 gives the results of this projection in terms of the resource gap in each country for the entire 1969–85 period, while table IV-4 indicates the figures corresponding to four selected years—1970, 1975, 1980, and 1985.

As observed in these tables, the size of the resulting gap is, obviously, excessively high and rapidly expanding; consequently, it does not appear compatible with a development strategy that must necessarily be directed toward helping the Latin American countries reach, as soon as possible, a stage of development in which their dependence on external financing in net terms would be reduced and eventually eliminated.

Table IV-3 also shows that, considering the 1969–85 period as a whole, and given the assumed growth of exports at an average rate similar to that recorded to date in this decade, the trade gap is dominant for all countries of the region—with a single exception, due to unusual behavior of the economy of that particular country in recent years. This implies that very little can be done to accelerate the development of most Latin American countries and to

Table IV-3. Cumulative Gaps for 1969–85 Using Alternative A (in Millions of $)

Country	Dominant Gap[a]		Algebraic[c]
	Positive[b]		
Argentina	C	–	–6,886
Bolivia	C	2,656	2,656
Brazil	C	8,788	8,788
Chile	C	5,310	5,310
Colombia	C	4,313	4,313
Costa Rica	C	174	170
Ecuador	C	2,069	2,069
El Salvador	C	1,550	1,550
Guatemala	C	181	175
Honduras	C	771	771
Mexico	C	4,527	4,527
Nicaragua	C	1,789	1,789
Panama	C	111	–61
Paraguay	C	1,427	1,427
Peru	C	6,237	6,237
Dominican Republic	A	1,594	1,594
Uruguay	C	165	165
Venezuela	C	3,208	–1,342
Total		44,870	33,252

[a]C (trade) or A (savings) were assigned to the previously predominating (in size) positive gaps throughout the period. The larger of the two gaps is construed to be dominant in each case. For a further breakdown, see appendix IV-B.

[b]Sum of resource deficits, not considering possible surplus years.

[c]Algebraic sum of all annual results obtained in calculations for each country, including both deficits and surpluses.

Table IV-4. Projected Resource Gap for Latin America in Selected Years Using Alternative A

Country	1970		1975		1980		1985	
	Dominant Gap	Millions of $	Dominant Gap	Millions of $	Dominant Gap	Millions of $	Dominant Gap	Millions of $
Argentina	C	-309	C	-376	C	-443	C	-537
Bolivia	C	70	C	122	C	191	C	281
Brazil	C	119	C	337	C	670	C	1,149
Chile	A	110	A	183	C	394	C	693
Colombia	C	163	C	209	C	286	C	417
Costa Rica	C	15	C	14	C	8	C	-4
Ecuador	C	29	C	81	C	157	C	267
El Salvador	C	30	C	66	C	115	C	183
Guatemala	A	20	C	13	C	9	C	-5
Honduras	C	15	C	33	C	57	C	91
Mexico	C	143	C	195	C	307	C	516
Nicaragua	C	47	C	83	C	129	C	186
Panama	C	19	C	8	C	-11	C	-45
Paraguay	C	36	C	64	C	103	C	155
Peru	A	151	C	259	C	457	C	728
Dominican Republic	A	61	A	80	A	107	A	143
Uruguay	A	5	A	7	C	8	C	25
Venezuela	A	-652	C	-388	C	147	C	958
Total countries with gap		1,033		1,754		3,145		5,792
Algebraic total		72		990		2,691		5,201
Algebraic total excluding Argentina		381		1,366		3,134		5,738

Note: (–) means surplus of resources; C: trade; A: savings.

[a] Although strictly speaking only the countries with positive gaps should be considered, the rest of this chapter uses certain countries with negative gaps (surplus of resources) for some years since projections for the countries still show balance-of-payments deficits on current account requiring net external financing.

Source: Appendix IV-B.

reduce, within a prudent period, their dependence on external financing, unless a sizable increase is achieved in exports and/or import replacement through domestic efforts aimed at this objective and through improvement of the external markets for regional export commodities.

Financing gap. The projections on dominant resource gaps in the various countries of Latin America, prepared in accordance with the parameters observed in the past and assuming a prudent evolution of exports of goods and services also consistent with historic experience, indicate an excessive rise in the amount of resources required to attain and maintain per capita income growth at the rate of 2.5 percent comtemplated in the Charter of Punta del Este.

As shown in table IV-5, within the context of these assumptions, such shortages of real resources would be twenty times the current levels by 1985, rising from a projected level equivalent to $329 million for 1970 to $5.863 billion at the end of the following fifteen years. In other words, the volume required under these circumstances would be equivalent to nearly $2.4 billion a year from 1969 to 1985. These figures do not consider Argentina, which throughout the entire period would have surplus resources available for achieving the proposed growth goal and could, consequently, attain a higher

Table IV-5. Latin America: Projected Resource and Financing Gaps Using Alternative A[a] (in Millions of $)

Resource and Financing Item	1970	1975	1980	1985	1969–85
Exports of goods and services	13,579	16,590	20,351	25,022	312,096
Dominant resource gap[b]	329	1,353	3,167	5,863	40,425
Receipts net of factors	2,293	2,409	2,490	2,627	41,536
Interest	504	329	191	90	4,913
Profits	1,789	2,080	2,299	2,537	36,629
Gap on current account	2,622	3,762	5,657	8,490	81,961
Amortization	947	685	501	407	10,877
Direct investment	736	898	1,101	1,365	17,102
Net capital requirements	2,833	3,549	5,057	7,532	75,736
Amortization of new debt	–	485	2,078	5,202	26,738
Interest on new debt	255	1,182	2,687	5,065	34,478
Gross capital requirements	3,088	5,216	9,822	17,799	136,952
Coefficient of service[c]	12.5	16.2	26.8	43.0	24.7

[a]Excludes Argentina, which would have a surplus of resources available in all years during 1969–85.

[b]Figures under this heading do not coincide exactly with the last line of table IV-4 because table IV-5 includes the gaps for Haiti, and Trinidad and Tobago, calculated by methods different from those used for the other countries in table IV-4 (see appendix IV-B).

[c]Service on existing debt and debt to be contracted as percentage of exports of goods and services.

rate of growth. In contrast, they envisage the situation of countries such as Panama, Trinidad and Tobago, and Venezuela, which alternated between recorded surpluses and deficits during the period. Inclusion of the surpluses slightly moderates the figures noted, which would otherwise be still more exorbitant.

The projections for dominant resource gaps have been integrated with projections of financial flows abroad. In other words, consideration has been given to payments of interest and amortization on the external debt existing at the end of 1968, and the flows of direct foreign investment and remittances of profits abroad have also been projected. This gives net external financing requirements, that is, in excess of payments for interest and amortization entailed by this new debt. In order to estimate the volumes of total gross financing required, it has been assumed that the conditions of this new financing would continue to be similar to those obtained by the various Latin American countries in the recent past from international financing agencies. These conditions, which would be more favorable than those actually obtained at present, taking into account the terms of suppliers' financing, would signify an average for Latin America of 4.8 percent in annual interest and growth and amortization periods of four and sixteen years, respectively (see table IV-5).

Even on these terms, given the level that would be reached by the resource gap, the growth financing requirements of the Latin American countries, excluding Argentina, would exceed the possibilities of any conceivable financial scheme for the next twenty years. These requirements, estimated at about $3 billion by the beginning of the next decade, would rise to almost $18 billion in 1985, representing more than $8 billion a year as an average for the entire period. Moreover, this would imply that the burden of external debt service would more than triple by the end of the period, reaching 43 percent of the value of exports.

In examining the evolution of the main variables in the different countries—the individual projections for which are presented in appendix IV-B—it is apparent that, with the exception of Argentina and Panama, their continued development within the framework of historic trends and of current external financing conditions would make it impossible to achieve the economic growth goal adopted, either because of the improbability of procuring the volume of financing resources required and/or because debt service would create intolerable balance-of-payments difficulties. Consequently, if the proposed growth is to be attained alternative courses of action must be proposed from the standpoints of both the resource and financing gaps.

The evolution projected would signify an increase in the external debt service coefficient during the period 1969 to 1985 by amounts ranging from duplication during the period, in the case of Mexico, to an increase eight and nine times over, in the cases of El Salvador and Ecuador, and up to ten and twenty times over in Paraguay and Venezuela. An apparent exception to this behavior is observed in Brazil, whose coefficient would rise from 21 to 25 percent between 1970 and 1985. Quite apart from the international liquidity problems this would involve for Brazil, the volume of financing required, $2.126 billion in 1985, makes it impossible to continue to accept the status quo. The results of projections for Venezuela, at first glance incredible, can be explained in part by the predicted deterioration in its current surplus of resources, which, if the projected trend is maintained, would be transformed into a deficit gap beginning in 1979, owing to the limited outlook for petroleum earnings and to the expansion of imports necessary in order to achieve the proposed improvement of income, given the country's high rate of population expansion. Contributing significantly to these trends would be the high volume of profit remittances; as a result, although the country will have a surplus of resources, increasing amounts of net external financing will be required starting immediately.

Graph IV-1 shows more clearly the implications of alternative A with reference to both the resource gap and gross capital requirements.

Reduction in Resource Gaps: Alternative B

Proposed policies and predicted effects. The preceding section has shown that the projection of resource and financing gaps based on historic behavior results in a nonfinanciable situation because of the heavy volumes of capital required and the possible balance-of-payments problems entailed. Consequently, policies must be designed to reduce both the resources and financing gaps. This section proposes policies aimed at reducing the resources gap and quantifies their possible effects. No detailed methodological explanation of the procedure used is presented here but a description appears in appendix IV-A. Along general lines, the proposed policies are based on reallocation of investment toward sectors directly contributing to a reduction of the trade gap, either through replacement of imports and/or expansion of exports, as well as on the generation of greater domestic savings.

Although the changes that have taken place in the relationships between trade and savings gaps throughout the projected period make it difficult to group the countries, four types of countries have been identified, taking into account the characteristics occurring most frequently during the period 1969–85. The first group (group A, table IV-6) contains those countries showing a deficit in the trade gap simultaneously with a surplus in domestic savings. For these countries, general policies were proposed in the projection

Graph IV-1. Latin America: Resource Gap and Gross Capital Requirements, Alternative A (in Millions of $)

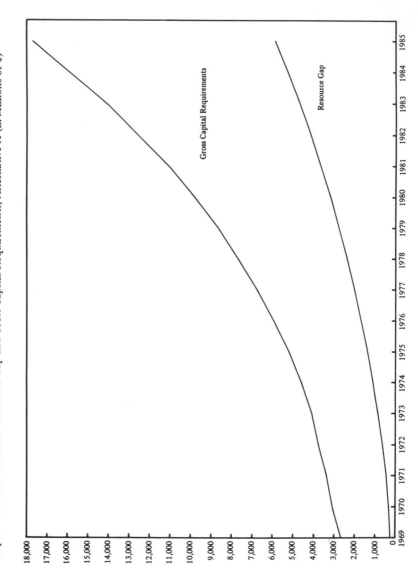

Table IV-6. Latin America: Reduction of Resource Gap (in Millions of $)

Country	Original Dominant Gap Positive	Original Dominant Gap Algebraic	Reduced Dominant Gap Positive	Reduced Dominant Gap Algebraic	Investment in Reduction of Trade Gap Absolute	Investment in Reduction of Trade Gap % of Total Investment	Alternative Effects on Trade Decrease in Imports	Alternative Effects on Trade Annual Growth of Exports
Group A								
Brazil	8,788	8,788	917	917	4,642	4.4	13.3	5.7
Colombia	4,313	4,313	1,461	1,461	1,505	5.7	13.4	5.3
Costa Rica	174	170	174	170	–	–	–	–
Ecuador	2,069	2,069	240	240	798	14.2	24.6	6.4
Guatemala	181	175	181	175	–	–	–	–
Honduras	771	771	141	141	236	13.8	13.5	6.7
Mexico	4,527	4,527	997	997	1,486	1.7	5.1	5.6
Panama	111	-61	111	-61	–	–	–	–
Venezuela	3,208	-1,342	–	-11,520	6,606	8.7	19.4	4.6
Group B								
Bolivia	2,656	2,656	1,203	1,203	1,187	28.6	21.4	7.3
Chile	5,310	5,310	1,311	1,311	3,465	10.9	12.8	5.6
El Salvador	1,550	1,550	474	474	584	13.4	12.8	7.1
Nicaragua	1,789	1,789	1,062	1,062	546	15.2	9.7	7.3
Paraguay	1,427	1,427	683	683	486	16.6	30.1	7.3
Peru	6,237	6,237	4,205	4,205	2,213	8.8	6.3	6.2
Uruguay	165	165	165	165	–	–	–	–
Group C								
Dominican Republic	1,594	1,594	513	513	–	–	–	–
Group D								
Argentina	–	-6,886	–	-513	–	–	–	–
Total	44,870	33,252	13,838	1,623	23,754	5.3	9.6	5.4

[a]For the methods followed, see appendix IV-A.

[b]To reduce the gap by the desired margin, projected exports would have to be increased by 5.4 percent a year as a regional average. Alternatively, projected imports would have to be reduced by the percentages indicated or export expansion and import replacement combined in such a way as to obtain, in net terms, the desired effects on the trade balance.

to reduce the trade gap with a view to its elimination by 1985. An exception within this group is Venezuela, for which the objective postulated was achievement of a surplus in the trade gap in order to offset the influence of profit remittances by petroleum companies on the predictable balance-of-payments position. The second group (group B, table IV-6) is composed of countries with a dominant trade gap combined with a domestic savings deficit. For these countries, the goal proposed was equalization of the gaps toward the end of the period, although in some of them (Chile and Paraguay), since these policies were insufficient, simultaneous reductions in both gaps were projected. The remaining two groups are composed of one country each. Group C represents the case of the Dominican Republic, a country revealing a dominant savings gap together with a trade deficit, for which a policy designed to equalize both gaps by 1985 was proposed. Finally, Argentina, the only country with a surplus of resources in both gaps throughout the period, constitutes group D. These surplus resources appear to suggest that Argentina would be able to expand at a higher than projected rate and would probably be able to achieve 3.5 percent a year in growth of the per capita product.

As shown in table IV-6, reduction in the cumulative positive gaps as a result of the proposed policies would amount to $31 billion, that is a cutback from $44.9 billion—the cumulative gap projected in alternative A—to $13.8 billion. Total investment earmarked for the sectors of import replacement and/or export expansion would amount to $23.8 billion, with Brazil, Chile, and Venezuela accounting for more than two-thirds of this amount.

Furthermore, the investment allocated for reducing the trade gap averaged 5.3 percent of total projected investment for all the countries considered, ranging from only 1.7 percent in the case of Mexico to 28.6 percent for Bolivia. Although no attempt was made to distribute the effect of the investment earmarked for reducing the trade gap between exports and imports, the limits within which this effect would be located are determined in table IV-6. Accordingly, if all of the investment is utilized to replace imports, this would entail a reduction of 9.6 percent in the import level. If, on the other hand, the entire investment is allocated to export sectors, exports would expand at a rate of 5.4 percent per annum. In view of the slim margin of import replacement at the national level apparently prevailing in most of the Latin American countries, it is estimated that the regional rate required as a minimum increase in exports is very close if not equal to the above-mentioned rate of 5.4 percent a year. This projection has not taken into account the import replacement at the regional level that should result from the process of integration; it is very possible that, at the level of individual countries, both export and import requirements will have to reach higher levels than those indicated here.

For all the countries of the region, except Argentina, the projection resulted in a significant increase in the coefficient of savings, as compared to
that projected, according to historic trends, under alternative A. For almost
all countries, this increase would signify a utilization of potential savings that
would be frustrated unless exports were expanded by at least the projected
margin, and for three of them—Chile, Paraguay, and the Dominican
Republic—it was necessary to postulate in *ex ante* increase in the savings rate,
that is, in the potential savings of those countries.

Financing gap. Assuming that the Latin American countries succeed in
making the larger effort programmed, the over-all gap in real resources for the
region would be considerably diminished (see table IV-7). The scope of the
proposed effort is more clearly apparent if Venezuela and Trinidad and
Tobago are excluded, since the definition of gap used in this study excludes
remittances of profits from direct foreign investment, while for these countries resource requirements are determined basically by the size of direct
profit remittances on foreign investments in activities relating to petroleum.[4]
In order to reduce their external financing requirements, these countries

[4]See appendix tables IV-C-18 and IV-C-20.

Table IV-7. Latin America: Projected Resource and Financing Gaps Using Alternative B[a]
(in Millions of $)

Resource and Financing Item	1970	1975	1980	1985	1969–85
Exports of goods and services	13,753	17,579	22,858	29,779	343,580
Dominant resource gap	233	56	-134	-439	-695
Gap on current account	2,526	2,465	2,356	2,188	40,841
Net capital requirements	2,737	2,251	1,746	1,231	34,632
Amortization of new debt	–	477	1,606	3,196	19,282
Interest of new debt	258	963	1,737	2,601	22,059
Gross capital requirements	2,995	3,691	5,089	7,028	75,973
Coefficient of service[b]	12.4	14.0	17.7	21.1	16.6
Dominant resource gap excluding Trinidad and Tobago and Venezuela	890	882	680	276	12,414

[a]Excluding Argentina.
[b]Amortization and interest on existing debt and debt to be contracted as percentage
of exports of goods and services.

Source: Appendix IV-C.

would need to attain heavy surpluses in that gap which distort the significance of the over-all concept for the region.[5] Excluding the two countries, it
is apparent that the resource gap would gradually decline from $890 million
in 1970 to $276 million in 1985. The average gap during the period, there-
fore, would drop to $730 million from the nearly $2.5 billion indicated in the
first projection of the gap for all of Latin America, excluding Argentina,
Venezuela, and Trinidad and Tobago.

This new estimate of the shortages of real resources has been integrated
with a projection of gross financing requirements that would be necessary to
cover the shortages of domestic funds. It has also been assumed, as in the first
projection, that the conditions of the new financing would be the same as
those recently obtained by Latin America from international financing agencies. Moreover, the projected flow of direct investments and profit remittances on investments remains unchanged at the same level as in alternative A,
and the projection of service payments on existing debt at the end of 1968 is,
of course, also included.

As shown in table IV-7, the reduction in resource gaps would lead to a
significant decline in gross growth-financing requirements; these requirements
would amount to $7.028 billion in 1985 and close to $4.469 billion as an
annual average during the period—almost 50 percent less than those deriving
from the first projection.

However, despite the size of the domestic effort programed, which would
result in declining resource gaps throughout the period cumulatively totaling
70 percent less than the original figure, the region would continue to need
external financing in rapidly increasing volumes (at an average rate of 5.5
percent a year between 1970 and 1985). This would also lead to a continuing
excessive increase in the regional coefficient of external debt service rising
from about 12 percent in 1970 to 21 percent toward the end of the period.
In addition, the over-all volume of gross financing required would continue to
far exceed any flow of funds that could reasonably be expected.

Examining the effects of gap reduction with regard to most financing
needs for the several countries, on the assumption that such financing would
continue to be granted on current terms, it is also observed (table IV-8) that,
except in the case of Brazil, the rest of the countries[6] would continue to

---

[5]Otherwise, it would be pointless for the projection of table IV-7 to show a surplus
of resources beginning in 1980, since it would be more logical to propose a higher rate of
growth for the region as a whole.

[6]With the exception of Costa Rica, Guatemala, Panama, and Uruguay; that is, those
countries which, under the assumptions adopted for these projections, would encounter
no significant restrictions with regard to resources and/or would have acceptable external
trade positions at the close of the period.

Table IV-8. Alternative B

Country	Gross Capital Requirements (Millions of $)			Coefficient of Service[a] (Percent)	
	1970	1985	Annual Average 1969–85	1970	1985
Bolivia	76	168	115	11.4	24.0
Brazil	532	615	513	20.5	12.7
Chile	391	1,121	681	17.2	38.6
Colombia	230	299	259	11.2	19.0
Costa Rica[b]	44	68	54	11.4	10.4
Dominican Republic	60	221	120	8.6	29.0
Ecuador	62	149	96	10.4	26.1
El Salvador	33	110	66	4.4	13.6
Guatemala[b]	52	98	68	8.9	10.9
Haiti	21	41	16	2.1	20.9
Honduras	30	69	47	5.6	13.8
Mexico	671	1,634	1,022	17.2	27.0
Nicaragua	66	207	119	7.8	19.8
Panama[b]	39	5	29	3.7	3.6
Paraguay	43	119	74	20.3	58.3
Peru	360	661	530	15.0	22.2
Trinidad and Tobago	21	7	9	3.3	3.5
Uruguay[b]	59	102	58	20.5	18.7
Venezuela	224	1,335	587	3.4	22.5
Total	2,995	7,028	4,469	12.4	21.1

[a] Amortization and interest on existing and contractable external debt as percentage of exports of goods and services.
[b] Results of first projection.

Source: See appendix IV-C.

require high and increasing amounts of financing, leading in all cases to an evolution of the debt service coefficient undoubtedly entailing serious balance-of-payments difficulties.

Reduction in Financing Gap: Alternative C

Reduction of the predominant resource gap, while a necessary condition, is not in itself sufficient in most countries to achieve a projection which could be financed without balance-of-payments problems. This section proposes alternative conditions for the additional financing that call for a softening of current interest rates together with longer grace periods and easier amortization terms. As in alternative B, work was done at the level of each country— see appendix IV-B—by endeavoring to determine the necessary conditions and amounts of additional financing required, taking into account the coefficient of creditworthiness (service on existing and uncontracted debt as a percentage of exports of goods and services), and the degree of comparative development in each country. Finally, total projections for the region as a whole were formulated by totaling the results obtained in each country.

As shown in table IV-9, the additional gross financing required by Latin America during the period 1969–85 as indicated by this projection is much lower than the needs presented in projecting historic trends and in reducing the resource gap. The $3.8 billion annual average that would be needed by Latin America compares very favorably with the $8 billion a year resulting from alternative A. This amount, which appears to be financially possible, combined with favorable conditions would make it possible to achieve the proposed goal without creating balance-of-payments liquidity problems.

Employing the indicator commonly accepted by financing agencies to evaluate the degree of solvency in each country, that is, coefficient of debt service to exports, it is apparent that limits close to those of the historic period are observed, producing a growth of 12 to 15 percent between 1970 and 1985. With regard to the determination of gross financing needs, annual requirements would point upward, as a result of financing the service costs on new debts alone, while the projected domestic effort would lead to a surplus of resources that would contribute in part to meeting financial needs.[7]

Finally, the necessary conditions of the additional financing required, taking into account the conditions established for each country, indicate that, on the average, such financing should be supplied at an interest rate of close to 4.5 percent, with a grace period of six years and amortization term of twenty-three years. These conditions lead to an aid component of over 35 percent, implying a slightly lower coefficient than that observed during the period 1961-67.[8] However, the estimate of the aid component of external financing received by Latin America includes only the financing granted by the United States and international agencies with headquarters in Washington, while the projected aid component refers to the total financing required. Consequently, it is more accurate to compare the amounts of aid received with those projected.[9] In this connection, it is estimated that Latin America

---

[7] As noted, while the surplus of resources derives from the inclusion of Trinidad and Tobago and Venezuela, their exclusion transforms this result into a deficit which will, however, decline rapidly throughout the period. The resource gap for 1985 is only 30 percent of that for 1970.

[8] See chap. II of this report. A discount rate of 8.5 percent was used for this calculation.

[9] This comparison assumes that the financing not included in the calculations of the historic period, that is, supplier credits and, to a lesser extent, financing from European governments, did not represent aid.

Table IV-9. Latin America: Projected Resource and Financing Gaps Using Alternative C[a]
(in Millions of $)

Resource and Financing Item	1970	1975	1980	1985	Cumulative Total 1970–85
Exports of goods and services	13,753	17,579	22,858	29,779	330,532
Dominant resource gap	233	56	-134	-439	-987
Net capital requirements	2,737	2,251	1,746	1,231	32,003
Amortization of new debt	–	259	956	1,083	11,108
Interest on new debt	219	839	1,488	2,180	18,791
Gross capital requirements	2,956	3,349	4,190	5,214	61,902
Coefficient of services	12.1	12.0	13.7	15.0	13.3

[a]Excludes Argentina.

Source: See appendix IV-C.

would need to increase its annual aid component from $754 million a year received during the period 1961–67 to $1.33 billion a year during the projected period, if the proposed growth goals are to be achieved.[10]

The projection presented in table IV-9 results from totaling the projections for each country, with the assumption that new debts would be contracted under similar conditions for the entire projection period. However, evolution of the resource gap in each country, with higher deficits at the beginning of the period, leads to the assumption that softer conditions are required in the first year, gradually hardening during the period. If we accept the conditions derived from the calculation by country as an average for the entire period and make a probable distribution of their evolution taking into account the foregoing considerations, the gross requirements to be covered would be as shown in table IV-10. According to this table, gross annual requirements would decrease slightly as compared to calculations for alternative C (see table IV-9) by $3.6 billion a year. Since the average component of required aid remains unchanged at about 35 percent, the annual amount of this component is close to $1.26 billion.

[10] The $1.33 billion figure is obtained by application of the aid component required (35 percent) to the $3.8 billion estimated as necessary for each year. For calculation of the $754 million, see chap. II.

Table IV-10. Latin America: Projected Resource and Financing Gaps Using Alternative C Revised (in Millions of $)

Item	1970	1975	1980	1985	Cumulative Total 1970–85
Net capital requirements[a]	2,737	2,251	1,746	1,231	32,003
Amortization of new debt[b]	–	–	567	1,252	6,448
Interest on new debt[b]	232	857	1,572	1,948	19,043
Gross capital requirements	2,969	3,108	3,885	4,431	57,494
Coefficient of service	12.2	10.6	12.4	12.4	12.0

[a]Excludes Argentina.
[b]The following conditions were assumed:
  1970–75 interest rate = 4.1, grace period = 7 years, amortization period = 26 years.
  1976–80 interest rate = 4.5, grace period = 6 years, amortization period = 23 years.
  1981–85 interest rate = 5.0, grace period = 4 years, amortization period = 17 years.

Finally, comparing gross requirements in 1985 with those for 1970, we can differentiate countries that would require current amounts from others which, in contrast, would diminish their gross requirements or maintain levels similar to those for 1979.[11] The results obtained for each country appear to follow a pattern based on the degree of comparative development. In this connection, the projections appear to underline the need for furnishing greater support in terms of financing to those countries with a lesser degree of development. Exceptions to this apparent trend are Venezuela, Mexico, and Chile, which, despite their comparatively high income level within the region, would require larger volumes and more favorable conditions during the next few years. The first two have traditionally received limited amounts of external financing on concessionary conditions, while Chile, in contrast, has been the country which has made the greatest use of external resources in the past. For the projected period, the three countries would require increasing amounts of financing. The rate of expansion of Venezuela's demands locate it, in terms of the need to improve conditions of the external financing received, in the same group as the less-developed countries of the region. Basically this is a result of the low initial level of external financing, which coincides with the comparatively unfavorable prospects for evolution of its petroleum exports and the high incidence of profit remittances by petroleum companies. Despite the domestic effort proposed for this country, which

[11]See the individual projections for each country in appendix IV-C.

would enable it to rise from a predicted deficit of $958 million in 1985 to a surplus of about $600 million, Venezuela must contract debts in the first years of the projected period, which will subsequently exert an effect on the corresponding amortization and interest payments. A similar situation occurs in Mexico, where the reduced level is combined with short-term balance-of-payments problems that will involve this country in a sizable debt. Finally, Chile, for which balanced resources are predicted in 1985, reveals growing needs owing to projected indebtedness until such time as the necessary investments begin to show their effects in reducing the resource gap.

With regard to the financing conditions required,[12] there is also a direct relationship between the country's degree of development and the "softness" of the financing. This results partly from the fact that the development level was taken into account in proposing conditions but also from consideration of the balance-of-payments position in each country. The relationship between the aid component and the degree of development has been so carefully observed in the past that the present study aims only at improving general conditions for all countries while maintaining the previous distribution. Apparently the only country that would move from the normal (hard) conditions group to the intermediate group is Uruguay, which though able to bear an indebtedness on current terms at the beginning of the decade, will require preferential treatment for the projected period in order to avoid generating pressures on the balance of payments.

Finally, evolution of the coefficient of solvency between 1970 and 1985 indicates that some of the countries with higher service coefficients, such as Brazil and Uruguay, could reduce those levels if the necessary financing is obtained on the conditions outlined here. In contrast, Chile, Colombia, and Peru, with a comparatively high coefficient of services in 1970, will still reveal a moderate increase. Likewise, Mexico and Venezuela will record a higher coefficient of services in 1985.

Graph IV-2 illustrates more clearly the implications of alternatives B and C with reference to the reduction of the resource gap and introduction of more favorable conditions for new indebtedness.

DETERMINATION OF THE GAP AND ITS POSSIBLE FINANCING[13]

Projection of Foreseeable Financing and its Conditions

So far, after reducing the resource and financing gaps by proposing policies related to the major macroeconomic variables in each country and indicating

[12] See tables by country in appendix IV-C.

[13] Throughout this section, totals for Latin America exclude Argentina, which is not expected to require external financing on noncommercial conditions.

Graph IV-2. Latin America: Resource Gap, Alternative B (with and without Trinidad–Tobago and Venezuela), and Gross Capital Requirements, Alternatives B and C (in Millions of $)

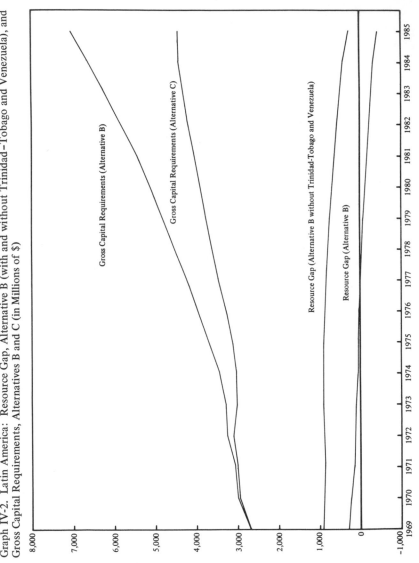

the need for improved external financing conditions in order to prevent balance-of-payments problems, we now have to determine gross capital requirements. This section aims at comparing this projection of needs with an autonomous projection of available funds by source, and it includes certain hypotheses about the composition of the proposed policies. The gap, and other possible alternatives for its financing, will be determined in a later section.

Table IV-11 projects foreseeable external funds for the period 1970–85, incorporating certain policies with regard to both volumes and conditions. The following hypotheses are inferred with reference to the volumes of external financing to be procured.

1. During the period 1970–75, Latin America would confine its indebtedness under credits from suppliers and EXIMBANK to amounts equivalent to the amortization on existing and future debts. Beginning in 1976, when various countries of the region would start to show the effects of the domestic effort in connection with resource gaps, this financing would increase until by the end of the period it would constitute almost the entire amount forecast.

2. World Bank financing would rise significantly over the next five years, as announced by the president of that institution. It has been estimated that the average volume of loans authorized by the World Bank between 1963 and 1967 will double in 1973. After that year, a moderate growth is assumed.

3. Although it is considered advisable for the IDA to increase its financing of the region, this projection has retained the level of the last two years.[14]

4. Financing by European governments and foreign investments have been projected assuming a moderate growth above current levels.

5. Financing granted under the Alliance for Progress itself has been projected with a significant increase for the period 1970–75. After 1975, such financing would gradually decline and reach fairly low levels toward the end of the period. It was initially assumed that AID loans would amount to nearly $500 million a year up to 1980, declining thereafter to only $100 million in 1985. For the IDB, accelerated growth of the Special Operations Fund was assumed up to 1980, declining thereafter to $100 million in 1985. At the same time it was

---

[14] A very substantial increase in IDA financing to Latin America would entail, as assumptions, a considerable increase in IDA resources and probably a change in the rule limiting the granting of funds by that agency to countries with certain levels of income. Since the Secretariat has not studied these questions in detail, it preferred to make no suggestions in this respect.

Graph IV-3. Latin America: Possible Financing by Source (in Millions of $)

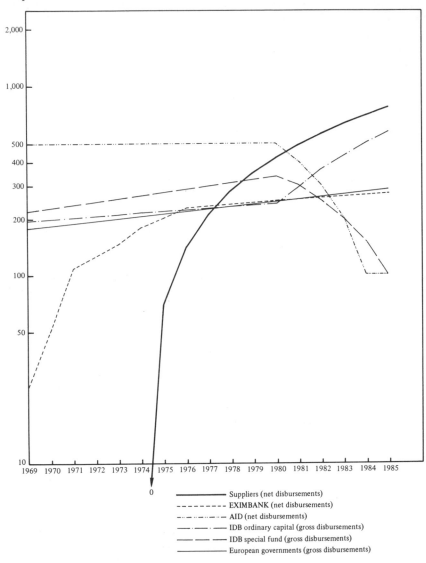

Table IV-11. Latin America: Possible Financing by Source[a] (in Millions of $)

Source	1970	1975	1980	1985	Cumulative Total 1970–85
World Bank	443	646	713	787	10,611
IDA	6	6	6	6	88
EXIMBANK	300	425	565	759	8,073
Suppliers	331	493	1,014	2,057	14,372
European governments	183	212	246	285	3,688
Inter-American Development Bank	424	494	577	675	8,636
Regular Operations Fund	(197)	(218)	(241)	(575)	(4,572)
Fund for Special Operations	(227)	(276)	(336)	(100)	(4,064)
AID	500	500	500	100	6,600
P.L. 480	75	75	–	–	600
Total	2,262	2,851	3,621	4,669	52,668

Note: For assumptions used, see pp. 99–101.

[a]Excludes Argentina.

assumed that the ordinary capital resources of the bank would expand normally up to 1980, absorbing thereafter the decline in operations proposed for the Special Operations Fund. No projections on the Social Progress Trust Fund were included, since this fund is exhausted, with only recoveries on loans made remaining as a source of income. The Canadian and United Kingdom funds have also been excluded, since available data do not allow for a trend prediction with any degree of accuracy. Operations carried out under P.L. 480 were projected at $75 million a year up to 1975, declining thereafter to the point of total elimination in 1980. With regard to their composition, the historic ratio of about 10 percent was maintained for loans under Title IV, as compared to the rest of the operations.

With reference to projected conditions, it was assumed, in general, that those prevailing during the historic period would continue, even though this implies an expectation of improvement in the capital markets, since current interest rates in the first months of 1969 exceed projections. It was also proposed that the supplier countries would in some way subsidize their exports to the region through the concession of preferential interest rates. Actually, this policy is already in force in some cases, for example, the subsidized suppliers' credit granted by KREDITANSTALT. For credits from suppliers and EXIMBANK, a reduction in the interest rate, as compared with average levels in recent years, from between 6 and 6.5 percent to 5 percent has been assumed. Likewise it was assumed that European suppliers will tend to adjust their terms to those currently granted by EXIMBANK, in other words, grace and amortization periods extended from two to three years and from nine to thirteen years, respectively.

For funds relating directly to the Alliance for Progress, that is, AID and IDB, no conditions were projected, since it was felt that they should be determined on the basis of the conditions required by the region. Nevertheless, an amount of $100 million a year of the projected AID funds was excepted from this treatment in the expectation, as outlined further on, that the United States will continue to utilize these resources—together with funds for P.L. 480 operations—bilaterally on conditions similar to those prevailing up to 1968. Synthesized, the conditions used as working hypotheses are as follows:

Source	Interest Rate	Grace Period	Amortization Period
IBRD	6	5	17
IDA	0.75	10	40
EXIMBANK	5	3	13
Suppliers	5	3	13
European governments	5	5	15
AID (bilateral loans)	2.5	9	30
P.L. 480 (10 percent Title IV)	2.5	2	20

Determination of the Gap and Necessary Conditions of External Financing

Taking into account the assumptions outlined above, a determination was made of the gap and of the conditions that should be offered for financing granted under the alliance in order to satisfy requirements estimated for the region as a whole, according to the needs of each country. As shown in table IV-12, the gap resulting from a comparison of foreseeable funds with gross requirements determined for the region as a whole amounts to a little over $4.8 billion for the period 1970-85. This gap is concentrated in the first years of the period; it begins to decline after 1970 and reaches a surplus of $238 million in 1985. Accordingly, 59 percent of the gap is concentrated in the 1970-75 subperiod, while 30 percent covers the years 1976 to 1980.

Graph IV-4 illustrates the evolution of the gap during the period 1970-85. Once the additional amount has been determined, consideration must be given to the conditions on which funds granted under the alliance as such

Table IV-12. Latin America: Determination of the Gap To Be Financed[a]
(in Millions of $)

Period	Gross Capital Requirements[b]	Foreseeable Funds[c]	Gap
1970–75	18,222	15,388	2,834
1976–80	17,955	16,513	1,442
1981–85	21,317	20,767	550
Cumulative total	57,494	52,668	4,826

[a]Excludes Argentina.
[b]See table IV-10.
[c]See table IV-11. Both cumulative totals differ from those of this table because they include 1969.

(IDB and AID less $100 million a year for bilateral operations) should be loaned, so that the average conditions of total external financing will approximate those required by the countries, that is, 4.5 percent interest, six years of grace and twenty-three years for the amortization.

As shown in table IV-13, using the hypothetical conditions described on page 101 as data for external financing, which in this study is not considered to be derived from the alliance as such, and comparing these conditions with those required by Latin American countries, it is concluded that, on the average for the projected 1970–85 period, the financing channeled through the IDB and the AID should be provided at 3.5 percent interest with nine years of grace and thirty-nine years for amortization. In other words, the financing should be furnished on terms similar to those apparently granted by IDA, but at an interest rate more than four times higher than the current rate for operations by that institution. In this way, the aid component of the financing would average about 50 percent for the entire period.

However, given the hypothetical changes in the composition of external financing for Latin America during the projected period, it is useful to determine the conditions required for various subperiods. Furthermore, given the evolution of the resource gaps in each country—with the highest deficits concentrated during the first five years while the policies designed to reduce them are maturing—it appears logical to assume that during the first three years more favorable conditions of external financing will be required, gradually settling to a normal level over the projected period.

As shown in table IV-13, financing granted under the alliance should average 3.1 percent interest with ten years of grace and forty years for amortiza-

Graph IV-4. Latin America: Gross Capital Requirements of Alternative C and Foreseeable Funds
(in Millions of $)

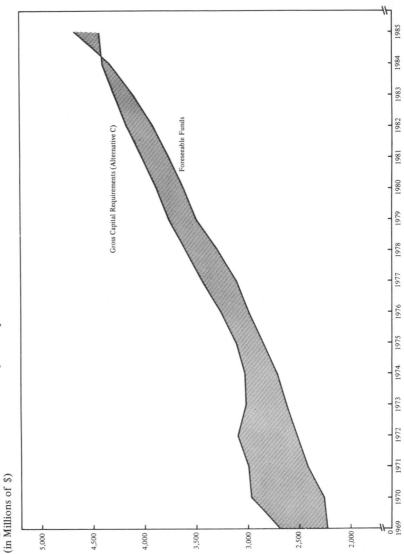

Table IV-13. Latin America: Determination of Necessary Conditions of Projected External Financing

Financing Source	Amounts (Millions of $)	Interest Rate	Grace Period	Amortization Period
1970–75				
Group I[a]	5,654	4.9	5	17
Group II[b]	4,581	5.0	3	13
Group III[c]	7,987	3.1	10	40
Amounts and conditions required	*18,222*	*4.1*	*7*	*26*
1976–80				
Group I	5,269	5.2	5	18
Group II	6,530	5.0	3	13
Group III	6,155	3.5	10	38
Amounts and conditions required	*17,955*	*4.5*	*6*	*23*
1981–85				
Group I	5,659	5.5	5	18
Group II	11,337	5.0	3	13
Group III	4,321	4.4	5	26
Amounts and conditions required	*21,317*	*5.0*	*4*	*17*
1970–85				
Group I	16,582	5.2	5	18
Group II	22,448	5.0	3	13
Group III	18,464	3.5	9	39
Amounts and conditions required	*57,494*	*4.5*	*6*	*23*

[a] IBRD, IDA, European governments, P.L. 480, and $100 million a year from AID.
[b] EXIMBANK and suppliers' credits.
[c] IDB (ordinary and special operations), AID less $100 million a year.

tion during the period 1970-75.[15] Subsequently, as the countries in the region gradually improve their position with regard to the resources gap, such financing could begin to be offered on conditions tending toward the current ones for ordinary operations. During the period 1976–80, only an increase in the interest rate is foreseeable, while grace and amortization terms should be similar to those in the first subperiod. However, the effect of the policies followed would make possible during the last five years of the projected

[15] This would assume a significant improvement in the average conditions of total external financing received by each of the countries in the region, though the extent will vary depending on individual circumstances.

period a substantial hardening of conditions so that an average of 4.4 percent interest, five years of grace and twenty-six years for amortization might be reached for this subperiod; in other words, the repayment schedules would be similar to those in force for program loans but with a higher rate of interest. These variations in the conditions of resources transferred under the Alliance for Progress would be reflected in a significant increase, during the period 1970–75, of the aid component, which would then gradually decline.

External Financing Strategy

The external financing strategy outlined in this study consists, in part, of a substantial increase in external financing granted during the next few years— during the 1970–75 period—by the financing institutions of the Alliance for Progress (AID, IDB) and possibly by other multinational agencies already established or to be set up in the future (such as subregional development banks).[16] The other basic factor in this strategy is an intensification of the domestic effort directed especially toward expanding exports and national savings. The expansion would make it possible, after 1975, to diminish gradually the net transfer of external resources and the net amount and aid component of financing furnished under the Alliance for Progress.

In order to achieve the increase in financing necessary under the Alliance for Progress during the coming years, various alternatives might be considered. These years coincide with the period during which a solution to the balance-of-payments problems of the United States can be expected, although these problems will probably continue to restrict United States financial cooperation—a circumstance that must be taken into account in the various solutions to be considered. Since this problem of increased financing is more fully analyzed in chapters V and VI, following an examination of the problems relating to tied aid, the following paragraphs present only one of the possible solutions, indicating subsequently other alternatives that could modify or complement the proposal made here.

The most widely-held theory in the United States is that this country should in the future channel its foreign aid more fully through multilateral institutions and reduce the share represented by bilateral assistance. Since this is also the majority opinion in Latin America, its implementation for the region in the immediate future would be desirable. To this end, according to the quantitative aspects of the solution suggested here, projected bilateral financing through AID for Latin America would be continued, beginning in

---

[16]The observations made in the rest of this section regarding the IDB can also be extended to those other multinational institutions already in operation or planned in the near future.

1970, at a much lower level than at present, which is established at $100 million a year by way of example. For its part, the United States would continue to assign bilaterally the funds projected under P.L. 480.

At the same time, the proposed solution calls for a sizable increase in United States contributions to the IDB. These contributions would rise from an annual average of $250 million during the years 1965-67 to $650 million during the period 1970-75, gradually dropping off in subsequent years almost to a vanishing point in 1985. This amount represents the nonreimbursable contribution that would be made by the United States to enable the IDB to expand its operations by an average of slightly over $1.3 billion[17] a year during the period 1970-75. Assuming that the IDB will have resources of its own available during the next few years, at a rate of $50 million a year for example, it would be necessary to procure about $600 million a year in the international capital markets.[18] Within the context of this example, the IDB could charge a commission of from 0.50 to 0.75 percent[19] and pay an interest rate of about 7 percent a year on its bond issues.[20] Appendix VII presents this example and compares it with the possible application of a measure such as the Horowitz Proposal.

The foregoing would permit IDB operations in the period 1970-75 to be carried out on the basis of the average conditions indicated in table IV-13, that is, 3.1 percent interest, ten years of grace, and forty years of amortization. Naturally, the volume of financing forecast here for the IDB would signify a substantial expansion of its operations, as well as its entry into new fields traditionally covered by AID, in its over-all or sectoral loan programs. It would be necessary both to expand and reorganize the IDB, and in this connection, to endeavor to rationalize, as a whole, the functions of all the

[17]According to the projection summarized in table IV-13, the annual average for the period would amount to $1.331 billion. In order to round off the figures involved, the text will continue to use $1.3 billion. If the exact amount resulting from the projections were used, the United States contribution to the IDB would total $665 million, with a similar amount for the total sum of other resources to be mobilized by the IDB according to the assumptions used here.

[18]Probably, owing to the lapse between attraction of resources and their subsequent utilization, a larger procurement than the average indicated here would be necessary during the first few years, since the projections imply an expansion of the current pipeline.

[19]This assumes a reduction in the current commission, on which basis it would be possible to decrease unit operating costs by expanding the total volume of loans.

[20]These conditions assume a slight reduction of the interest rate in the immediate future, which for the most recent IDB bond issues amounted to about 7.5 percent during the first months of 1969. This example also assumes that all IDB credits will be serviced from now on in dollars. If part of these amounts were to be recovered in local currency, it would probably be necessary to raise the average interest rate projected here for future loans.

inter-American mechanisms already in operation through their mutual coordination.

Considering the experience of the recent past, it would also, at first glance, appear difficult for the IDB to obtain $600 million in the international capital markets, particularly if, as in this case, the aim would be to procure these funds, at least for the most part, outside the United States. However, it should be pointed out that the industrial countries, including the United States, could be motivated to permit and promote this attraction of resources by the IDB through a liberalization of tied aid procedures, as explained in chapters V and VI. Such procurement of resources in the international capital markets could also be facilitated if all the member governments of the IDB would jointly guarantee the bond issues of that agency.

Basically the proposal formulated here consists of increasing the United States contribution to the IDB while decreasing, though to a lesser extent, the operations heretofore carried out bilaterally. This increased contribution would compensate the IDB for the higher interest rate it would necessarily have to pay in the capital markets. The proposed system represents, in fact, no more than a consolidation and expansion of the present system. In order to permit better programing of IDB operations and of the development policy of the Latin American countries, it would be desirable for the amounts required over several years to be authorized jointly, even if their delivery to the IDB were scheduled on a year-to-year basis.

In practice, the system suggested here would comply with the objectives of the scheme presented by the Governor of the Bank of Israel, Dr. Horowitz, since the IDB could lend at lower rates than those prevailing in the capital markets. There is a difference, however, between the methods of operation of the two schemes, for if the required $1.3 billion a year is financed by the Horowitz procedure, it would be necessary to float issues on the capital markets for that amount, while in the scheme outlined here only one-half of that amount or less is scheduled for procurement on those markets. Furthermore, within the context of the volumes and assumptions indicated earlier, implementation of the Horowitz Proposal would entail a United States contribution similar to, and probably—depending on the operational formula adopted—higher than the one indicated in the scheme suggested in this study, as is shown in greater detail in appendix VII. For all these reasons, it would appear that the suggestion presented here offers greater possibilities of implementation than the Horowitz Proposal.[21]

---

[21] It should also be considered that reduction of the interest rate charged by EXIM-BANK and on suppliers' credits, proposed in earlier pages for the projections presented here, may make it necessary for the exporting countries to subsidize those interest rates, thus adopting—each one separately and for comparatively small amounts—a modified version of the Horowitz Proposal.

The amounts, conditions, and terms suggested in these pages attempt only to indicate an integral system that would serve to satisfy the minimum external financing needs of Latin America during the next few years. If a proposal such as the one suggested were to be adopted, analysis of the projection and assumptions adopted in this study would clearly have to be explored in greater depth.

The proposal outlined above is not the only one possible for achieving the desired ends; the following two possibilities which would to some extent alter the assumptions suggested here could also be considered, for example.

1. The cost of the resources obtained by the IDB in the international capital markets could be reduced significantly if the industrialized countries would exempt from their domestic taxes the yield on securities of that institution. This would be equivalent in practice to a subsidy of the interest rates at which these resources are obtained.

2. The financing required on concessionary conditions would also be significantly reduced if the developing countries were assigned a higher proportion of the special drawing rights (SDR's) to be established in the International Monetary Fund.[22]

Finally, a determination should be made of the aid component of financing to be granted by the United States during the period 1970–75, pursuant to the assumptions of the projections and suggestions presented in this report. This component would amount to $837 million a year, with $650 million corresponding to contributions to IDB, $70 million to P.L. 480, $44 million to bilateral AID operations, and $73 million to EXIMBANK loans. Determination of the contributions to P.L. 480, EXIMBANK, and the bilateral loans to be granted by AID were made utilizing a discount rate of 6 percent, maintaining the conditions for such operations described in the previous section.

---

[22] In a report prepared by the new administration in the United States, the President's General Advisory Committee (U.S.) on Foreign Assistance Programs stated as follows: "One is the idea of devoting to development assistance some of the Special Drawing Rights (SDR's) to be created by the International Monetary Fund. The immediate objective is to get the SDR system itself into operation. But in a second round of creation of SDRs, the possibility should be considered of allotting a portion of them either to the International Development Association (IDA) as a supplement to its soft lending, or directly to less developed member countries. This would provide a new truly international source of financing for development assistance, and also enable the developed countries to earn new holdings of SDRs in the course of their exporting." *Development Assistance in the New Administration*, Report of the President's General Advisory Committee on Foreign Assistance Programs, 25 October 1968.

Appendixes to Chapter IV

APPENDIX IV-A: METHODOLOGY

THE METHOD USED

Models of two gaps for each of the Latin American countries were used for the projections contained in chapter IV. Analysis of the gaps makes it possible to determine capital requirements[1] which must be met in order to attain the growth objective established. Analysis of two gaps assumes that the amounts of required capital may be estimated either through the savings gap or through the trade gap.

In order to determine the savings gap, an estimate is made first of the amount of the minimum gross internal investment needed to reach the growth rate established. At the same time, an estimate is made of maximum potential internal savings. The difference between the two constitutes the savings gap. The trade gap is determined on the basis of an estimation of the minimum amount of imports needed, and a comparison of this with the maximum amount of potential exports.

According to the definition of national accounts, the trade and savings gaps should be identical, *ex-post*. Both indicate the surplus of resources that an economy has used with respect to those which it produces internally and the net amount of resources received from abroad. *Ex-ante*, however, the gaps are not necessarily equal. When insufficient savings pose the major obstacle for growth, the savings gap will be larger or predominant. When strangulation of the capacity to import is greater, the trade gap will be predominant. When adjusted to the same level *ex-post*, it is assumed that the smaller gap must be raised to the level of the larger or predominating gap from the *ex-ante* standpoint.

This adjustment process may be seen more clearly from the fact that the internal resources gap and the difference between the savings and trade gaps are identical. In other words:

$$\text{internal resources gap} = \text{savings gap} - \text{trade gap}$$
$$(C + I - M) - (Y - X) = (I - Y + C) - (M - X)$$

in which $(C + I - M)$ represents the demand for internal resources for consumption and investments, and $(Y - X)$ represents the available supply of said resources. When the *trade gap* predominates, i.e., $(M-X) > (I-Y+C)$, the

---

[1]The requirements "must be met" in the sense that the dominating gap must be covered if there is a desire to obtain the growth rate established. Nevertheless such requirements may be "insufficient" since they must be considered in addition to the other movements in the balance of payments.

internal resources gap is negative. This situation is referred to as "frustrated savings," since the surplus of internal resources is spent on unplanned consumption.

If financing is obtained to fill the trade gap, the actual savings will be greater than the potential savings. On the other hand, if the *savings gap* predominates, $(I-Y+C) > (M-X)$, the internal resources gap is positive. If available external financing covers only the smaller gap, the planned growth rate will not be achieved owing to insufficient internal resources. If available external financing covers the predominant savings gap, it will be possible to attain the growth rate planned; however, the adjustment of the trade and savings gaps so as to make them identical *ex-post* will result in a "superfluous imports" situation, in which actual imports may be greater than needed to achieve the growth rate planned. In both cases, identical levels *ex-post* implies that the difference between the two gaps is equal to zero, and the demand for internal resources is equal to the supply.[2]

A line of reasoning similar to the foregoing is followed when one of the gaps is negative and the other is positive. In such a case, the positive gap predominates. When both gaps are negative, there is a surplus both of savings as well as of exports (foreign exchange). Although in this case the smaller surplus is taken as the predominant gap, the accounting implication is that an outflow of capital will be caused. Nevertheless, since only the so-called surplus resources gap is considered, it could be absorbed through payments to factors abroad (interest and profits), and through amortization payments on the outstanding external debt, resulting in net capital requirements equal to zero, which could even develop into a deficit. In terms of the planned rate of growth, savings and trade gaps which present a surplus, and are not absorbed by other outflow on the balance of payments, imply that the economy is operating below its optimum level, i.e., other things being equal, the planned growth objective is smaller than that which potentially could be achieved with available resources.

Lastly, it should be noted that if available external financing is not sufficient to cover the predominant gap, the planned objective may be attained only if *policies are implemented* either to increase exports or reduce imports, if the trade gap predominates, or through increases in capital productivity or in the tendency to save, if the savings gap is the predominating one. If success is not achieved through the implementation of these policies, the result will be a growth rate lower than the one planned.

---

[2] Furthermore, it is possible to define a "balanced growth rate" which would produce equalization *ex-ante* of both gaps. At that rate, the demand for goods and services will be equal to the supply thereof—a "full employment" situation in which the growth objective plan is achieved, and in which internal resources are used simultaneously to the fullest extent.

HUNT LIBRARY
CARNEGIE-MELLON UNIVERSITY

EQUATIONS USED

The model computed in the recent study on the two gaps prepared by the Panel of Experts of CIAP in *The External Gap in Latin America, 1968–1973* was used as a basis for projection to the year 1985. Nevertheless, certain parameters were changed in some countries, and the basis for the 1968 projection was updated. In connection with the changes made in the parameters, this procedure was followed only when, in the light of new available data and alternative estimates, it was observed that the estimated parameters presented considerable differences.

Changes were specifically introduced in the following cases:

1. The import function for Brazil, for which a marginal trend to import at a level equal to the median and equal to 0.076 was used because historical data and the relationships between imports and product and investment made it impossible statistically to use a more elaborate regression equation.

2. Import function for Chile,

   $M_t = -0.704 + 0.1877 \ Y_t \quad R^2 = 0.94$

3. Import function for Costa Rica,

   $M_t = 0.285 \ Y_t$ in which the median import tendency was derived from the projected trend in the most recent country review conducted by CIAP. Observations made during the 1950–1968 period did not reveal any significant relationship.

4. Import function for Mexico,

   $Mu = 5.400 + 0.0899 \ Y_t \quad R^2 = 0.97$

5. In the case of Venezuela, the investments, savings, and import functions were recomputed because new data from national accounts were available for the 1950–1968 period. The following equations were used:

   $I_t = 0.2090 \ Y_t$
   $S_t = 0.2535 \ Y_t$
   $M_t = 0.1400 \ Y_t$

The following table shows the parameters used in each country.

METHODOLOGY FOR GAP REDUCTION: ALTERNATIVE B

The procedure followed to reduce the predominant gap may be described as a hybrid combination of the methodologies used in the following papers:

   a. H. B. Chenery, *Toward a More Effective Alliance for Progress*, Discussion Paper No. 13, AID, Office of Program Coordination, March 1967.

   b. H. B. Chenery and I. Adelman, "Foreign Aid and Economic Development: The Case of Greece," *The Review of Economics and Statistics*, February 1966, no. 1.

Appendix Table IV-A-1. Parameters Used

Country	Investment Functions				Savings Functions				Import Functions				Units in Millions of
	Constant	Y_t	Y_t	P_t	Constant	Y_t	P_t	X_t	Constant	Y_t	C_t	I_t	
Argentina	192.13	0.3684	—	—	—	0.3501	-7.487	—	—	0.1124	—	—	Billions of 1960 pesos
Bolivia	872.38	—	0.2769	55.715	-728.1	0.2744	—	—	-364.63	0.684	0.2574	—	1963 pesos
Brazil	-268.08	0.3366	—	9.2477	-56.38	0.1480	—	0.3901	—	0.076[a]	—	—	1960 new cruzeiros
Colombia	1.1961	—	0.1498	—	—	0.2042	—	—	2.29	0.0878	—	—	Billions of 1958 pesos
Costa Rica	-29.3	—	0.1027	60.281	—	0.3295	-53.327	—	—	0.285[a]	—	—	1960 dollars
Chile	-0.4965	—	0.2093	—	—	0.1716	—	—	-0.704	0.1877[a]	—	—	Billions of 1965 escudos
Ecuador	186.35	—	0.1327	—	—	0.1807	-122.93	—	-81.536	—	0.08	0.736	1960 sucres
El Salvador	-23.936	—	0.1727	—	—	0.1974	-18.273	—	-50.039	0.3139	—	—	1960 dollars
Guatemala	-78.836	0.2481	—	48.203	-21.112	0.1194	—	—	-59.209	0.2112	—	—	1960 dollars
Honduras	18.513	0.2163	—	18.062	—	0.1424	—	—	-49.219	—	0.2224	1.117	1960 dollars
Mexico	-20.781	0.2395	—	1.1686	-0.2648	0.2067	—	—	5.400	0.0899[a]	—	—	Billions of 1960 pesos
Nicaragua	-31.214	—	0.2546	—	-13.657	0.1921	—	—	-37.996	—	0.2412	1.2018	1960 dollars
Panama	-127.6	0.5402	—	-191.45	—	0.2913	-50.732	—	10.7	0.3842	—	—	1960 balboas
Paraguay	-3.310.5	—	0.2383	—	—	0.1264	—	—	—	0.1622	—	—	1962 guaranies
Peru	0.7856	—	0.2247	—	—	0.1984	—	—	-5.66	—	0.2011	0.587	Billions of 1963 soles
Dominican Republic	—	—	—	—	—	0.152	—	—	43.09	0.1466	—	—	
Uruguay	—	0.2873	—	—	—	0.1521	—	—	—	0.151	—	—	1962 pesos
Venezuela	—	0.2090[a]	—	—	—	0.2535[a]	—	—	—	0.1400[a]	—	—	1963 pesos 1957 bolivares

[a]Changed parameters: Y = gross geographical product, P = population, C = consumption, I = investment.

Source: See text.

    c. H. B. Chenery and P. Eckstein, *Development Alternatives for Latin America,* Memorandum No. 19 (rev.), AID, Office of Program Coordination, June 1965.

    d. H. B. Chenery and A. M. Strout, *Foreign Assistance and Economic Development,* Discussion Paper No. 7 (rev.), AID, Office of Program Coordination, June 1965.

In general, four basic procedures were used in order to reduce the gaps of the countries dealt with in this paper.

1. When the trade gap was predominant and positive, and the savings gap presented a surplus throughout the projection period, that gap was reduced to zero in 1985, the last year in the period. Subsequently, the investment needed to reduce the trade gap was assigned to each year lineally, with a one-year maturity period, i.e., it was assumed that there would be equal annual increases in investment which would have a cumulative effect as time passed (Chenery-Strout, p. 42).

This procedure was followed for five countries: Brazil, Colombia, Ecuador, Honduras, and Mexico.

2. When both gaps were positive, and the trade gap predominated, different procedures were applied, depending on the situation in each country: (*a*) It was reduced to a point where it was equal to the *ex-ante* savings gap in the last year of the projection period. Once again, investment was assigned lineally following the same procedure indicated in par. 1. The countries for which this method was followed were El Salvador, Nicaragua, and Peru. (*b*) The predominant trade gap was reduced in order to cover only a part of the difference from the originally estimated savings gap. This procedure was applied in the case of Bolivia. (*c*) The procedure indicated in (*a*) was followed for some countries as the tendency to save increased, thus establising an *ex-ante* situation identical with the reduced trade gap for each year in the period. For 1985, a gap equal to zero was planned for Chile, and a gap at an arbitrary level between the original level and zero was established in the case of Paraguay.

3. When the savings gap predominated throughout the period, it was reduced anually *ex-ante* until it equaled the trade gap originally projected. The Dominican Republic was the only country to which this procedure was applied.

In the cases of Costa Rica, Guatemala, Panama, and Uruguay, no changes were proposed for the original projection because of the fact that in some of these countries, the gaps originally estimated were approaching zero, and in others the resulting amounts were within the estimates of financing expected. Argentina and Venezuela were also dealt with in a special manner. In the case of Argentina, the original projection resulted in a surplus in both gaps throughout the period, with this surplus not being absorbed by the outflows predicted in the balance of payments. Hence, a rate of growth higher than the original one (3.5 percent) was set for Argentina. In the case of Venezuela, the trade gap, which went from a surplus in the beginning of the period to a deficit toward the end, was reduced to a surplus for the entire period. This goal was established taking into account the fact that profit remittances were absorbing the entire surplus.

A more detailed description of the assumptions made in computing the reduction of the trade gap and investment needed for that purpose incorporates the following:

1. The expansion of exports and/or the substitution of the imports would require a marginal capital-product relationship equal to Kb, in which:

K = median capital-product relationship for 1970, 1975, 1980, and 1985.

b = coefficient applied to the capital-product relationship for investment in reducing the trade gap (b = 1.2). This coefficient reflects "the possibility that the local currency may have been overvalued, in which case the returns from exports would be smaller, and imports would be more competitive with national substitutes than would be the case with a balanced rate of exchange. In order to meet the requirements for additional investments (extra cost) it would then be necessary to obtain internal savings close to the potential levels" (Chenery, bp. 7).

2. The additional investment required for each year due to the greater capital-product relationship will be:

$\left(1 - \dfrac{1}{b}\right)$ $^{I}m_t$ in which $^{I}m_t$ = estimated annual investment for expansion

of exports and/or substitution of imports. A restriction was established according to which additional investments may not exceed 30 percent of the originally projected investment.

3. The annual reduction of the trade gap is equal to:

$$h \sum_{0}^{b-1} {}^{I}m_t/Kb$$

In which:

$$\sum_{0}^{t-1} {}^{I}m_t = \text{investment in reducing the accumulated trade gap with a}$$

delay of one year.

h = coefficient increasing between .5 and 1.0. Said coefficient introduces an adjustment through steady increases in the use of installed capacity beginning in the first year of investment. This would appear to be in accordance with the main assumption involved in the two-gap model according to which most of the reduction of the trade gap is achieved by reallocating current investment. Furthermore, it implicitly raises the capital-product relationship during the first few years of the investment period. Moreover, the increasing value of h insures that there will be no changes in the predominant gaps throughout the period.

4. $\displaystyle\sum_{0}^{t-1} {}^{I}m_t$ when $t = n$, is equal to: $\begin{bmatrix} F^m & - & F^m \\ 0 & & 1 \end{bmatrix}_n$ Kb, in which

$\begin{bmatrix} F^m & - & F^m \\ 0 & & 1 \end{bmatrix}_n$ = reduction planned for the trade gap in 1985.

APPENDIX IV-B: TABLES SUMMARIZING PROJECTIONS

Appendix Table IV-B-1. Projections for 1970–85[a] (in Millions of $)

Country	1969		1970		1971		1972		1973		1974	
Argentina	C	−295	C	−309	C	−322	C	−336	C	−336	C	−362
Bolivia	C	61	C	70	C	79	C	89	C	99	C	110
Brazil	C	83	C	119	C	158	C	195	C	244	C	288
Chile	A	96	A	110	A	123	A	138	A	151	A	167
Colombia	C	159	C	163	C	170	C	178	C	186	C	197
Costa Rica	C	16	C	15	C	16	C	16	C	15	C	14
Ecuador	C	21	C	29	C	38	C	48	C	58	C	70
El Salvador	C	25	C	30	C	37	C	44	C	50	C	58
Guatemala	A	21	A	20	A	17	A	16	C	12	C	12
Honduras	C	13	C	15	C	19	C	22	C	25	C	29
Mexico	C	140	C	143	C	149	C	156	C	169	C	181
Nicaragua	C	42	C	47	C	55	C	61	C	68	C	76
Panama	C	21	C	19	C	18	C	16	C	13	C	11
Paraguay	A	32	C	36	C	41	C	47	C	52	C	59
Peru	A	146	A	151	A	161	C	170	C	195	C	227
Dominican Republic	A	56	A	61	A	61	A	67	A	73	A	76
Uruguay	A	5	A	5	A	6	A	6	A	5	A	6
Venezuela	A	−615	A	−652	C	−674	C	−612	C	−544	C	−470
Total Positive Gaps		937		1,033		1,148		1,269		1,415		1,581
Algebraic Sum		30		72		152		321		535		749

Appendix Table IV-B-1. *Continued*

Country	1975		1976		1977		1978		1979		1980	
Argentina	C	-376	C	-376	C	-403	C	-416	C	-429	C	-443
Bolivia	C	122	C	135	C	148	C	161	C	176	C	191
Brazil	C	337	C	398	C	455	C	523	C	595	C	670
Chile	A	183	C	214	C	255	C	298	C	346	C	394
Colombia	C	209	C	220	C	234	C	248	C	266	C	286
Costa Rica	C	14	C	13	C	13	C	11	C	10	C	8
Ecuador	C	81	C	94	C	108	C	124	C	140	C	157
El Salvador	C	66	C	75	C	83	C	93	C	104	C	115
Guatemala	C	13	C	13	C	12	C	11	C	10	C	9
Honduras	C	33	C	37	C	41	C	46	C	51	C	57
Mexico	C	195	C	211	C	230	C	253	C	278	C	307
Nicaragua	C	83	C	92	C	100	C	109	C	118	C	129
Panama	C	8	C	4	C	1	C	-2	C	-7	C	-11
Paraguay	C	64	C	71	C	79	C	86	C	95	C	103
Peru	C	259	C	295	C	330	C	369	C	413	C	457
Dominican Republic	A	80	A	84	A	90	A	96	A	101	A	107
Uruguay	A	7	A	6	A	7	A	7	A	7	A	8
Venezuela	C	-388	C	-299	C	-201	C	-95	C	71	C	147
Total Positive Gaps		1,754		1,962		2,186		2,435		2,731		3,145
Algebraic Sum		990		1,287		1,582		1,922		2,295		2,691

Country	1981		1982		1983		1984		1985	
Argentina	C	-456	C	-483	C	-497	C	-510	C	-537
Bolivia	C	207	C	224	C	242	C	261	C	281
Brazil	C	756	C	845	C	936	C	1,037	C	1,149
Chile	C	447	C	504	C	562	C	629	C	693
Colombia	C	306	C	331	C	358	C	385	C	417
Costa Rica	C	6	C	5	C	2	C	0	C	-4
Ecuador	C	176	C	197	C	219	C	242	C	267
El Salvador	C	127	C	139	C	153	C	168	C	183
Guatemala	C	8	C	5	C	2	C	-1	C	-5
Honduras	C	63	C	70	C	76	C	83	C	91
Mexico	C	339	C	337	C	419	C	464	C	516
Nicaragua	C	139	C	150	C	161	C	173	C	186
Panama	C	-17	C	-23	C	-30	C	-37	C	-45
Paraguay	C	111	C	122	C	132	C	142	C	155
Peru	C	503	C	556	C	610	C	667	C	728
Dominican Republic	A	113	A	122	A	129	A	135	A	143
Uruguay	C	11	C	15	C	18	C	21	C	25
Venezuela	C	285	C	434	C	594	C	769	C	958
Total Positive Gaps		3,597		4,096		4,613		5,176		5,792
Algebraic Sum		3,124		3,590		4,086		4,628		5,201

[a]Projections with an assumed low rate of growth for exports; see table IV-2, alternative A. Predominant Gap: C = trade, A = savings.

Source: Projections by OAS Secretariat.

Appendix Table IV-B-2. Accumulated Predominant Trade Gap (in Millions of $)

Country	Years	Positive Trade Gap	Savings Gap	Investment	Savings	Frustrated Savings (2) – (3)	Actual Savings (5) – (6)	Ex-post Savings Gap (4) – (7)
	(1)	(2)	(3)	(4)	(5)	(6)	(7)	(8)
Argentina	–	–	–	–	–	–	–	–
Bolivia	1969/85	2,656	264	4,354	4,090	2,392	1,698	2,656
Brazil	1969/85	8,788	-14,221	113,474	127,695	23,009	104,686	8,788
Chile	1976/85	4,342	2,922	23,692	20,770	1,400	19,350	4,342
Colombia	1969/85	4,313	-5,760	28,852	34,612	10,073	24,539	4,313
Costa Rica	1969/85	174	-803	4,608	5,411	977	4,434	174
Ecuador	1969/85	2,069	-682	6,026	6,708	2,751	3,957	2,069
El Salvador	1969/85	1,550	327	4,681	4,354	1,223	3,131	1,550
Guatemala	1973/83	107	-150	3,371	3,521	257	3,264	107
Honduras	1969/85	771	-817	1,809	2,626	1,588	1,038	771
Mexico	1969/85	4,527	-22,241	93,316	115,557	26,768	88,789	4,527
Nicaragua	1969/85	1,789	762	3,864	3,102	1,027	2,075	1,789
Panama	1969/77	111	-244	1,959	2,203	355	1,848	111
Paraguay	1970/85	1,395	1,178	3,032	1,854	217	1,637	1,395
Peru	1972/85	5,779	3,205	23,942	20,737	2,574	18,163	5,779
Dominican Republic	–	–	–	–	–	–	–	–
Uruguay	1980/85	98	48	2,462	2,414	50	2,364	98
Venezuela	1979/85	3,208	-9,357	43,945	53,302	12,565	40,737	3,208
Total		41,677	-45,569	363,387	408,956	87,246	321,710	41,677

Source: Projections by OAS Secretariat.

Appendix Table IV-B-3. Accumulated Predominant Savings Gap (in Millions of $)

Country	Years	Positive Savings Gap	Trade Gap	Imports	Exports	Superfluous Imports (2) – (3)	Actual Imports (4) – (6)	Ex-post Trade Gap (7) – (5)
	(1)	(2)	(3)	(4)	(5)	(6)	(7)	(8)
Argentina	—	—	—	—	—	—	—	—
Bolivia	—	—	—	—	—	—	—	—
Brazil	—	—	—	—	—	—	—	—
Chile	1969/75	968	537	8,902	8,365	431	9,333	968
Colombia	—	—	—	—	—	—	—	—
Costa Rica	—	—	—	—	—	—	—	—
Ecuador	—	—	—	—	—	—	—	—
El Salvador	—	—	—	—	—	—	—	—
Guatemala	1969/72	74	39	1,344	1,305	35	1,379	74
Honduras	—	—	—	—	—	—	—	—
Mexico	—	—	—	—	—	—	—	—
Nicaragua	—	—	—	—	—	—	—	—
Panama	—	—	—	—	—	—	—	—
Paraguay	1969	32	31	88	57	1	89	32
Peru	1969/71	458	354	3,530	3,176	104	3,634	458
Dominican Republic	1969/85	1,594	513	5,669	5,156	1,081	6,750	1,594
Uruguay	1969/79	67	69	3,215	3,284	136	3,351	67
Venezuela	—	—	—	—	—	—	—	—
Total		3,193	1,405	22,748	21,343	1,788	24,536	3,193

Source: Projections by OAS Secretariat.

APPENDIX IV-C: ALTERNATIVES A, B, AND C BY COUNTRY

Appendix Table IV-C-1. Argentina: Projections of Resource and Financial Gaps[a]
(in Millions of $)

Item	1970	1975	1980	1985	1969–85
Alternative A					
1. Exports of goods and services	1,289	1,625	1,975	2,402	30,237
2. Predominant resources gap	−309	−376	−443	−537	−6,886
3. Net income from factors	183	142	128	137	2,462
Interest	83	32	6	2	508
Profits from direct investment	100	110	122	135	1,954
4. Gap in current account	−126	−234	−315	−400	−4,424
5. Amortizations	284	103	17	12	1,634
6. Net direct investments	−100	−125	−150	−175	−2,270
7. Net capital requirements	58	−256	−448	−563	−5,060
8. Servicing of new debt	−	13	13	13	165
9. Interest on new debt	11	10	6	3	128
10. Gross capital requirements	69	−233	−429	−547	−4,767
11. Service factor[b]	29.3	9.7	2.1	1.2	8.1

[a]1. *Alternative A:*
    a. Projection of the resource gap according to the parameters and growth of exports, observed historically. See chap. IV, p. 81.
    b. Terms for additional financing similar to those in effect in recent years: interest, 5 percent; grace period, 4 years; amortization period, 16 years.

[b]Service factor: amortization and interest on current and future debts, as a percentage of the exports of goods and services.

Appendix Table IV-C-2. Bolivia: Projections of Resource and Financial Gaps[a]
(in Millions of $)

Item	1970	1975	1980	1985	1969–85
Alternative A					
1. Exports of goods and services	181	220	268	327	4,028
2. Predominant resources gap	70	122	191	281	2,656
3. Net income from factors	8	10	11	13	175
Interest	6	6	5	4	90
Profits from direct investment	2	4	6	9	85
4. Gap in current account	78	132	202	294	2,831
5. Amortizations	11	9	9	8	151
6. Net direct investments	-10	-13	-16	-19	-235
7. Net capital requirements	79	128	195	283	2,747
8. Servicing of new debt	–	3	26	70	334
9. Interest on new debt	4	23	54	103	686
10. Gross capital requirements	83	154	275	456	3,767
11. Service factor[b]	11.6	18.6	35.0	56.6	31.3
Alternative B					
1. Exports of goods and services	185	249	338	454	4,900
2. Predominant resources gap	63	74	75	69	1,203
3. Gap in current account	71	84	86	82	1,378
4. Net capital requirements	72	80	79	71	1,294
5. Servicing of new debt	–	3	21	46	246
6. Interest on new debt	4	17	33	51	411
7. Gross capital requirements	76	100	133	168	1,951
8. Service factor[b]	11.4	14.1	20.1	24.0	18.3
Alternative C					
1. Exports of goods and services	185	249	338	454	4,900
2. Net capital requirements	72	80	79	71	1,294
3. Servicing of new debt	–	–	5	19	72
4. Interest on new debt	4	17	33	52	417
5. Gross capital requirements	76	97	117	142	1,783
6. Service factor[b]	11.4	12.9	15.4	18.3	14.9

[a]1. *Alternative A:*
   a. Projection of the resource gap according to the parameters and growth of exports, observed historically. See chap. IV, p. 81.
   b. Terms for additional financing similar to those in effect in recent years: interest, 3 percent; grace period, 6 years; amortization period, 23 years.

2. *Alternative B:*
Differs from alternative A only with respect to the projection for the resource gap, which incorporates the policies suggested in order to reduce it. See chap. IV, p. 87.

3. *Alternative C:*
Differs from alternative B with respect to the terms for additional financing: interest, 3 percent; grace period, 10 years; amortization period, 30 years.

[b]Service factor: amortization and interest on current and future debts, as a percentage of the exports of goods and services.

Appendix Table IV-C-3. Brazil: Projections of Resource and Financial Gaps[a]
(in Millions of $)

Item	1970	1975	1980	1985	1969–85
Alternative A					
1. Exports of goods and services	2,222	2,703	3,287	3,999	50,610
2. Predominant resource gap	119	337	670	1,149	8,788
3. Net income from factors	296	261	250	243	4,487
Interest	130	80	49	22	1,253
Profit from direct investments	166	181	201	221	3,234
4. Gap in current account	415	598	920	1,392	13,275
5. Amortizations	291	167	114	87	2,754
6. Net direct investments	−180	−200	−220	−243	−3,542
7. Net capital requirements	526	565	814	1,236	12,487
8. Servicing of new debt	−	−	140	342	1,664
9. Interest on new debt	43	172	362	548	4,444
10. Gross capital requirements	569	737	1,316	2,126	18,595
11. Service factor[b]	20.9	15.5	20.2	25.0	20.0
Alternative B					
1. Exports of goods and services	2,254	2,936	3,856	5,033	57,694
2. Predominant resource gap	83	78	38	−	917
3. Gap in current account	379	339	288	243	5,404
4. Net capital requirements	490	306	182	87	4,616
5. Servicing of new debt	−	−	120	230	1,290
6. Interest on new debt	42	136	220	298	2,824
7. Gross capital requirements	532	442	522	615	8,730
8. Service factor[b]	20.5	13.0	13.0	12.7	14.1

[a]1. *Alternative A:*
   a. Projection of the resource gap according to the parameters and growth of exports, observed historically. See chap. IV, p. 81.
   b. Terms for additional financing similar to those in effect in recent years: interest, 4 percent; grace period, 7 years; amortization period, 21 years.

2. *Alternative B:*
   Differs from alternative A only with respect to the projection for the resource gap, which incorporates the policies suggested in order to reduce it. See chap. IV, p. 87.

[b]Service factor: amortization and interest on current and future debts, as a percentage of the exports of goods and services.

Appendix Table IV-C-4. Chile: Projections of Resource and Financial Gaps[a]
(in Millions of $)

Item	1970	1975	1980	1985	1969–85
Alternative A					
1. Exports of goods and services	1,113	1,322	1,570	1,865	24,417
2. Predominant resource gap	110	183	394	693	5,310
3. Net income from factors	196	197	193	196	3,329
Interest	54	42	25	16	609
Profits from direct investment	142	155	168	180	2,720
4. Gap in current account	306	380	587	889	8,639
5. Amortizations	106	99	64	49	1,394
6. Net direct investments	−27	−20	−20	−20	−525
7. Net capital requirements	385	459	631	918	9,564
8. Servicing of new debt	–	43	232	564	2,892
9. Interest on new debt	32	171	383	724	4,920
10. Gross capital requirements	417	673	1,246	2,206	17,376
11. Service factor[b]	17.3	26.9	44.8	72.5	40.2
Alternative B					
1. Exports of goods and services	1,113	1,400	1,839	2,489	27,797
2. Predominant resource gap	85	89	95	0	1,311
3. Gap in current account	281	286	288	196	4,640
4. Net capital requirements	360	364	332	225	5,561
5. Servicing of new debt	–	41	199	436	2,386
6. Interest on new debt	31	146	291	460	3,637
7. Gross capital requirements	391	551	822	1,121	11,584
8. Service factor[b]	17.2	23.4	31.5	38.6	28.9
Alternative C					
1. Exports of goods and services	1,113	1,400	1,839	2,489	27,797
2. Net capital requirements	360	364	332	225	5,561
3. Servicing of new debt	–	24	113	231	1,318
4. Interest on new debt	24	106	210	322	2,605
5. Gross capital requirements	384	494	655	778	9,484
6. Service factor[b]	16.5	19.4	22.4	24.8	21.3

[a]1. *Alternative A:*
  a. Projection of the resource gap according to the parameters and growth of exports, observed historically. See chap. IV, p. 81.
  b. Terms for additional financing similar to those in effect in recent years: interest, 5 percent; grace period, 5 years; amortization period, 15 years.

2. *Alternative B:*
Differs from alternative A only with respect to the projection for the resource gap, which incorporates the policies suggested in order to reduce it. See chap. IV, p. 87.

3. *Alternative C:*
Differs from alternative B with respect to the terms for additional financing: interest, 4 percent; grace period, 5 years; amortization period, 25 years.

[b]Service factor: amortization and interest on current and future debts, as a percentage of the exports of goods and services.

Appendix Table IV-C-5. Colombia: Projections of Resource and Financial Gaps[a]
(in Millions of $)

Item	1970	1975	1980	1985	1969–85
Alternative A					
1. Exports of goods and services	785	930	1,105	1,312	17,191
2. Predominant resource gap	163	209	286	417	4,313
3. Net income from factors	73	75	76	79	1,279
Interest	37	29	20	13	429
Profits from direct investment	36	46	56	66	850
4. Gap in current account	236	284	362	496	5,592
5. Amortizations	34	53	43	39	729
6. Net direct investments	–45	–59	–73	–87	–1,093
7. Net capital requirements	225	278	332	448	5,228
8. Servicing of new debt	–	–	62	157	756
9. Interest on new debt	19	80	168	295	2,144
10. Gross capital requirements	244	358	562	900	8,129
11. Service factor[b]	11.5	17.4	31.5	38.4	23.6
Alternative B					
1. Exports of goods and services	797	1,015	1,312	1,687	19,758
2. Predominant resource gap	150	115	56	0	1,461
3. Gap in current account	223	190	132	79	2,740
4. Net capital requirements	212	184	102	31	2,376
5. Servicing of new debt	–	–	55	116	620
6. Interest on new debt	18	66	113	152	1,409
7. Gross capital requirements	230	250	270	299	4,405
8. Service factor[b]	11.2	14.6	17.6	19.0	16.1
Alternative C					
1. Exports of goods and services	797	1,015	1,312	1,687	19,758
2. Net capital requirements	212	184	102	31	2,376
3. Servicing of new debt	–	–	46	97	519
4. Interest on new debt	18	66	113	152	1,411
5. Gross capital requirements	230	250	261	280	4,306
6. Service factor[b]	11.2	14.6	16.9	17.8	15.6

[a]1. *Alternative A:*
   a. Projection of the resource gap according to the parameters and growth of exports, observed historically. See chap. IV, p. 81.
   b. Terms for additional financing similar to those in effect in recent years: interest, 4 percent; grace period, 7 years; amortization period, 21 years.

2. *Alternative B:*
Differs from alternative A only with respect to the projection for the resource gap, which incorporates the policies suggested in order to reduce it. See chap. IV, p. 87.

3. *Alternative C:*
Differs from alternative B with respect to the terms for additional financing: interest, 4 percent; grace period, 7 years; amortization period, 25 years.

[b]Service factor: amortization and interest on current and future debts, as a percentage of the exports of goods and services.

Appendix Table IV-C-6. Costa Rica: Projections of Resource and Financial Gaps[a]
(in Millions of $)

Item	1970	1975	1980	1985	1969–85
Alternative A					
1. Exports of goods and services	229	321	450	632	6,598
2. Predominant resource gap	15	14	8	- 4	170
3. Net income from factors	25	29	32	36	513
Interest	8	5	3	2	79
Profit from direct investments	17	24	29	34	434
4. Gap in current account	40	43	40	32	687
5. Amortizations	15	8	7	6	149
6. Net direct investments	−14	−19	−23	−28	−352
7. Net capital requirements	41	32	24	10	480
8. Servicing of new debt	—	4	15	29	177
9. Interest on new debt	3	11	21	29	257
10. Gross capital requirements	44	48	60	68	916
11. Service factor[b]	11.4	8.7	10.2	10.4	10.0
Alternative C					
1. Exports of goods and services	229	321	450	632	6,598
2. Net capital requirements	41	32	24	10	480
3. Servicing of new debt	—	4	15	27	167
4. Interest on new debt	2	8	14	20	181
5. Gross capital requirements	43	44	53	57	828
6. Service factor[b]	10.9	7.8	8.7	8.7	8.7

[a]1. *Alternative A:*
   a. Projection of the resource gap according to the parameters and growth of exports, observed historically. See chap. IV, p. 81.
   b. Terms for additional financing similar to those in effect in recent years: interest, 4 percent; grace period, 5 years; amortization period, 20 years.

2. *Alternative C:*
   Differs from alternative A with respect to the terms for additional financing: interest, 3 percent; grace period, 5 years; amortization period, 20 years.

[b]Service factor: amortization and interest on current and future debts, as a percentage of the exports of goods and services.

Appendix Table IV-C-7. Dominican Republic: Projections of Resource and Financial Gaps[a] (in Millions of $)

Item	1970	1975	1980	1985	1969–85
Alternative A					
1. Exports of goods and services	210	267	341	435	5,156
2. Predominant resource gap	61	80	107	143	1,594
3. Net income from factors	34	42	50	57	767
Interest	5	4	4	3	72
Profits from direct investment	29	38	46	54	695
4. Gap in current account	95	122	157	200	2,361
5. Amortizations	8	9	11	9	165
6. Net direct investments	-6	-8	-10	-12	-156
7. Net capital requirements	97	123	158	197	2,370
8. Servicing of new debt	–	4	30	72	364
9. Interest on new debt	8	35	76	133	962
10. Gross capital requirements	105	162	264	402	3,696
11. Service factor[b]	10.0	19.5	35.5	49.9	30.3
Alternative B					
1. Exports of goods and services	210	267	341	435	5,156
2. Predominant resource gap	19	24	34	53	513
3. Gap in current account	53	66	84	110	1,280
4. Net capital requirements	55	67	85	107	1,289
5. Servicing of new debt	–	3	17	40	209
6. Interest on new debt	5	20	43	74	544
7. Gross capital requirements	60	90	145	221	2,042
8. Service factor[b]	8.6	13.5	22.0	29.0	19.2
Alternative C					
1. Exports of goods and services	210	267	341	435	5,156
2. Net capital requirements	55	67	85	107	1,289
3. Servicing of new debt	–	2	13	30	157
4. Interest on new debt	4	14	30	50	377
5. Gross capital requirements	59	83	128	187	1,823
6. Service factor[b]	8.1	10.9	17.0	21.1	15.0

[a]1. *Alternative A:*

   a. Projection of the resource gap according to the parameters and growth of exports, observed historically. See chap. IV, p. 81.

   b. Terms for additional financing similar to those in effect in recent years: interest, 4 percent; grace period, 6 years; amortization period, 24 years.

2. *Alternative B:*

   Differs from alternative A only with respect to the projection for the resource gap, which incorporates the policies suggested in order to reduce it. See chap. IV, p. 87.

3. *Alternative C:*

   Differs from alternative B with respect to the terms for additional financing: interest, 3 percent; grace period, 6 years; amortization period, 30 years.

[b]Service factor: amortization and interest on current and future debts, as a percentage of the exports of goods and services.

Appendix Table IV-C-8. Ecuador: Projections of Resource and Financial Gaps[a]
(in Millions of $)

Item	1970	1975	1980	1985	1969–85
Alternative A					
1. Exports of goods and services	254	294	341	345	5,307
2. Predominant resource gap	29	81	157	267	2,069
3. Net income from factors	32	32	32	33	546
Interest	7	5	3	1	70
Profits from direct investment	25	27	29	32	476
4. Gap in current account	61	113	189	300	2,615
5. Amortizations	14	14	8	7	185
6. Net direct investments	−11	−15	−18	−22	−273
7. Net capital requirements	64	112	179	285	2,527
8. Servicing of new debt	−	9	51	127	616
9. Interest on new debt	6	35	88	165	1,073
10. Gross capital requirements	70	156	318	577	4,216
11. Service factor[b]	10.6	21.4	44.0	87.0	36.6
Alternative B					
1. Exports of goods and services	260	336	444	532	6,587
2. Predominant resource gap	21	21	10	0	240
3. Gap in current account	53	53	42	33	786
4. Net capital requirements	56	52	32	18	698
5. Servicing of new debt	−	8	35	70	405
6. Interest on new debt	6	24	42	61	529
7. Gross capital requirements	62	84	109	149	1,632
8. Service factor[b]	10.4	15.2	19.8	26.1	18.1
Alternative C					
1. Exports of goods and services	260	336	444	532	6,587
2. Net capital requirements	56	52	32	18	698
3. Servicing of new debt	−	5	18	32	199
4. Interest on new debt	3	13	22	29	269.8
5. Gross capital requirements	59	70	72	79	1,166.8
6. Service factor[b]	9.2	11.0	11.5	13.0	11.0

[a]1. *Alternative A:*
   a. Projection of the resource gap according to the parameters and growth of exports, observed historically. See chap. IV, p. 81.
   b. Terms for additional financing similar to those in effect in recent years: interest, 5 percent; grace period, 5 years; amortization period, 14 years.

2. *Alternative B:*
   Differs from alternative A only with respect to the projection for the resource gap, which incorporates the policies suggested in order to reduce it. See chap. IV, p. 87.

3. *Alternative C:*
   Differs from alternative B with respect to the terms for additional financing: interest, 3 percent; grace period, 5 years; amortization period, 25 years.

[b]Service factor: amortization and interest on current and future debts, as a percentage of the exports of goods and services.

Appendix Table IV-C-9. El Salvador: Projections of Resource and Financial Gaps[a]
(in Millions of $)

Item	1970	1975	1980	1985	1969–85
Alternative A					
1. Exports of goods and services	267	349	456	596	6,421
2. Predominant resource gap	30	66	115	183	1,550
3. Net income from factors	10	11	12	14	199
Interest	3	2	1	1	32
Profits from direct investment	7	9	11	13	167
4. Gap in current account	40	77	127	197	1,749
5. Amortizations	5	5	4	3	74
6. Net direct investments	-11	-15	-18	-22	-274
7. Net capital requirements	34	67	113	178	1,549
8. Servicing of new debt	–	6	28	76	371
9. Interest on new debt	4	24	67	144	865
10. Gross capital requirements	38	97	208	399	2,786
11. Service factor[b]	4.5	10.6	21.9	37.6	20.9
Alternative B					
1. Exports of goods and services	271	374	517	708	7,174
2. Predominant resource gap	25	31	28	23	474
3. Gap in current account	35	42	40	37	673
4. Net capital requirements	29	32	26	18	473
5. Servicing of new debt	–	5	18	37	217
6. Interest on new debt	4	17	34	55	428
7. Gross capital requirements	33	54	78	110	1,118
8. Service factor[b]	4.4	7.8	11.0	13.6	10.5
Alternative C					
1. Exports of goods and services	271	374	517	708	7,174
2. Net capital requirements	29	32	26	18	473
3. Servicing of new debt	–	2	10	19	113
4. Interest on new debt	2	8	13	19	167
5. Gross capital requirements	31	42	49	56	753
6. Service factor[b]	3.7	4.5	5.4	5.9	5.4

[a]1. *Alternative A:*
   a. Projection of the resource gap according to the parameters and growth of exports, observed historically. See chap. IV, p. 81.
   b. Terms for additional financing similar to those in effect in recent years: interest, 6 percent; grace period, 4 years; amortization period, 19 years.

2. *Alternative B:*
   Differs from alternative A only with respect to the projection for the resource gap, which incorporates the policies suggested in order to reduce it. See chap. IV, p. 87.

3. *Alternative C:*
   Differs from alternative B with respect to the terms for additional financing: interest, 3 percent; grace period, 5 years; amortization period, 25 years.

[b]Service factor: amortization and interest on current and future debts, as a percentage of the exports of goods and services.

Appendix Table IV-C-10. Guatemala: Projections of Resource and Financial Gaps[a]
(in Millions of $)

Item	1970	1975	1980	1985	1969–85
Alternative A					
1. Exports of goods and services	315	432	592	811	8,732
2. Predominant resource gap	20	13	9	–5	175
3. Net income from factors	24	29	35	41	547
Interest	5	3	2	1	52
Profit from direct investments	19	26	33	40	495
4. Gap in current account	44	42	44	36	722
5. Amortizations	16	6	3	3	109
6. Net direct investments	–13	–17	–21	–25	–313
7. Net capital requirements	47	31	26	14	518
8. Servicing of new debt	–	7	21	39	247
9. Interest on new debt	5	17	30	45	386
10. Gross capital requirements	52	55	77	98	1,151
11. Service factor[b]	8.9	7.6	9.5	10.9	9.1
Alternative C					
1. Exports of goods and services	315	432	592	811	8,732
2. Net capital requirements	47	31	26	14	518
3. Servicing of new debt	–	7	19	34	221
4. Interest on new debt	3	10	16	22	205
5. Gross capital requirements	50	48	61	70	944
6. Service factor[b]	7.6	6.0	6.8	7.4	6.7

[a]1. *Alternative A:*
    a. Projection of the resource gap according to the parameters and growth of exports, observed historically. See chap. IV, p. 81.
    b. Terms for additional financing similar to those in effect in recent years: interest, 5 percent; grace period, 4 years; amortization period, 20 years.

2. *Alternative C:*
    Differs from alternative A with respect to the terms for additional financing: interest, 3 percent; grace period, 4 years; amortization period, 20 years.

[b]Service factor: amortization and interest on current and future debts, as a percentage of the exports of goods and services.

Appendix Table IV-C-11. Haiti: Projections of Resource and Financial Gaps[a]
(in Millions of $)

Item	1970	1975	1980	1985	1969–85
Alternative A					
1. Exports of goods and services	46	52	62	92	987
2. Imports of goods and services	66	84	106	134	1,609
3. Resource gap	20	32	44	62	642
4. Profit remittances	3	3	3	3	51
5. Private transfers	15	15	15	15	255
6. Gap in current account	8	20	32	50	438
7. Amortizations	1	1	–	–	8
8. Direct investment	-1	-1	-1	-1	-17
9. Government grants	4	4	4	4	68
10. Net capital requirements	4	16	28	46	365
11. Servicing of new debt	–	–	5	15	65
12. Interest on new debt	–	3	8	19	109
13. Gross requirements	4	19	41	80	539
14. Service factor[b]	2.2	7.7	21.0	37.0	18.4
Alternative B					
1. Exports of goods and services	48	58	70	86	1,086
2. Imports of goods and services	66	81	100	125	1,549
3. Resource gap	19	23	30	39	463
4. Gap in current account	6	11	18	24	259
5. Net requirements	2	7	14	23	186
6. Servicing of new debt	–	–	3	8	34
7. Interest on new debt	–	2	4	10	56
8. Gross requirements	2	9	21	41	277
9. Service factor[b]	2.1	5.2	10.0	20.9	9.0
Alternative C					
1. Net requirements	2	7	14	23	186
2. Servicing of new debt	–	–	–	1	4
3. Interest on new debt	–	1	3	7	40
4. Gross requirements	2	8	17	31	230
5. Service factor[b]	2.1	3.4	4.3	9.3	4.8

[a]1. *Alternative A:*

   a. Projection of the resource gap according to the parameters and growth of exports, observed historically. See chap IV, p. 81.

   b. Terms for additional financing similar to those in effect in recent years: interest, 4 percent; grace period, 5 years; amortization period, 15 years.

2. *Alternative B:*

Differs from alternative A only with respect to the projection for the resource gap, which incorporates the policies suggested in order to reduce it. See chap. IV, p. 87.

3. *Alternative C:*

Differs from alternative B with respect to the terms for additional financing: interest, 3 percent; grace period, 10 years; amortization period, 30 years.

[b]Service factor: amortization and interest on current and future debts, as a percentage of the exports of goods and services.

Appendix Table IV-C-12. Honduras: Projections of Resource and Financial Gaps[a]
(in Millions of $)

Item	1970	1975	1980	1985	1969–85
Alternative A					
1. Exports of goods and services	158	202	258	330	3,897
2. Predominant resource gap	15	33	57	91	771
3. Net income from factors	18	22	25	30	401
Interest	3	3	2	2	49
Profits from direct investment	15	19	23	28	352
4. Gap in current account	33	55	82	121	1,172
5. Amortizations	4	5	4	4	75
6. Net direct investments	-6	-8	-10	-12	-156
7. Net capital requirements	31	52	76	113	1,091
8. Servicing of new debt	–	1	11	31	145
9. Interest on new debt	2	13	30	59	386
10. Gross capital requirements	33	66	118	203	1,622
11. Service factor[b]	5.7	10.9	18.2	29.1	16.8
Alternative B					
1. Exports of goods and services	160	215	289	385	4,275
2. Predominant resource gap	12	12	6	0	141
3. Gap in current account	30	34	31	30	542
4. Net capital requirements	28	31	25	22	461
5. Servicing of new debt	–	1	9	20	106
6. Interest on new debt	2	10	18	27	227
7. Gross capital requirements	30	42	52	69	794
8. Service factor[b]	5.6	8.8	11.4	13.8	10.7
Alternative C					
1. Exports of goods and services	160	215	289	385	4,275
2. Net capital requirements	28	31	25	22	461
3. Servicing of new debt	–	1	7	13	74
4. Interest on new debt	2	7	12	19	161
5. Gross capital requirements	30	39	44	54	696
6. Service factor[b]	5.6	7.4	8.7	9.9	8.4

[a]1. *Alternative A:*
   a. Projection of the resource gap according to the parameters and growth of exports, observed historically. See chap. IV, p. 81.
   b. Terms for additional financing similar to those in effect in recent years: interest, 4 percent; grace period, 6 years; amortization period, 22 years.

2. *Alternative B:*
   Differs from alternative A only with respect to the projection for the resource gap, which incorporates the policies suggested in order to reduce it. See chap. IV, p. 87.

3. *Alternative C:*
   Differs from alternative B with respect to the terms for additional financing: interest, 3 percent; grace period, 6 years; amortization period, 30 years.

[b]Service factor: amortization and interest on current and future debts, as a percentage of the exports of goods and services.

Appendix Table IV-C-13. Mexico: Projections of Resource and Financial Gaps[a]
(in Millions of $)

Item	1970	1975	1980	1985	1969–85
Alternative A					
1. Exports of goods and services	2,654	3,385	4,321	5,515	65,282
2. Predominant resource gap	143	195	307	516	4,527
3. Net income from factors	462	485	553	667	8,980
Interest	146	82	40	9	1,213
Profits from direct investment	316	403	513	658	7,767
4. Gap in current account	605	680	860	1,183	13,507
5. Amortizations	246	170	130	128	2,973
6. Net direct investments	-232	-325	-456	-641	-6,681
7. Net capital requirements	619	525	534	670	9,799
8. Servicing of new debt	–	207	563	1,134	6,951
9. Interest on new debt	68	256	483	802	6,237
10. Gross capital requirements	687	987	1,580	2,606	22,989
11. Service factor[b]	17.3	21.1	28.1	37.6	26.6
Alternative B					
1. Exports of goods and services	2,668	3,489	4,577	5,979	68,459
2. Predominant resource gap	127	79	23	–	997
3. Gap in current account	589	564	576	667	9,977
4. Net capital requirements	603	409	250	154	6,269
5. Servicing of new debt	–	199	500	913	6,034
6. Interest on new debt	68	235	395	567	5,066
7. Gross capital requirements	671	843	1,145	1,634	17,369
8. Service factor[b]	17.2	19.7	23.3	27.0	22.3
Alternative C					
1. Exports of goods and services	2,668	3,489	4,577	5,979	68,459
2. Net capital requirements	603	409	250	154	6,269
3. Servicing of new debt	–	139	334	581	3,989
4. Interest on new debt	68	234	395	567	5,065
5. Gross capital requirements	671	782	979	1,302	15,323
6. Service factor[b]	17.2	17.9	19.6	21.5	19.3

[a]1. *Alternative A:*
   a. Projection of the resource gap according to the parameters and growth of exports, observed historically. See chap. IV, p. 81.
   b. Terms for additional financing similar to those in effect in recent years: interest, 5 percent; grace period, 3 years; amortization period, 14 years.

2. *Alternative B:*
Differs from alternative A only with respect to the projection for the resource gap, which incorporates the policies suggested in order to reduce it. See chap. IV, p. 87.

3. *Alternative C:*
Differs from alternative B with respect to the terms for additional financing: interest, 5 percent; grace period, 5 years; amortization period, 20 years.

[b]Service factor: amortization and interest on current and future debts, as a percentage of the exports of goods and services.

Appendix Table IV-C-14. Nicaragua: Projections of Resource and Financial Gaps[a]
(in Millions of $)

Item	1970	1975	1980	1985	1969–85
Alternative A					
1. Exports of goods and services	215	287	384	514	5,711
2. Predominant resource gap	47	83	129	186	1,789
3. Net income from factors	21	26	31	36	469
Interest	5	4	3	2	56
Profits from direct investment	16	22	28	34	413
4. Gap in current account	68	109	160	222	2,258
5. Amortizations	7	5	4	3	74
6. Net direct investments	-11	-15	-18	-22	-274
7. Net capital requirements	64	99	146	203	2,058
8. Servicing of new debt	—	6	30	75	380
9. Interest on new debt	5	23	58	111	741
10. Gross capital requirements	69	129	234	389	3,179
11. Service factor[b]	7.9	13.2	24.7	37.2	21.9
Alternative B					
1. Exports of goods and services	217	307	433	602	6,293
2. Predominant resource gap	44	58	68	76	1,038
3. Gap in current account	65	84	99	112	1,507
4. Net capital requirements	61	74	85	93	1,307
5. Servicing of new debt	—	6	25	54	301
6. Interest on new debt	5	12	32	60	417
7. Gross capital requirements	66	92	142	207	2,025
8. Service factor[b]	7.8	8.8	14.8	19.8	13.5
Alternative C					
1. Exports of goods and services	217	307	433	602	6,293
2. Net capital requirements	61	74	85	93	1,307
3. Servicing of new debt	—	2	14	32	168
4. Interest on new debt	4	16	32	51	400
5. Gross capital requirements	65	92	131	176	1,875
6. Service factor[b]	7.4	8.8	12.2	14.6	11.1

[a]1. *Alternative A:*
   a. Projection of the resource gap according to the parameters and growth of exports, observed historically. See chap. IV, p. 81.
   b. Terms for additional financing similar to those in effect in recent years: interest, 4 percent; grace period, 5 years; amortization period, 21 years.

2. *Alternative B:*
   Differs from alternative A only with respect to the projection for the resource gap, which incorporates the policies suggested in order to reduce it. See chap. IV, p. 87.

3. *Alternative C:*
   Differs from alternative B with respect to the terms for additional financing: interest, 3 percent; grace period, 6 years; amortization period, 30 years.

[b]Service factor: amortization and interest on current and future debts, as a percentage of the exports of goods and services.

Appendix Table IV-C-15. Panama: Projections of Resource and Financial Gaps[a]
(in Millions of $)

Item	1970	1975	1980	1985	1969–85
Alternative A					
1. Exports of goods and services	356	488	668	916	9,862
2. Predominant resource gap	19	8	–11	–45	–61
3. Net income from factors	28	33	40	50	627
Interest	5	3	2	2	53
Profits from direct investment	23	30	38	48	574
4. Gap in current account	47	41	29	5	566
5. Amortizations	6	7	4	3	85
6. Net direct investments	–16	–21	–26	–31	–392
7. Net capital requirements	37	27	7	–23	259
8. Servicing of new debt	–	3	11	17	116
9. Interest on new debt	2	7	11	11	132
10. Gross capital requirements	39	37	29	5	507
11. Service factor[b]	3.7	4.1	4.2	3.6	3.9

[a]1. *Alternative A:*
  a. Projection of the resource gap according to the parameters and growth of exports, observed historically. See chap. IV, p. 81.
  b. Terms for additional financing similar to those in effect in recent years: interest, 3 percent; grace period, 5 years; amortization period, 25 years.

[b]Service factor: amortization and interest on current and future debts, as a percentage of the exports of goods and services.

Appendix Table IV-C-16. Paraguay: Projections of Resource and Financial Gaps[a]
(in Millions of $)

Item	1970	1975	1980	1985	1969–85
Alternative A					
1. Exports of goods and services	57	60	63	66	1,042
2. Predominant resource gap	36	64	103	155	1,427
3. Net income from factors	7	7	7	7	116
Interest	4	3	2	1	44
Profits from direct investment	3	4	5	6	72
4. Gap in current account	43	71	110	162	1,543
5. Amortizations	5	7	5	4	87
6. Net direct investments	−5	−6	−8	−9	−115
7. Net capital requirements	43	72	107	157	1,515
8. Servicing of new debt	–	2	16	44	206
9. Interest on new debt	3	27	54	96	686
10. Gross capital requirements	46	100	177	297	2,407
11. Service factor[b]	21.1	65.0	122.2	219.7	98.2
Alternative B					
1. Exports of goods and services	59	74	99	132	1,488
2. Predominant resource gap	33	40	43	45	683
3. Gap in current account	40	47	50	52	799
4. Net capital requirements	40	48	47	47	771
5. Servicing of new debt	–	2	13	28	150
6. Interest on new debt	3	13	27	44	341
7. Gross capital requirements	43	63	87	119	1,262
8. Service factor[b]	20.3	33.8	47.5	58.3	47.1
Alternative C					
1. Exports of goods and services	59	74	99	132	1,488
2. Net capital requirements	40	48	47	47	771
3. Servicing of new debt	–	–	3	11	41
4. Interest on new debt	2	10	19	30	237
5. Gross capital requirements	42	58	69	88	1,049
6. Service factor[b]	18.6	27.0	29.3	34.8	27.5

[a]1. *Alternative A:*
    a. Projection of the resource gap according to the parameters and growth of exports, observed historically. See chap. IV, p. 81.
    b. Terms for additional financing similar to those in effect in recent years: interest, 4 percent; grace period, 6 years; amortization period, 23 years.

2. *Alternative B:*
    Differs from alternative A only with respect to the projection for the resource gap, which incorporates the policies suggested in order to reduce it. See chap. IV, p. 87.

3. *Alternative C:*
    Differs from alternative B with respect to the terms for additional financing: interest, 3 percent; grace period, 6 years; amortization period, 30 years.

[b]Service factor: amortization and interest on current and future debts, as a percentage of the exports of goods and services.

Appendix Table IV-C-17. Peru: Projections of Resource and Financial Gaps[a]
(in Millions of $)

Item	1970	1975	1980	1985	1969–85
Alternative A					
1. Exports of goods and services	1,058	1,349	1,722	2,198	26,020
2. Predominant resource gap	151	259	457	728	6,237
3. Net income from factors	99	91	80	72	1,471
Interest	37	28	16	7	394
Profits from direct investment	62	63	64	65	1,077
4. Gap in current account	250	350	537	800	7,708
5. Amortizations	94	59	41	23	896
6. Net direct investments	-12	-15	-18	-22	-276
7. Net capital requirements	332	394	560	801	8,328
8. Servicing of new debt	–	51	170	381	2,121
9. Interest on new debt	28	115	250	463	3,227
10. Gross capital requirements	360	560	980	1,645	13,676
11. Service factor[b]	15.0	18.8	27.7	39.8	25.5
Alternative B					
1. Exports of goods and services	1,058	1,399	1,959	2,780	28,990
2. Predominant resource gap	151	196	160	0	2,524
3. Gap in current account	250	287	240	72	3,995
4. Net capital requirements	332	331	263	73	4,615
5. Servicing of new debt	–	51	160	302	1,883
6. Interest on new debt	28	111	203	286	2,516
7. Gross capital requirements	360	493	626	661	9,014
8. Service factor[b]	15.0	17.8	21.4	22.2	19.6
Alternative C					
1. Exports of goods and services	1,058	1,399	1,959	2,780	28,990
2. Net capital requirements	332	331	263	73	4,615
3. Servicing of new debt	–	43	134	248	1,562
4. Interest on new debt	28	111	202	286	2,515
5. Gross capital requirements	360	485	599	607	8,692
6. Service factor[b]	15.0	17.2	20.1	20.3	18.5

[a]1. *Alternative A:*
   a. Projection of the resource gap according to the parameters and growth of exports, observed historically. See chap. IV, p. 81.
   b. Terms for additional financing similar to those in effect in recent years: interest, 4 percent; grace period, 4 years; amortization period, 21 years.

2. *Alternative B:*
   Differs from alternative A only with respect to the projection for the resource gap, which incorporates the policies suggested in order to reduce it. See chap. IV, p. 87.

3. *Alternative C:*
   Differs from alternative B with respect to the terms for additional financing: interest, 4 percent; grace period, 5 years; amortization period, 25 years.

[b]Service factor: amortization and interest on current and future debts, as a percentage of the exports of goods and services.

Appendix Table IV-C-18. Trinidad and Tobago: Projections of Resource and Financial Gaps[a] (in Millions of $)

Item	1970	1975	1980	1985	1969–85
Alternative A					
1. Exports (f.o.b.)	−414	−476	−546	−627	−8,624
2. Imports (c.i.f.)	405	504	628	783	9,578
3. Services (net)	−63	−73	−83	−93	−1,309
4. Resource gap					
(surplus: minus sign)	−72	−45	−1	63	−355
5. Net income from factors	122	130	138	147	2,262
Interest	6	4	2	1	52
Profits	116	126	136	146	2,210
6. Gap in current account					
(surplus: minus sign)	50	85	137	210	1,907
7. Amortizations	8	6	4	2	85
8. Direct investment	−37	−42	−47	−50	−745
9. Net capital requirements	21	49	94	162	1,247
10. Servicing of new debt	−	4	24	76	341
11. Interest on new debt	2	16	48	113	634
12. Gross capital requirements	23	69	166	351	2,222
13. Service factor[b]	3.4	5.5	12.4	26.7	11.2
Alternative B					
1. Exports (f.o.b.)	−416	−482	−559	−648	−8,787
2. Imports (c.i.f.)	405	469	540	626	8,507
3. Services (net)	−63	−73	−83	−93	−1,309
4. Resource gap					
(surplus: minus sign)	−74	−86	−102	−115	−1,589
5. Gap in current account	48	44	36	32	673
6. Net capital requirements	19	8	−7	−16	13
7. Servicing of new debt	−	4	10	16	112
8. Interest on new debt	2	7	9	7	109
9. Gross capital requirements	21	19	12	7	234
10. Service factor[b]	3.3	3.8	3.9	3.5	3.5
Alternative C					
1. Net capital requirements	19	8	−7	−16	13
2. Servicing of new debt	−	2	6	9	64
3. Interest on new debt	2	6	8	−6	101
4. Gross capital requirements	21	16	7	−1	178
5. Service factor[b]	3.3	3.2	3.1	2.4	3.0

Notes to table are given on following page.

Notes to Appendix Table IV-C-18

[a]In this case, only the trade gap has been projected, because of the fact that background data on national accounts were not available.

1. *Alternative A:*
    a. Projection of the resource gap according to the parameters and growth of exports, observed historically. See chap. IV, p. 81.
    b. Terms for additional financing similar to those in effect in recent years: interest, 6 percent; grace period, 4 years; amortization period, 14 years.

2. *Alternative B:*
   Differs from alternative A only with respect to the projection for the resource gap, which incorporates the policies suggested in order to reduce it. See chap. IV, p. 87.

3. *Alternative C:*
   Differs from alternative B with respect to the terms for additional financing: interest, 5 percent; grace period, 5 years; amortization period, 20 years.

[b]Service factor: amortization and interest on current and future debts, as a percentage of the exports of goods and services.

Appendix Table IV-C-19. Uruguay: Projections of Resource and Financial Gaps[a]
(in Millions of $)

Item	1970	1975	1980	1985	1969–85
Alternative A					
1. Exports of goods and services	264	306	355	412	5,601
2. Predominant resource gap	5	7	8	25	165
3. Net income from factors					
Interest	8	3	1	–	50
Profit from direct investments					
4. Gap in current account	13	10	9	25	215
5. Amortizations	41	9	5	2	196
6. Net direct investments					
7. Net capital requirements	54	19	14	27	411
8. Servicing of new debt	–	10	23	40	275
9. Interest on new debt	5	14	22	35	299
10. Gross capital requirements	59	43	59	102	985
11. Services factor[b]	20.5	11.8	14.4	18.7	14.0
Alternative C					
1. Exports of goods and services	264	306	355	412	5,601
2. Net capital requirements	54	19	14	27	411
3. Servicing of new debt	–	5	14	24	161
4. Interest on new debt	4	11	16	26	223
5. Gross capital requirements	58	35	44	77	795
6. Service factor[b]	20.1	9.2	10.1	12.6	11.2

[a]1. *Alternative A:*
   a. Projection of the resource gap according to the parameters and growth of exports, observed historically. See chap. IV, p. 81.
   b. Terms for additional financing similar to those in effect in recent years: interest, 5 percent; grace period, 3 years; amortization period, 18 years.

2. *Alternative C:*
   Differs from alternative A with respect to the terms for additional financing: interest, 4 percent; grace period, 5 years; amortization period, 20 years.

[b]Service factor: amortization and interest on current and future debts, as a percentage of the exports of goods and services.

Appendix Table IV-C-20. Venezuela: Projections of Resource and Financial Gaps[a]
(in Millions of $)

Item	1970	1975	1980	1985	1969–85
Alternative A					
1. Exports of goods and services	2,781	3,147	3,562	4,030	56,630
2. Predominant resource gap	−652	−388	147	958	−1,342
3. Net income from factors	827	923	911	903	15,263
Interest	35	23	11	3	316
Profits from					
direct investments	792	900	900	900	14,947
4. Gap in current account	175	535	1,058	1,861	13,921
5. Amortizations	35	46	41	27	652
6. Net direct investments	−80	−80	−80	−80	−1,360
7. Net capital requirements	130	501	1,019	1,808	13,213
8. Servicing of new debt	–	125	620	1,913	8,717
9. Interest on new debt	16	140	473	1,168	6,253
10. Gross capital requirements	146	766	2,112	4,889	28,183
11. Service factor[b]	3.1	10.6	32.1	77.2	28.1
Alternative B					
1. Exports of goods and services	2,810	3,358	4,077	4,965	63,034
2. Predominant resource gap	−583	−740	−712	−600	−11,520
3. Gap in current account	244	183	199	303	3,743
4. Net capital requirements	199	149	160	250	3,035
5. Servicing of new debt	–	130	351	755	4,473
6. Interest on new debt	25	98	189	330	2,469
7. Gross capital requirements	224	377	700	1,335	9,977
8. Service factor[b]	3.4	8.8	14.5	22.5	12.5
Alternative C					
1. Exports of goods and services	2,810	3,358	4,077	4,965	63,034
2. Net capital requirements	199	149	160	250	3,035
3. Servicing of new debt	–	20	74	149	873
4. Interest on new debt	5	58	119	213	1,519
5. Gross capital requirements	204	227	353	612	5,427
6. Service factor[b]	2.7	4.4	6.0	7.9	5.3

[a]1. *Alternative A:*
  a. Projection of the resource gap according to the parameters and growth of exports, observed historically. See chap. IV, p. 81.
  b. Terms for additional financing similar to those in effect in recent years: interest, 6 percent; grace period, 2 years; amortization period, 10 years.

2. *Alternative B:*
Differs from alternative A only with respect to the projection for the resource gap, which incorporates the policies suggested in order to reduce it. See chap. IV, p. 87.

3. *Alternative C:*
Differs from alternative B with respect to the terms for additional financing: interest, 5 percent; grace period, 5 years; amortization period, 20 years.

[b]Service factor: amortization and interest on current and future debts, as a percentage of the exports of goods and services.

CHAPTER V

Some Problems in the Negotiation and Utilization of External Public Financing

TYING OF EXTERNAL FINANCING AND THE CRITERION OF ADDITIONALITY

General Background

Use of most of the external public financing received by Latin America is currently restricted to payment for imports from the country granting the funds. Only the ordinary resources of international banking institutions— IBRD and IDB—are not bound by that condition. Bilateral financing, both from the United States and from other industrialized countries, is already virtually wholly "tied," and even multilateral aid granted on concessionary conditions is covered by this type of restriction. In the IDB, utilization of the Social Progress Trust Fund is contingent upon payment of imports from the United States, while the Special Operations Fund is subject to bidding in which only companies from the IDB member countries, that is, the United States and Latin America, may participate. Furthermore, it appears likely that the projected new United States contribution to the IDA will also be subject to a special "tying" procedure.[1]

An earlier chapter of this study presents certain tentative estimates of the effect of this tying on United States financing to Latin America,[2] inasmuch as it generally tends to reduce the aid component of such financing. However, further mention of this topic should be made here, since other aspects must also be considered in some depth.

There are two different types of bilateral financing operations which, in turn, result in two different kinds of tying. On the one hand, there are credits in kind, such as those under P.L. 480 and those granted mainly for direct promotion of exports by the country contributing the resources; this is the case, for example, of credits from the United States EXIMBANK, most of the

---

[1] According to this proposal, for as long as IDA receives funds from sources other than the United States and for at least the following three years, the funds contributed by the United States could only be used to finance purchases in that country.

[2] See chap. II.

public credits received by Latin America from Europe and Japan, and, generally speaking, suppliers' credits. In these instances, with the exception of operations under P.L. 480, the aid component of the financing is almost nonexistent and its advantages and disadvantages for the recipient country depend on circumstantial balance-of-payments conditions.

The other type of bilateral external financing is generally characterized by concessionary conditions with respect to interest rate and grace and amortization terms and by the fact that a substantial portion of the funds granted is not tied to the importation of specific capital goods for a given investment project. This group includes almost all AID financing operations: its overall and sectoral program loans and project loans. In these cases, all or part of the matching funds and local currency of the foreign exchange received under the external credit is used to pay local costs of the investment programs carried out or promoted by the governments. The AID operations represent the most acute current problem of tied aid.

When the seriousness of the United States balance-of-payments problem first became apparent at the end of the last decade, long-term development financing began to be contingent upon its use to pay for imports from the United States, and by the time the Alliance for Progress was launched, tying of aid had become the general rule for AID operations. Since the United States balance-of-payments problem has worsened, and since foreign aid has lost favor in Congress and in public opinion, the criterion that such aid can only be justified if it is shown to have no harmful effects on the balance of payments has been gaining ground. To this end, it has been proposed that "additional" exports from the United States should be financed, that is, export transactions that would not have been carried out if such aid had not existed. Consequently, mechanisms have been evolved in an attempt to prevent the United States from financing exports from that country that would have been exported in the normal course of events, chargeable to the "regular" foreign exchange earnings of the recipient countries.

The criterion of additionality, as applied to AID operations, is designed to ensure that United States exports will at least maintain their previous participation in the total imports of beneficiary countries under normal trade conditions. For a better appreciation of what the application of this criterion involves, we must first review briefly the development of the major conditions during this decade that have governed the use of foreign exchange derived from program credits. This type of operation most clearly illustrates the implications of the change that the criterion of additionality has brought about in the United States bilateral aid system, although, as shown elsewhere, these implications are not confined to this one category of credit.

Use of Foreign Exchange Derived from Program Credits[3]

During the first few years of the Alliance for Progress, when it was anticipated that over-all external financing for national development programs would reach a much higher level than it actually has, the conditions applied to the use of foreign exchange deriving from program credits were simple and easily applied as compared to their subsequent evolution.

On the dates stipulated at the time each loan was arranged, AID opened letters of credit in favor of the beneficiary country which could be used to pay for the acquisition of all types of merchandise in the United States—with the exception of those expressly included on the "negative list," consisting mainly of luxury articles—and to pay for freight and insurance on those imports. The greatest problem in utilization of the letters of credit at that time was the condition that at least 50 percent of the imported merchandise should be transported in United States bottoms. For this reason, a substantial share of imports from the United States did not qualify for use of the letters of credit, since the importers very often preferred to employ other means of transportation, either because of their lower cost or, occasionally, because no United States ships were available on the date required or such ships did not transport the goods to the port of entry most convenient to the importer. The fact that the terms during which the letters of credit could be used were fairly long facilitated compliance with the stipulated conditions. Moreover, the original and main purpose of the program credits was to help finance national development programs, and the local currency counterpart of these loans could be used by the governments concerned on dates predetermined in the agreements, which were generally earlier than the dates on which the foreign exchange was utilized.

The conditions summarized above gradually changed until the current status was reached. Various administrative requirements have been established, such as stamping the imported goods with the emblem of the Alliance for Progress, submitting the imports desired to a system of prior bids, the establishment of a term of forty-five days for the receipt of proposals after

[3]The analysis contained in this section is based primarily on the Secretariat's study of the experiences of various countries in this area. The slight differences in such evolution in each of the three countries are not mentioned here, since they are not significant as regards the questions posed by this study, even though the comparative importance of the effects of application of tied aid procedures may vary according to specific circumstances in each beneficiary country. It should be pointed out that for various other countries receiving aid credits not directly tied to the importation of specific goods during these years, procedures similar to those described here were also followed; however, the Secretariat has not analyzed in detail the evolution of foreign-exchange use for these countries.

publication by AID of the list of merchandise in the *Small Business Bulletin*, and making successive changes in the documentation required for each shipment.

Much more important than this development of administrative requirements are the changes which have been gradually made in the negative list as the number and importance of items whose importation could not be financed chargeable to the letters of credit expanded significantly. Such financing was prohibited, for example, for imports made by a certain company,[4] and the list began to include, especially after 1966, articles with a clear competitive advantage for the United States, in terms of price and quality, or those with a comparatively secure market because of particularly appropriate distribution systems, consumer familiarity with trademarks, linkage between future imports and features of the existing productive structure (in the case of spare parts), etc. Also about the middle of the decade, minimum limits were specified on the value of each shipment (i.e., $1,000) eligible for financing under the letters of credit.

It should also be pointed out that, due mainly to the new restrictions introduced in the system and to various administrative difficulties involved in its operation, utilization of the letters of credit gradually dropped off in several countries. As a result the United States, especially after 1966, began to encourage the governments of the beneficiary countries to offer certain incentives to importers acquiring United States merchandise under the conditions stipulated in the program credit agreements.

The Criterion of Additionality and Overall and Sectoral Credits[5]

The criterion of additionality, already present in the expanding negative list, together with the insistence on incentives to importers of United States merchandise after about 1966, substantially altered the system of United States bilateral aid to Latin America and to the rest of the world as well, starting in 1967–68 when the fundamental changes summarized in the following paragraphs were made.

[4] For example, in the case of Chile, it was stipulated that imports by the Gran Minería del Cobre could not be paid for under these letters of credit.

[5] This section, like the preceding one, endeavors to generalize the experience of Latin American countries that have received program loans. Application of the criterion of additionality is not confined to overall program credits but also extends, in the same manner though to an extent varying in each case, to other AID operations, such as sectoral credits. For this reason, and considering the increase in the comparative importance of sectoral credits within total AID operations in recent years, the Secretariat has, in preparing this section, carefully analyzed the operation of both overall and sectoral program credits in the majority of the Latin American countries. As also indicated in the previous section, evolution in this field has varied by country, since the criterion of

In 1967, the Committee on the Balance of Payments operating at the cabinet level in the United States set up a work group on additionality which, with participation by AID, the Treasury Department, and the Department of Commerce, was instructed to find ways of making this principle operational. With regard to program loans, and to sectoral credits and other AID financial operations not directly tied to imports of specific goods for given investment projects, the most important of the new conditions are as follows:

1. The negative lists have been replaced by positive lists, which specify a very limited number of items eligible for financing with letters of credit issued under loan contracts.

2. The major criterion for selecting items to be included in the positive lists has been that the United States, in the recent past, must have had a minority participation in total imports of the beneficiary countries for each of those items.[6]

3. Composition of the positive lists and terms for utilization of the letters of credit are now determined in accordance with the additional United States exports to be promoted with a view toward maintaining their participation in the market. If the usual rate of importation from the United States of the items included in a positive list amounted during the previous period,[7] for example, to $4 million a month and the aim is to expand by 50 percent United States exports of these items to the country benefiting from the credit, the letters of credit—valid only to pay for imports included on the positive lists—should be used at a rate of $6 million a month. If the amount of credit covered by the system is $60 million, it will be stipulated, therefore, that the corresponding letters of credit will have to be used within ten months. The over-all result of application of the principle of additionality in this example would be. to increase by $20 million United States exports of these items.[8]

---

additionality has not been evenly applied by the United States in every case, but, in the opinion of the Secretariat, these differences are comparatively insignificant and do not alter the conclusions that may be drawn from this analysis. It should, however, be noted that the negative effect of application of the principle of additionality may be greater in some countries than in others, owing to the various characteristics of import trade and of import, exchange, and credit policies in each.

[6] In some negotiations held during the first few months of 1969, this rule was relaxed to some extent, allowing for inclusion on the positive list of certain items in which prior United States participation in total imports was higher than 50 percent.

[7] The previous period for comparison purposes varies from one country to another and from loan to loan.

[8] The percentages of additionality, terms, and other conditions vary from country to country. The example given in the text is designed solely to illustrate the method employed and does not refer directly to any specific case.

4. In cases where the beneficiary countries have sufficiently complete exchange and/or tariff controls, the system of additionality assumes that the country utilizes those controls in such a way as to reorient toward the United States imports of the items indicated in pars. 1 and 2 in the number and terms prescribed by the procedure outlined in par. 3.

5. In several cases, the United States has requested that preferential exchange treatment be granted to its exporters included in the positive lists. In at least one country, this treatment has been granted as a preferential rate of exchange. In another country the same concession was agreed upon in practice by supplying credits to importers and guaranteeing their purchase of the corresponding foreign exchange, upon expiration of the term of those credits, at the same exchange rate as that prevailing at the time the original operation was carried out. In several other cases, no agreement has been reached on such an incentive because of a refusal by the beneficiary countries.

6. For countries without the control systems mentioned in par. 4, a series of tariff and/or administrative incentives is established by mutual agreements between the United States and the countries receiving the credit in order to encourage purchases of the selected items in the United States. These incentives, whose specific type varies depending on the circumstances of each beneficiary country, may include exemptions from prior deposits, reduction of tariff duties, and other similar advantages.[9] It should be noted that, in order to comply with commitments at the world level with regard to trade and international payments, these incentives are not authorized directly for imports made from the United States. Instead, provisions are issued establishing the concession of these advantages when imports of merchandise included on the positive lists are paid for abroad with resources deriving from credits granted, for example, at more than twenty-five years term and no more

---

[9]Since the system of additionality is already in general effect, many examples of tariff "incentives" can be cited. Among operations analyzed by the Secretariat, mention may be made of the following cases: (a) utilization of import licenses as an instrument for achieving the desired goal of United States imports, together with elimination of prior deposits and the granting of credits referred to in par. 6; (b) elimination of prior import deposits combined with credit incentives; and (c) reduction of tariff duties by the equivalent of 25 percent of the c.i.f. value of capital goods included in the positive list and as chargeable against external credits granted at more than twenty-five years term (AID credits), simultaneously with a reduction of 15 percent on those goods paid against credits of eight to twenty-five years, 10 percent for imports against credits of five to eight years, and 5 percent for credits of between one and five years. In this case, before applying the criterion of additionality, all capital goods imported on credit benefited from the 25 percent reduction of customs duties.

than 2.5 percent interest—in other words, on the conditions on which AID has granted the credit.[10]

7. Supplementing the incentives outlined above, others relating to credits have also been established. Among the various cases analyzed by the secretariat in this connection, the two following examples may be cited:

   a. In one of the countries studied, a minimum of 180 days of credit was granted to all importers acquiring goods in the United States under this system, with the further offer of a preferential rate (4 percent a year).

   b. In another country, the minimum credit limit was fifty days, with a maximum of up to five years for capital goods (decided on a case-by-case basis by the monetary authorities) and without a preferential interest rate.

8. In order to secure better support from all government agencies of the beneficiary countries for the most rapid utilization possible of letters of credit, AID has been introducing the system of "letters of commitment" by which the counterpart funds may not be delivered to the government to finance spending programs until the import operation is carried out or until the importer pays the corresponding value. This system varies in the different countries and in some the earlier procedure of delivering counterpart funds to the government before the importation and/or payment of its value by the importer is still allowed.

9. Finally, mention should be made of another instrument proposed for application of the criterion of additionality, which in general calls for promoting the liberalization of restrictive import trade practices. In these cases, it can be assumed that such general liberalization would promote additional exports from the United States only to the extent that such exports are competitive with those of other exporting countries and provided that reduction of the restrictions also reduces the comparative importance of national production and/or increases total consumption of the goods involved.[11]

---

[10] As a result at least one European country (West Germany) has extended credit to a Latin American country under the conditions stipulated in the regulations issued on this aspect by the government of the beneficiary country. Also one complaint from a European country has already been submitted to the pertinent international agencies on the grounds that these incentives, in the case of a specific Latin American country, violate current agreements on international payments and trade.

[11] The general liberalization of trade referred to here obviously contradicts the incentives mentioned in previous paragraphs, which are in the main based precisely on the existence of general restrictions that permit preferential treatment to the United States. Among all the Latin American countries which the Secretariat has been able to study in

The Criterion of Additionality and Project Loan Priorities

As already pointed out, the criterion of additionality is not applicable solely to cases of over-all program loans but extends, in one way or another, to all AID operations. For example, some of the sectoral credits not allocated to specific imports for the projects or programs to be financed[12] are subject to the same procedures as the program loans. In fact, agreements on utilization of letters of credit by countries receiving both types of credit usually include both the total amount of the over-all loans and the amount not assigned to specific imports under sectoral loans.

No less important is the fact that the criterion of additionality also influences selection of the specific projects and programs financed by AID. Instead of presenting here any specific observation or analysis, this point is best illustrated by the following sentence by Mr. William S. Gaud, AID administrator up to the beginning of this year, in his statement of January 14, 1969, to the Subcommittee on International Exchange and Payments of the United States Congress Joint Economic Committee: "Beginning in 1964, special provisions were written into a number of loan agreements which required that the funds be used only for imports in excess of the recipient country's normal marketing requirements for certain commodities, such as fertilizer. In 1965 we further modified our financing policies to *include U.S. export promotion as an explicit criterion for selecting capital projects* and commodities for AID financing. Moreover, we have been giving *increasing weight to choosing capital projects which have a follow-on export potential.*"[13]

In other words, according to Mr. Gaud, the possibility of promoting United States exports is one of the explicit criteria determining the projects to be financed by AID. We may ask ourselves at this point to what extent this criterion has been and continues to be contradictory to the priorities that should govern the composition of public investment in the beneficiary countries. And, though Mr. Gaud does not refer to this, it should also be considered whether this criterion has influenced the general conditions—for example, sectoral composition of public spending, subsidies of inputs for farmers, etc.—agreed upon in negotiating certain over-all and sectoral loans.

---

this respect, only one can be said to have evolved a general and significant liberalization of import trade during the last two years, that is, during the period in which the criterion of additionality has been in full force.

[12] As an example of imports specified in the sectoral credits, mention may be made of fertilizers and farm machinery in credits for the agricultural sector.

[13] Statement of the Honorable William S. Gaud, administrator, Agency for International Development, before the Subcommittee on International Exchange and Payments of the Joint Economic Committee, January 14, 1969 (mimeographed). Underlining by the Secretariat.

The Criterion of Additionality and
the United States Balance of Payments

An evaluation, within the multilateral context of the Alliance for Progress, of the effects of the criterion of additionality should take into account, on the one hand, the extent to which this criterion has contributed to the aim of promoting additional United States exports—and thus maintaining that country's higher participation in the total import trade of the recipient countries—and, on the other, the consequences of its application for the Latin American countries.

This evaluation must necessarily be based on recognition of the existence of an unfavorable balance-of-payments position in the United States. However, such recognition does not imply the need to agree with the procedures adopted or to be adopted by that country to protect its balance of payments. Nor does it imply that it will be impossible to encounter formulas reconciling the interests of the United States and Latin America in the field of financial transactions.

Since the end of the last decade the United States has been tying its financial aid to the purchases of its goods and services. This tying significantly reduces the aid component of external financing and, from the standpoint of the recipient countries, it would be highly advisable to encounter more flexible and less costly procedures than those in effect, to which end certain suggestions are made in the final chapter of this study. However, from the standpoint of the United States balance of payments, it appears that aid tying has undoubtedly helped to prevent a greater deterioration than that occurring in recent years in this country's external position. In a way, it can be said that the part of the aid component absorbed by finance tying is converted into a general subsidy of United States exports.

However, a different conclusion is reached when the analysis refers not to tied aid as a whole but specifically to application of the principle of additionality. In the first place, its effect as an instrument to promote United States exports appears to have been very limited. At this point we may cite again Mr. Gaud's aforementioned statement to Congress:

It is difficult to say what the record would have been if we had not followed the policies we did. But let me begin making two assumptions.

First, if we had not introduced effective tying in the early sixties we could reasonably expect that only 40 percent of all commodity credits would be spent in the United States, as was the case in FY 1960.

The direct result on Gold Budget outflows might have been an increase of about $800 million a year from FY 1965 through FY 1968. Taking into

account indirect respending effects, the net increase in balance of payments costs might have been approximately $500 million a year.[14]

Second, let us assume that we had continued tying but had not imposed
additionality restrictions since 1964. Accepting the validity of the 10 percent substitution figure which we calculated for 1963–64, and taking
respending into account, it appears that all our additionality efforts only
saved us about $35 million a year over the last four years. It is striking that
the balance of payments benefits of additionality efforts are so much
smaller than those of the original tying.[15]

That is, according to Mr. Gaud, the net benefit to the United States
balance of payments of aid tying is about $500 million a year, while that of
the principle of additionality is only $35 million a year. Since these figures
refer to all AID operations throughout the world, the absolute amount of
benefit to the United States balance of payments from adoption of these
methods for AID operations with Latin America is, obviously, much less. The
impact of application to the region of the additionality principle according to
the method employed by Mr. Gaud would not exceed a level of from $10 to
$15 million a year.

While general aid tying tends to convert part of the cost of such aid into a
subsidy, also general, of United States exports, the additionality criterion
concentrates its subsidy on various items in which United States production is
less competitive on the world markets. In other words, a portion of the cost
of foreign aid to the United States taxpayer is used to subsidize the most
inefficient part of his country's productive structure, mainly, that part unable to compete adequately with the outside world.[16] We may ask whether,
in the long range, this comparatively expensive policy of export promotion
will not have harmful effects on the maintenance of high levels of efficiency
in the exporting sectors of this country and, ultimately, on over-all participation of United States exports in world trade.

[14]Taking into account these "respending effects," the percentage of untied financing
that would be spent to pay for goods and services in the United States amounts to 50
percent, as expressed by Mr. Gaud in another paragraph of this same statement.

[15]For a fuller explanation of the methods employed by Mr. Gaud and the AID in
arriving at these figures, see the complete text of this statement to the U.S. Congress on
January 14, 1969.

[16]To cite Mr. Gaud again: "Commodities on these (positive) lists are selected jointly
by AID, Commerce and Treasury according to several criteria. We attempt to identify
particular commodities where we believe we have a competitive advantage, but which are
not yet well represented in the recipient country's markets. We also seek to finance items
which will engender a follow-on demand, often for industrial spare parts. For the most
part, however, positive lists are made up of commodities in which the United States is
relatively less competitive, and which we would otherwise be unlikely to export in any
great volume."

Finally, among the negative aspects for the United States of the criterion of additionality, special mention must be made of the fact that, in view of the administrative difficulties and inflexibilities in the sound management of economic policy involved,[17] its application creates an unfavorable attitude among government officials and businessmen in the recipient countries toward United States aid and, more generally, toward the foreign economic policy of the United States.

Effect of the Criterion of Additionality on Latin American Countries

While application of the additionality criterion does not appear to have produced significant benefits for the United States, information available to the Secretariat indicates that it has led to a sizable reduction in aid utilization by the recipient countries.

Among the main determining factors in this reduction, the following may be cited:

1. Application of many of the incentives and regulations promoted on the basis of the principle of additionality is obviously contrary to the liberalization of foreign trade by the recipient countries, and to a better allocation of resources in those countries and in international trade in general, through proper operation of market mechanisms.[18] In countries in which direct exchange and/or tariff control systems are currently operating, the application of this principle would tend to diminish, in practice, the possibilities of liberalizing these controls. In countries where international trade is freer, the incentives promoted by the United States actually represent the establishment of direct or indirect import controls, depending on the case. We may cite the example of a Latin American country whose experience in this aspect has been studied in detail by the Secretariat. In the period 1964-67, this country made a significant effort to liberate its foreign trade by eliminating most of the established control systems. Because of the pressing conditions of its operations with AID, the monetary authorities of this country have been forced to devote a great deal of their efforts to reorienting toward the United States imports of items included on the positive list, through application of the incentives agreed upon in this

---

[17]See the following section on the effects of additionality on the recipient countries.

[18]Referring to the various instruments used to promote additionality, Mr. Gaud, in his above-mentioned statement to the U.S. Congress, said: "All of these efforts except the removal of discriminatory barriers, are restrictions on the operation of free market forces."

connection. Accordingly, before importation of capital goods included on the list can be approved from another source, the importer must present comparable offers from United States exporters and prove that the cost of the United States goods is significantly higher than for the other alternatives. This documentation is submitted for consideration to an interdepartmental government committee which, after taking into account all the circumstances of the case, decides which of the alternatives should be approved. In the same country, the Secretariat knows of a case in which the importation of certain articles chargeable to external credits not granted by AID has been prohibited unless such imports comply with certain requisites that are apparently beyond the reach of the other exporting countries.[19]

2. In cases where incentives are granted in the form of preferential exchange treatment, the damages are probably even greater than when the direct controls mentioned in the previous paragraph are employed, since this provides an incentive to maintain (or establish) systems of multiple exchanges that tend to distort the allocation of resources in general. When this preferential treatment takes the form of a guarantee of exchange rates for fairly extensive periods, a speculative factor—expectations of devaluation—is also introduced that can lead to unnecessary imports harmful to the short-range evolution of the balance of payments in the recipient country.

3. Application of the principle of additionality represents a reduction in the aid component of credit extended by AID. An earlier section of this study quantified the effects of tying on this aid component and, though no adequate quantitative analysis is available in this respect, it appears logical to assume that when imports financed by AID credits are confined to those items in which the United States position is least competitive, that is, when the criterion of additionality is applied, reduction of the aid component must be more intensive than under the earlier procedure. An indication that this is actually so is the fact that, in many of the recipient countries, the incentives originally agreed upon when the criterion of additionality was first applied have failed to stimulate purchases from the United States to the extent expected; consequently, an attempt has been made to increase these incentives to the level necessary to offset sufficiently the higher cost to the individual importer.

[19]In this case, the country competing with the United States was Latin American. Further reference to this specific case will be made elsewhere.

4. Another way of evaluating the reduction in the net benefit to the Latin American countries resulting from application of the additionality criterion would be to consider that in exchange for receiving credits on concessionary conditions from the United States, the aid recipients extend that country preferential treatment for certain imports which the United States wishes to expand. This is equivalent to the establishment in developing Latin American countries of "inverse preferences" in favor of the United States. In other words, it is the same procedure explicitly opposed by the United States when employed in trade relations between Europe and the developing countries of other regions.

5. The administrative cost to the recipient country of applying the incentives agreed upon pursuant to the principle of additionality is also considerable. A sizable portion of the skilled personnel employed by the institutions operating the system—primarily central banks and also, to an extent that varies in each country, planning offices, development banks, and various ministries—must be devoted to this task. The Secretariat has been able to confirm directly that a very high percentage of the available time of the higher executive personnel of those institutions must be employed in solving the domestic and external problems arising from reorientation of import trade toward the United States. Obviously, the caliber and sound management of economic policy can be undermined by withdrawing this technical and executive personnel from the highest priority tasks.

6. The general efficiency of economic activity in the recipient country is also adversely affected by the fact that businessmen importing goods included in the positive lists, especially those endeavoring to make their purchases outside the United States, must devote time and effort to the administrative processing, quotation requests, and other requisites of this system. The Secretariat has ascertained, through interviews with private importers in various Latin American countries, that the principle of additionality has caused those importers no less irritation than it has government officials.

7. Another important problem is the sluggishness which application of this principle entails in trade relations between the recipient countries and the rest of the world. It may even be stated that trade among the Latin American countries is adversely affected by application of the incentives and/or controls through which the system operates. In this respect, the Secretariat has examined in detail a specific case in which the measures agreed upon between the Latin American country and the United States to expand United States exports prevented a fairly sizable

sale by another Latin American country, which, except for application of these measures, appeared to occupy a favorable competitive position for this operation in terms of quality and price.[20]

8. The establishment of preferential interest rates for banking credit to importers acquiring goods included on the positive list from the United States and the concession of credits for purposes which, at times, do not appear to correspond to the priorities of development policy—for example, concession of credits for 180 days at 4 percent interest for importers of such consumer and capital goods—represent, at least potentially, a sizable distortion in the economy that is unjustified from the domestic standpoint of the process of allocating resources by market mechanisms.

9. The volume of domestic credit expansion sometimes required for application of the principle of additionality may significantly obstruct the management of monetary and credit policy, particularly in countries that are trying to control inflationary processes. For example, the Secretariat was able to examine in detail a case in which the expansion of credit incentives requested by the United States—extension from fifty to 180 days of the minimum credit limit granted to all importers of United States goods included in the positive list—would have signified that a very high proportion, from about 30 percent to 50 percent, depending on the time limit set for utilization of the letters of credit in this specific operation, of the total credit expansion planned for the private sector in the following year would have to be assigned to the importers following the system under discussion.

10. Finally, the fact that the United States is using the principle of additionality as one of the criteria determining the selection of specific investment projects financed by AID suggests the possibility that occasionally the purposes for which external financing is used are not wholly consistent with the priorities of national development policy in the recipient countries. Some United States officials responsible for applying the system of additionality frequently complain that it does not operate as efficiently as expected because the authorities of the recipient countries do not always make the efforts required to achieve the agreed upon aims. The Secretariat, in its study of experience in this area in various Latin American countries, has confirmed that there are indeed cases in which the incentives have not been applied with the

[20]This specific case refers to a sale by Argentina to another Latin American country of water pumps and other articles for agricultural use which could not be arranged because of the application of regulations agreed upon by the importing country with AID.

diligence projected and in which administrative processing has been unnecessarily complicated. In view of the unfavorable aspects of this system, it is not surprising that such cases should exist and that, in fact, a somewhat vacillating attitude should occasionally develop with regard to the application of measures whose economic justification is highly debatable, if not patently nonexistent, and whose consonance with the objectives of national development policy is also inadequate.

Conclusions

Two main conclusions can be derived from this analysis of tied aid and of the criterion of additionality. Firstly, tying of credits from AID generally leads to difficulties in the countries receiving the financing and sizably reduces the aid component. On the other hand, from the standpoint of the United States, such tying exerts favorable effects on that country's balance of payments. Secondly, application of the criterion of additionality does not appear to benefit the United States balance of payments significantly, while at the same time it sharply accentuates the problems already caused by tying for the recipient countries. It tends also to alienate the goodwill which from the point of view of the United States should be one of the favorable effects of its foreign aid programs.

It would, therefore, be advisable to eliminate immediately the criterion of additionality, and at the same time institute studies and negotiations at the national, inter-American, and international levels as soon as possible to seek formulas directed toward the total untying of external financing granted under the Alliance for Progress. On this point, certain further suggestions are made in the final chapter of this study.

EXTERNAL FINANCING AND NATIONAL DEVELOPMENT PRIORITIES

Objectives of External Financing in Latin America

At the start of the Alliance for Progress, it was expected, and so stated in the Charter of Punta del Este, that each country would prepare long-range national development programs which, following a multilateral evaluation, would serve as a basis for procuring external financing, especially from the United States government and the IDB. The Charter of Punta del Este itself indicated the basic objectives of economic and social development which, adapted to the circumstances of each country, should guide both the preparation of those plans and the concession of external financing, with a sizable part of this financing to be granted in the form of over-all program credits. As everyone now knows, this planning has failed to operate as anticipated,[21] and external financing, partly because of planning deficiencies, has not in general been extended on the basis of long-range development plans.

Since in many cases there was no clear, operational definition of the objectives and instruments of national development policy in specific plans suitable for execution, the initial concept of program loans lost much of the comparative importance originally assigned to it under the alliance, and each of the various financing agencies began to define *its* own priorities with a view to loans to be offered to each Latin American country. At present, these external financing institutions have prepared or are preparing, each agency separately, a medium-range program covering about five years of its future financing operations with each Latin American country.

The existence of these programs of each agency poses the need for co-ordinating them in terms of national priorities under the development policy of each country. That is, we must return to some extent to the pertinent provisions of the alliance at the time of its inception, though under different procedures that incorporate the experience of recent years. The final chapter of this study presents certain suggestions in this respect, while the remainder of this chapter examines the evolution under the alliance of the relations between external financing and development priorities.

Evolution of Priorities for the Use of External Financing

An earlier section of this study examined in detail evolution of the sectoral composition of external public financing received by Latin America during the period covered by the Alliance for Progress. Without attempting to repeat that analysis here, we should nevertheless repeat some of its conclusions, together with other observations on the priorities governing the concession of such financing:

1. Throughout the entire period, participation by the manufacturing sector in the total financing received by Latin America from external public institutions remained at a comparatively low level, less than the share corresponding to the power, transportation, and agricultural sectors; mining, including the petroleum industry, also failed to receive sizable volumes of resources from those financing agencies. Generally speaking, the criterion adopted appears to be that in the goods-producing sectors—with the exception of agriculture—where international private enterprises operate with

---

[21] See "Problems and Perspectives of Economic and Social Development" (CIES/1380) and "Estado de la Planificación en la América Latina" (CIES/1383). See also the reports presented by the Panel of Nine to the First (document CIES/17), Second (CIES/631), and Fourth (CIES/853 and 854) Annual Meetings of the IA-ECOSOC.

greater efficiency, those enterprises should be the ones to channel most of the transfer of capital and technological resources to Latin America.

2. In the first years of the alliance, some division of work was observed among the external financing agencies: IBRD specialized mainly in economic infrastructure; IDB allocated a sizable amount of its total resources to social development; and AID, as "residual" lender, preferred program credits, budget support credits, and certain priority projects, which for one reason or another were not covered by the two banks mentioned. Recently, this specialization has been less marked, with more similar sectoral priorities observed in the three institutions cited, though the IDB still places a greater emphasis on the social field.

3. Excluding EXIMBANK, there are very few instances—in some projects of the agricultural sector and of small and intermediate industry—of external public financing being used to promote export activities. Since an increase in exports is one of the basic priorities for development of the Latin American countries, it is essential for the external financing institutions to give greater attention to this aspect in programing their future activities.

4. Finally, we should recall at this point the statement already cited by Mr. William Gaud that promotion of United States exports is one of the criteria used in selecting investment projects financed by AID. The Secretariat has no information available on the extent to which this criteria may have influenced the allocation of financing granted by AID to Latin America. However, we should express here the advisability of encountering formulas to prevent criteria such as this from changing the orientation which, according to the Charter of Punta del Este and the Declaration of the Presidents of America, should be given to external financing granted under the Alliance for Progress.

External Financing and Development Policies

The external financing received by Latin America in this decade has not generally been extended in terms of formal long-range development plans, except on very few occasions, generally during the initial years of the alliance. However, AID continued to grant program credits to some countries and it was considered necessary to seek procedures through which the concession of these over-all credits could be based on orderly expression of the economic policy to be adopted by the recipient countries.

When CIAP was established in 1964, it was believed that the annual country reviews conducted by subcommittees of that agency could provide a proper framework for multilateral discussion of the economic and social policies of the Latin American countries; their conclusions would thus serve as a basis for granting external financing under the alliance, especially in the case of program credits. Without attempting to present here an evaluation of the extent to which the country reviews have actually achieved this objective, it should be mentioned that, on the one hand, the IDB usually abstains from separate general evaluations of the economic and social policy of recipient countries, on the grounds that the country reviews already perform this function within the context of the inter-American system. On the other hand, AID is obliged, pursuant to current United States legislation, to grant its financing in accordance with the conclusions and recommendations of the CIAP subcommittees.

In the case of program credits, an additional procedure supplementing the country reviews is involved. The corresponding national authorities send a letter to the CIAP chairman specifically stating the most important aspects of the government program for the following year. This letter constitutes the policy basis for the authorization of program credits. Occasionally, this letter has been replaced by a copy—also sent to the CIAP chairman—of a declaration on economic policy made internally in the country by the corresponding authorities or by a copy of a memorandum sent by the government to another international agency.

These letters to the CIAP chairman constitute a unilateral and voluntary statement by the respective governments on the guidelines of the economic policy programed for the immediate future. However, they do not usually cover the entire field of this economic policy but tend rather to concentrate on those areas in which AID requests a definition of the government's intentions before agreeing to the respective loan. It is of interest to observe, in general, which these areas are and how they have evolved, since they are indicative of the national development priorities which the United States appears to support through its financing operations. In this respect, the following points may be made:

    a. There is a growing concentration on areas of interest to short-range policy, especially in recent years, in countries with intensive inflation. Accordingly, explicit mention is made of government programing with regard to public finances, monetary expansion, movement of international reserves, and other aspects of the stabilization policy, indicating as well the government's proposals with regard to the concerting and implementation of standby agreements with the International Monetary Fund.

    b. During the last few years, in indicating the programed composition of public expenditures, specific mention has been made of the percentage of those expenditures proposed for use in certain sectors, especially agriculture and education, coinciding with AID's interest in providing financial support for programs in which the percentage of public spending allocated to the sectors tends to increase. In addition, the anticipated volume of public savings and the proportion of total public spending expected to be used for investment are usually indicated.

c. Emphasis is usually placed on what the government plans to do with regard to liberalization of tariff protection for national production, with a view to increasing its efficiency.

Depending on specific circumstances in each country, plans for certain other priority action areas are outlined.

These areas generally correspond to the points usually most emphasized by AID representatives during the discussions held at meetings of the CIAP subcommittees, not only in cases where program credits exist, but in the other countries as well.

In all these aspects of AID activity, it is apparent that certain long-range topics given preferential attention in the Charter of Punta del Este and in operations during the first years of the alliance—as for example agrarian reform—are now assigned a significantly much lower priority. At the same time, it is evident that major concern is currently centered on short-range financial stability, both for countries where inflation now exists and in those areas where potential inflationary tensions have been emerging in these past few years.

CONCLUSIONS

The various problems examined in this chapter emphasize the need, in programing the external cooperation to be received by Latin America over the next few years, for giving attention not only to the amounts required and to the urgent need for improving conditions on which financing is granted with regard to interest rates and grace and amortization terms, but also to the changes that must be made in other aspects of this external cooperation.

It appears obvious that the criterion of additionality must be eliminated as soon as possible and that it is also necessary to find solutions to the more general problem of the tying of financing granted by the United States. In addition, procedures will have to be employed to ensure that the priorities governing the concession of external financing are defined by taking into stricter account the specific circumstances in each country and the orientation each government decides to give to its development policy.

CHAPTER VI

Project Loan Tying

INTRODUCTION

Chapter V has discussed the AID policies intended to assure that disbursements from that agency's program and sector loans be used exclusively for purchases of additional United States goods and services (i.e., the principle of additionality). However, the United States balance-of-payments problem, ever since the beginning of this decade, has given rise to similar policies in connection with project loans. In fact, such tying is an almost universal aspect of development assistance given bilaterally to Latin America. Sweden is the only country known to abstain completely from such practices. All other developed countries—at least occasionally or marginally—attach to their loans a provision that projects for which they provide the financing must serve the purpose of purchasing goods or services provided by this country, and may do so in an equally or more restrictive manner than United States agencies, even though there is no balance-of-payments problem.[1]

At its fifth annual meeting, IA-ECOSOC expressed the request that CIAP undertake a thorough quantitative and qualitative study of these practices.[2] In its attempt to provide CIAP with the necessary data, the Secretariat encountered difficulties similar to those encountered in earlier studies.[3] It

---

[1] The special tying conditions of the various financing institutions are presented in appendix VI-A.

[2] The Action Program of Viña del Mar, Heading B: External Financing, Point 18, reads as follows: "18. CIAP shall present, to the next meeting of IA-ECOSOC, a cost analysis of medium- and long-term tied loans, through weighted sampling of the lending countries, in consultation with the countries, taking cases of representative projects, both by sectors and by sources and types of financing. This study shall consider not only the differences resulting from costs of materials and equipment, but also from the costs of financing and the terms of the loans. A similar analysis will be made of program loans with official guarantees."

[3] Mahbub ul Haq, "Tied Credits—a Quantitative Analysis," International Economic Association, Conference on Capital Movements and Economic Development, July 21–31, 1965, Washington, D.C. UNCTAD, "Growth, Development, Finance and Aid Report on Tied Aid Credits: Chile," UNCTAD TD/7/Supp. 8/Add 1, New Delhi, India, February 1968.

proved impossible to obtain comparable cost data, on a sufficiently broad and representative spectrum of transactions, and therefore it is impossible to establish with any degree of certainty, either through census methods or through a representative sample, what, in general, is the price differential between goods or services purchased from the source specified by lenders insisting on tying and the same goods or services when purchased from the cheapest source. The main reasons for this difficulty are as follows:

1. Often, when there was general agreement that the cost of purchases from the tying source was substantially higher than from the best alternative source, no competitive international bidding had taken place.

2. Comparisons based on alternate price quotations do not correctly reflect true cost differentials from the buyer's viewpoint, when the goods or services in question are not homogeneous; and goods or services, that need be obtained from industrialized countries for carrying out development projects, quite often are not simple, homogeneous products. More likely than not, different industrialized countries have developed alternative types of capital goods or services which vary in price, depending on their suitability from the viewpoint of the individual Latin American country. These goods and services may have a different scale of output or a different economic life span.

While these factors made it impossible to prepare a meaningful, general quantification of tying costs, the Secretariat, nevertheless believes it will be useful to submit the findings of sixteen cases which it was able to investigate. It will be noted that lending activities by AID, EXIMBANK, and the Social Progress Trust Fund of the IDB (another United States tied financial resource) account for all but one of the transactions discussed. The reason is not necessarily the greater cost differential of such tying in comparison with tying by other bilateral lenders; it is explained by the predominance of the lenders mentioned among those which provide project financing in Latin America. It is also stressed, once more, that these cases do not form a representative sample from the viewpoint of Latin American borrowers. Finally, it should be noted that the inclusion of certain EXIMBANK credits among the cases shown in table VI-1 serves only to indicate the magnitude of cost differentials resulting from tying. It was not considered feasible for loans granted by an institution whose primary purpose is to promote United States exports to be untied.

COST DIFFERENTIAL BETWEEN TIED AND COMPETITIVE SOURCES

Table VI-1 presents the findings for the sixteen cases studied, which are set forth in greater detail in appendix VI-B.

Table VI-1. Summary of Cases Studied

Case	Agency	Loan Amount ($) (A)	Value of Goods		Cost of Tying for the Goods Studied ($) (B) −(C) (D)	Cost of Tying as Percentage of	
			Purchase from Tied Source ($) (B)	Price Quoted in More Competitive Source ($) (C)		Value of Categories Analyzed (%) (D) ÷ (B) (E)	Amount of Credit Authorized (%) (D) ÷ (A) (F)
I	EXIMBANK	8,000,000	1,524,222	1,056,199	468,023	30.7	5.8
II	IDB–SPTF	5,500,000	1,853,500	1,182,533	670,967	36.2	12.2
III	AID–IDB(CO)–IDA–IBRD	39,000,000	n.a.	n.a.	n.a.	n.a.	n.a.
IV	AID	650,000	n.a.	n.a.	n.a.	n.a.	n.a.
V	AID–EXIMBANK	5,050,000	n.a.	n.a.	1,300,000	n.a.	25.7
VI	AID	700,000	1,450,800	1,170,000	280,800	19.4	19.4
	(Local)	750,800					
VII	AID	1,200,000	n.a.	n.a.	n.a.	n.a.	n.a.
VIII	IDB–SPTF	1,100,000	244,890	138,477	106,413	43.5	9.7
IX	AID	2,000,000	291,191	161,519	129,672	44.5	6.5
X	IDB–SPTF	3,500,000	15,668	11,656	4,012	25.6	1.1
XI	AID	500,000	n.a.	n.a.	n.a.	n.a.	n.a.
XII	IDB–SPTF	3,020,000	1,291,252	1,169,000	122,252	9.5	4.0
XIII	IDB–SPTF	5,300,000	399,724	n.a.	n.a.	n.a.	n.a.
XIV	KFW	17,500,000	8,382,531	8,284,101	98,430	1.2	0.6
XV	AID	23,000,000	n.a.	n.a.	n.a.	n.a.	n.a.
XVI	AID	3,300,000	215,649	191,375	24,274	11.3	0.7

Horizontal continuation of Table VI-1

(A) × (E) Total Cost of Tying ($)	Financial Aid Component		Aid Component (Optimistic Hypothesis)		Cleared (Pessimistic Hypothesis)	
	Value ($)	(H) ÷ (A) (%)	(H) − (D) ($)	(J) ÷ (A) (%)	(H) − (G) ($)	(L) ÷ (A) (%)
(G)	(H)	(I)	(J)	(K)	(L)	(M)
2,456,000	303,421	3.8	−164,601	−2.1	−2,152,579	−26.9
1,991,000	1,291,084	23.5	620,117	11.3	−699,916	−12.7
n.a.	15,730,671	40.3	n.a.	n.a.	n.a.	n.a.
n.a.	424,003	65.2	n.a.	n.a.	n.a.	n.a.
280,800	591,397	11.7	−708,603	−14.0	n.a.	n.a.
n.a.	436,408	62.3	155,608	22.2	n.a.	n.a.
260,700	521,856	43.5	n.a.	n.a.	n.a.	n.a.
n.a.	331,431	30.1	225,018	20.5	70,731	6.4
896,000	1,334,227	66.7	n.a.	n.a.	n.a.	n.a.
n.a.	1,214,500	34.7	1,213,143	34.7	321,155	9.2
285,944	262,137	52.4	n.a.	n.a.	n.a.	n.a.
n.a.	713,841	23.6	591,589	19.6	427,847	14.2
n.a.	2,156,893	40.7	n.a.	n.a.	n.a.	n.a.
n.a.	1,545,220	8.8	1,446,790	8.3	n.a.	n.a.
n.a.	10,002,239	43.5	n.a.	n.a.	n.a.	n.a.
372,900	2,152,631	65.2	2,128,357	64.0	1,779,731	53.9

Source: Appendix VI-B.

165

Column B shows the total value of the goods purchased from tied sources in the cases for which information was available; column C shows the total value of the same goods had they been purchased in the alternative market where costs are lower. Column D sets out the cost of tying; that is, the difference between the amounts corresponding to the tied and to the competitive markets.

The study revealed that the cost of tying (column E) varied between 1.2 percent and 44.5 percent of the value of goods purchased in the tied sources; which represents a variation from 0.6 percent to 25.7 percent of the authorized amount of the loan. If a given case of tied loans is analyzed under the assumption that there were no additional purchases that would represent higher costs because of the tying, then the percentages in column B represent the direct monetary cost of the tying. It is likely, however, that in the additional purchases there may be price differences as between the tied source and the more competitive source, although it was not possible to measure them. Hence it may be deduced that the percentages in column F represent a minimum cost.

If it is assumed that the price difference found between the items for which information was available is representative of the other goods charged against the loan, then the cost of tying would be the amount appearing in column G.

From the standpoint of the borrower the aid component[4] in the loans analyzed varies between 3.8 percent and 66.7 percent of their value (columns H and I). To calculate the net proceeds obtained from the utilization of tied credits, the cost of tying must be subtracted from the aid component. These results are shown in columns J-M. If the minimum estimates (column F) are accepted, the aid component (columns J-K) would vary from -14 percent to 64 percent. If, on the other hand, the hypothesis presented in column G is accepted, the aid component would be smaller, fluctuating between -27 percent and 54 percent.

The case studies also lend themselves to some analysis concerning the extent of the price increase of specific imports when obtained from high-cost countries, rather than the cheapest source. For this purpose, table VI-2 is included. This table shows that higher prices almost invariably resulted from the obligation to buy in the United States rather than in Europe or Japan,

---

[4]The concept is defined in chap. II of the main document. However, in contradistinction to the calculation in that chapter, it is assumed in the attached table that the interest rate is 6 percent instead of 9 percent. This difference is explained by the fact that according to explanations proffered by officials of various Latin American countries, there was a possibility of obtaining credits from suppliers at this lower rate when the tied loans were negotiated.

Table VI-2. Various Examples of Tying Cost in Development Plans

Case	Cost of Goods Purchased Tied Source ($) (A)	Lower Bid ($) (B)	(A) − (B) Cost due to Tying ($) (C)	(C) ÷ (A) (%) (D)	No. of Categories	Type of Goods	Country of Purchase	Source of Lower Bid
I	1,524,222	1,056,199	468,023	30.7	9	Equipment for electric power stations	U.S.	Germany, Chile, Belgium
II	461,074	294,174	166,900	36.2	11	Cement pipe and other items for potable water	Colombia, Mexico and U.S.	Italy and the Federal Republic of Germany
VIII	244,890	138,477	106,413	43.5	3	Passenger elevators	U.S.	Japan and Europe
IX	291,191	161,519	129,672	44.5	1	Cement	U.S.	Latin American country
X	15,668	11,656	4,012	25.6	6	Misc. building materials	U.S.	Japan and/or Europe
XII	1,291,252	1,169,000	122,252	9.5	7	Cast-iron pipe	U.S.	France
XVII	215,649	191,375	24,274	11.3	17	Misc., necessary for electrification project	U.S.	Various European countries and Japan

Source: Appendix VI-B.

although higher cost also came about in one case because of the decision to buy in Latin America.

Another way of evaluating the increment in the cost of commodities derived from the tying of credits would be to analyze the competitiveness of the main lending countries in the categories usually imported by Latin America.

Unfortunately, there are no studies that take up all aspects of the problem of tying. For example, the results are presented below of a partial study[5] on the competitiveness of United States products measured in price indices in comparison to similar English, German, and Japanese goods on the European Common Market. The study covered 1,300 international bids and analyzed 200 products; in four important groups of products[6] the United States was found to be in an unfavorable price position vis-à-vis products of other markets examined in this study (see table VI-3).

Table VI-3. Relative Export Price Levels of Four Industrialized Areas

SITC	Category	International Price Levels, 1964[a]			
		U.S.	U.K.	EEC	Germany
		(A)	(B)	(C)	(D)
67	Iron and steel	100	81	80	81
68	Non-ferrous metals	100	98	98	100
71	Non-electrical machinery	100	92	98	95
73	Transportation equipment except highway motor vehicles (except 732)	100	91	92	91

[a]These indices are average indices for smaller groups corresponding to the level of three, four, five digits of the SITC weighted by the importance of each group in world trade.

Source: Krevis and Lipsey, "Measurement of Price Exchange," p. 485.

Cost of Using Non-Latin American Consultants

In the survey made, many of the officials of the borrowing countries pointed out that, in their opinion, the major excess costs arose not from the

[5]Irving B. Krevis and Robert E. Lipsey, "The Measurement of Price Exchange: A Report on the Study of International Price Competitiveness," American Economic Review, May 1967, vol. 2.

[6]Corresponding to groups 67, 68, 71, and 73 (except 732 of the Standard International Trade Classification of the United Nations [SITC]).

tying of the commodity purchasing market, but from the requirement that extraregional consulting firms be hired.

1. The salaries of the foreign consultants are higher than those of local consultants because of the differential in professional fees between developing and industrialized countries.
2. In many instances, the lender requires the hiring of services that the borrower considers unnecessary.
3. Because of the low level of the experts sent and the lack of knowledge of local conditions, the efficiency of the service rendered is not all it should be.

Tying in Relation to Services

Reference was made in most of the countries visited to the economic damage arising from the United States legal regulations as regards the hiring of services, especially in the areas of transportation and insurance. For example, in general, 50 percent of the goods purchased against EXIMBANK and AID credits must be shipped in vessels of United States registry and insured by United States companies. Since this 50 percent must be applied article by article, it turns out in practice that in most cases it does not pay to ship the remainder in bottoms of other nations.

In various countries, the damage most frequently mentioned was the delay arising from the infrequency with which United States ships touch their ports. Under these circumstances, there is a possibility of release from this shipping requirement but full advantage has not been taken of it because of lack of foresight or ignorance of this alternative. Another point mentioned was the damage produced by the underutilization of national or regional merchant fleet capacity.

Even though it has been impossible to obtain data that would permit assessing the magnitude of each type of damage, it should be pointed out that Haq[7] found that the rates charged by ships of United States registry were 43 to 113 percent higher than those of other countries. It was also impossible to obtain figures on the cost attached to the obligation of taking out insurance abroad.

THE OVERALL ECONOMIC EFFECTS OF TYING

An attempt should be made to estimate the over-all effects of tying procedures on the economies of the borrowing and lending countries. No precise

[7]Haq, "Tied Credits," p. 3.

calculations are possible and the following ones represent only rough guesses of the magnitudes involved.

Effects on Borrowers

For purposes of illustration, it is assumed that, on the average, tying adds somewhere between 12.5 and 25 percent to the cost of purchases made in relation to development assistance. Likewise, merely for the purpose of illustration, this percentage is considered specifically in relation to assistance given by AID. This agency of the United States government is singled out because it is, by far, the most important source of tied development assistance and lends itself most easily to illustrative purposes. Its selection does not imply that its tying procedures, in relative terms, are more costly to borrowers than such practices by other bilateral lenders, all of whom follow tying practices of comparable nature. The tying practices of EXIMBANK—the second most important development lender that restricts all uses of its resources to a given source of supply—have been omitted from this analysis. Since this agency was established, specifically, for the purpose of promoting the foreign trade of the United States, there is little likelihood that it will finance large-scale purchases in other areas.

In 1968, loan disbursements by AID in all countries participating in the Alliance for Progress amounted to about $380 million. While $201 million of this represents the flow of resources under program loans, in order to avoid complicating the illustration, it is assumed that the lower limits of cost increases resulting from tying this type of loan, too, were also of the magnitude of 12.5 and 25 percent. It follows that the requirement that AID funds must all be spent on United States goods and services had the same effect as reducing the value of United States assistance by about $40–85 million in one year. Inversely, untying might have automatically increased United States assistance in that one year by the amounts stated. In fact, untying would have had a greater benefit to the borrowing countries than an increase of AID loans by the amount mentioned, as it would have accomplished such increase of assistance *without* a corresponding future rise in payments of amortization and interest.

Other effects of tying on the borrowing country cannot be quantified but are equally significant. When borrowers are not allowed to purchase goods and services in the borrowing country or other Latin American countries—admittedly at a somewhat higher cost than in the United States in many instances—an important stimulant to development is lost. In the first place, there is no corresponding increase in demand for domestic resources which, to the extent they have heretofore been less than fully employed, would have brought about an increase in real national income. Secondly, as this demand for goods and services, required in connection with development projects and programs, is often of a highly sophisticated nature, it would have led, in particular, to the growth of those sectors whose expansion is most essential for development. This effect could have been felt either directly in the country borrowing for development purposes, or indirectly through the stimulation of integrating area industries.

Effects on Lenders

The alleged benefits to the lender of tied aid are primarily of two types: benefits accruing to domestic suppliers of specific goods and services—thus benefiting the respective economies in general; and secondly, improvement of the balance of payments of the lender.

The case of countries with a balance-of-payments surplus. In view of the situation in these countries no significant full employment or national income benefits can be assured in the respective developed country from the use of tying practices, although, evidently, special interest groups may benefit. As for balance-of-payments benefits, the situation of all but three countries tying development loans (France, the United Kingdom, and the United States), is such that improving the balance of payments is not a major policy concern. In fact, in one of the countries (Germany) it, admittedly, is in the lender's interest to reduce its net trade surplus.

On the other hand, the enlightened self-interest of lenders demands that recipients of their development assistance are able to make the best possible use of such aid; and any policy that reduces the purchasing power of development funds by a considerable percentage surely has the opposite effect. If this adverse result is weighed against the at best negligible benefits of tying aid to purchases in developed countries whose balance of payments are in a comfortable state and which are fully employed, the argument in favor of abolishing such tying should be self-evident. In short, there are only three countries (France, the United Kingdom, and the United States) where tying aid does not reveal itself, a priori, as an indefensible practice.

The case of countries with a balance-of-payments deficit. The balance of payments of Latin America with the United States during the last thirteen years has been consistently unfavorable.[8] Furthermore, since 1963, the balancing item (Errors and Omissions and Transfers between Areas) has consistently shown a negative sign. During the 1961–68 period, the average of these entries amounted to $274 million.

[8] *Problems and Perspectives of Economic and Social Development* (CIES/1380).

Part of this amount surely reflects statistical deficiencies: errors and omissions. But the relative and absolute size of the annual figures strongly support the assumption that much of it results from transfers between foreign areas. And since the sign is negative, this would mean that Latin America received funds from areas other than the United States which went to swell the assets of Latin American countries vis-à -vis the United States or to pay for the Latin American current account deficit. In short, Latin America, for the last five years, has supported the United States balance of payments.

What actually would be the effect of complete untying on the United States balance of payments? For purposes of illustration once more, the tying practices of AID are singled out in order to analyze the effect of such practices on the lending country. Again, it should be noted that this selection does not imply that the tying policies of this agency are more harmful from the viewpoint of the borrowing countries than those of other agencies following tying practices.

This agency disbursed $380 million in 1968. According to various studies, the average propensity to import by Latin American countries from the United States together with its import multiplier has been estimated to range from 0.50 to 0.55.[9] AID tying, therefore, saved the United States, at most, $180 million in 1968 (45 percent of $380 million). But this conclusion is based on the unrealistic assumption that present AID tying practices were *completely* effective, in the sense that every penny of the $380 million disbursed by AID in 1968 was spent in the United States, and that none of these expenditures liberated Latin American exchange-holding for expenditures in other regions (which, in the absence of AID assistance, would have been spent in the United States). Secondly, United States exports to Latin America brought about by tying embody a certain amount of foreign inputs (raw materials and components) and also cause an increase of income in the United States, causing a further increase in United States imports due to the multiplier effect. These additional imports would not have taken place had there been no tying, and the exchange loss thus induced must therefore be subtracted from the balance-of-payments benefit of tying. As a rough guess, it may be assumed that tied assistance to Latin America granted through AID is likely to have saved the United States—in terms of short-term balance-of-payments accounting—between $100 and $130 million in 1968.

It would be an oversimplification, nevertheless, to state that the United States authorities should decide whether or not to continue tying develop-

---

[9] It has been stated in *The United States Balance of Payments in 1968* (Washington, D.C.: Brookings Institution, 1963): "If the United States gives $1,000 in totally untied aid to Latin America . . . $550 will ultimately be spent for U.S. exports."

ment assistance in the case of the AID operations in Latin America solely by considering such quantifiable results as the increase of $40–85 million (if all AID tying were abolished) against the loss of approximately $100–130 million per year. Other factors should be kept in mind. The image of the United States suffers in Latin America as a result of tying procedures—particularly in connection with the rules governing the retaining of United States consulting services. Furthermore, delays in project or program execution, ascribable to tying provisions, further blemish this image.

Tying, invariably, reduces the aid component or increases the cost of development loans to borrowers; this effect is approximately quantifiable. Complete untying would—in some instances—solve the problem of the borrower, but it would involve, for certain lenders, a short-term balance-of-payments cost that, likewise, is approximately quantifiable. It is not for the Secretariat to recommend a simple trade-off, where this situation prevails. From the point of view of the philosophy of development aid itself, the elimination of tied aid is the only satisfactory solution. This would lead to a real increase in the flow of financing, which is scarce at the present time, with a corresponding decline in balance-of-payments income which can be considered to be marginal.

REDUCTION OF THE ADVERSE IMPACT OF TIED AID

In the cases of Canada, the Federal Republic of Germany, Italy, and Japan—that is, economies in near or full employment, with no balance-of-payments problems—it is recommended that tied aid, given either directly or channeled through a trustee, such as the IDB, should be abandoned completely. In the case of countries such as the United States, France, or the United Kingdom, it is understandable that, in relation to their external transactions, great concern is shown for the resulting balance-of-payments effect. But the balance-of-payments problem of any country, in the final analysis, is the result of a fundamental disequilibrium in the economic and financial situation of that country or of other countries with which the country in question has economic or financial relations. Specific balance-of-payments measures which result in an allocation of resources which is less than optimum cannot solve this underlying problem. Just as price control or rationing cannot solve inflation and only makes the use of resources less effective, so will tying of development loans decrease the effectiveness of development assistance without solving the fundamental balance-of-payments problem of the lender and/or borrower.

The only genuine solution to the United States balance-of-payments problem—or that of any other deficit country—is the reestablishment of external equilibrium through appropriate economic and monetary policies by deficit and surplus countries alike. This is also the one and only complete and permanent solution to the tied aid problem. Everything else is merely a stopgap.

Recent United States policies and advances in international financial co-operation give hope that these underlying economic problems will be solved. But this will take time. In the meantime, to allow early dismantling of tying prior to the complete solution of the balance-of-payments problem of deficit countries, surplus countries should increase considerably, at an early occa-sion, in relative and absolute terms, their untied development assistance. Given the fact that the United States continues to offer many goods and services on the international market at competitive prices, this country is likely to benefit sufficiently, from the increase of its own exports in the wake of liberalization of assistance by surplus countries, to permit untying of its own development assistance. This would be a multilateral action which, as with the expansion or integration of a market, would make everybody gain and nobody lose.

While the preceding suggestions seem to be the only ones offering a genuine and permanent solution of the problem at hand, their complete implementation may not be considered feasible at this time. While stressing that they are the best solutions, the following section considers possible means of lessening the effects of tied aid until a final solution is found.

Modification of Aid Tying Procedures

The adverse effect of tying procedures could be further modified by allow-ing Latin American countries to utilize development assistance funds for purchase not only in the United States but also in other Organization of American States member countries. This would imply extension to all of Latin America of the "regional" criterion used at present only in the case of AID loans to Central America. It thus would not create a precedent. It also would not have a greatly adverse impact on the United States balance of payments.

It may be assumed that any additional income in Latin American coun-tries, resulting from additional exports to neighboring countries, would be spent in its entirety—that is, nothing would be hoarded—and that the same would happen with all subsequent income rounds created by the initial in-crease in export incomes. Let it further be assumed that in Latin America taken as a whole, the marginal propensity to import from the United States is approximately the same as the propensity to import from the rest of the world. If these hypotheses are realistic, a change in policy allowing Latin American countries to utilize development funds received from the United

States for purchase anywhere in the Latin American area would divert no more than 50 cents out of each United States assistance dollar into extracontinental areas. An increase in income in any Latin American country almost invariably translates itself into imports of capital goods and other items furnished to a considerable extent by the United States. Therefore, while such liberalization might benefit Latin American development to a considerable extent—particularly in the so-called integration industries—the adverse effects on the United States balance of payments of such partial liberalization is bound to be limited.

Exemptions from Tying Procedures

It is suggested that any purchase exceeding a certain minimum, say $20,000, be submitted for bids open to all interested, regardless of domicile and nationality. The most favorable bid submitted by a supplier in the country tying development assistance could then be compared with the most favorable alternate bid. If the difference between these two bids were to exceed for example: (1) 10 percent of the total project; or (2) 20 percent of the group of items submitted, simultaneously, to international bidding; or (3) more than 25 percent of any individual item worth more than $10,000, the source of development assistance funds could be asked to give a waiver with regard to purchases in question.[10] Instances in which a waiver would be called for because of the existence of large price differentials are likely to be limited. On the other hand, this procedure would eliminate those instances— probably relatively few—of very high price differentials in the purchase of projects and programs financed by foreign official development assistance lenders or donors. In turn, such cost reform would eliminate cases which are most harmful to the image of the lender or donor.

Furthermore, the mere existence of this procedure is likely to eliminate monopolistic abuses that can exist whenever there are few suppliers of a given item in the lender or donor countries and when these sources know that they can operate under the umbrella of tying procedures.

Technical Assistance to Assure Optimum Purchasing Procedures

It is suggested that a technical advisory system be created which would help government agencies in Latin America to take advantage of the expertise possessed by such United States agencies as the General Services Administra-

---

[10] Percentage values given were chosen for purposes of illustration only, in a somewhat arbitrary fashion. It is realized, of course, that the minimum size of project justifying the additional cost of international bidding, as well as the decision of what are unjustifiably large price differentials, are matters which will have to be examined further and most likely would be modified in the light of thorough technical analysis.

tion or others responsible in that country for large-scale government purchases.

The *modus operandi* of United States firms, in some respects, is different from that of Latin American businesses with which the government officials in the country receiving development assistance are accustomed to deal. This may well put these officials at a negotiating disadvantage. Furthermore, many of the highly sophisticated and expensive capital goods required in connection with the execution of development projects and programs have no easily ascertainable market price. It requires technically highly qualified purchasing agents, who have dealt over a prolonged period of time with suppliers of such specialized items in the market in question, to negotiate an optimum purchase contract. Such lack of expertise by Latin American purchasing agents may not be so crucial whenever there is world-wide open bidding, with greater competition among suppliers, but it is indispensable when purchasing is limited to one country only; that is, when the limited number of suppliers enhances the disadvantage in which a less sophisticated buyer finds himself.

Such technical assistance could take the form of a special course or seminar, offered by United States agencies to Latin American government officials. It may also be advisable to establish a system which would allow Latin American purchasing agencies to undertake periodic consultation with their United States counterparts.

Appendixes to Chapter VI

APPENDIX VI-A: BILATERAL FINANCING

This section describes the special tying conditions of the bilateral and multilateral financing agencies. United States agencies, which in recent years have granted more than 80 percent of all development loans to Latin America, stipulate that the total amount of money lent must be spent on goods and services from the United States, except in the case of Central America, which is permitted to use the funds for imports from the other member states of the CACM. Also, at least 50 percent of the goods purchased must be transported in United States ships, excepting in cases in which this is impossible because of lack of services under the United States flag. The mechanism of additionality serves to ensure that foreign exchange will not be diverted to third countries, in the case of loans for programs.

Next in importance as a lender for development under the Alliance for Progress is the Federal Republic of Germany, which, through its Reconstruction Corporation (KFW), has authorized approximately 8 percent of all bilateral development loans to Latin America in recent years. There is generally no formal tying on the part of this institution, but in the opinion of some observers, German authorities give preference to projects requiring the importation of goods and services that can be obtained under more favorable conditions in Germany. Also, in some cases, the borrower has been obliged to make imports from Germany to promote German industries that are partially idle. Thus, it is estimated that no more than 30 percent of the funds lent by KFW to Latin America are spent outside of Germany. Technical and consulting services are financed by KFW when provided by Germans. Generally, the agency does not finance freight charges for goods purchased with the loans that it grants.

The Italian government confines its bilateral financial aid to Latin America (approximately 5 percent of the total) to guaranteeing credits from Italian suppliers, when they are discounted by Medio Crédito.[1] In other words, official Italian aid to Latin America is completely tied.

Canada provides development loans (2 percent of the total bilateral aid received by Latin America) subject to the requirement that they be used for purchasing goods and services that are at least 80 percent of Canadian origin.

The French government's credit for Latin America (from 1 to 2 percent of the bilateral aid received by the region) is for the most part not tied formally. It is customary, however, to conclude agreements for financial aid together with bilateral trade agreements for purchasing French goods and services which are called "development projects." Hence this aid is completely tied.

[1] Italian rediscount agency.

Japan—whose development credits have in recent years been between 1 and 2 percent of the total of this type of capital received by Latin America—performs these operations almost entirely through its export bank. It has extended credits mainly to finance sales of its shipping industry when these operations could not be financed through private banks.

Britain, which has in recent years supplied about 1 percent of the official credit aid received by Latin America, stipulates that the credits can be utilized for expenditures outside the United Kingdom only when the prices of English suppliers are unreasonably high. Thus it is considered that British credits to Latin America have for the most part been completely tied.[2]

To sum up: bilateral aid from the industrialized countries is entirely tied.

The most important multilateral agency for extending development credits to Latin America is the IDB, which is required to tie part of the financial aid it grants. Credits granted from its ordinary capital resources may generally be used to finance imports from the IDB member countries and from those nonmember countries which have issued bonds or have made direct loans to the bank. Loans charged to the Special Operations Fund can be used only for acquisition of goods in the member countries of the bank. All of the loans charged to the Social Progress Trust Fund and those made with the funds administered by the IDB for several developed countries have tying conditions similar to those indicated for bilateral loans.

APPENDIX VI-B: SAMPLE CASE STUDIES IN LATIN AMERICAN COUNTRIES

To illustrate the characteristics and relative magnitude of the cost of tied aid and financing for economic development, this appendix will present sixteen case studies. Each case corresponds to a loan granted by a bilateral or multilateral official agency. The purpose of the analysis is to quantify the level of each loan, the size of the aid component, and the effect of conditioning such loans upon certain special requirements or prerequisites.

The aid component in each loan is calculated as the difference between the face value of the authorized loan and the real value of the future commitments for amortization and interest. This difference is generally expressed as

[2] Andrzey Krasawski, "Aid and the British Balance of Payments," *Moorgate and Wallstreet Review*, Spring Issue, London, 1965.

a proportion of the face value of the loan, to indicate the relative amount of the grant in the financial operation. The formula proposed by Pincus[1] was used to calculate the aid component.

Amortization and interest commitments are updated by means of a discount rate equal to the interest rate that is asssumed to represent the capital opportunity cost in the financial markets of the industrial countries. By way of illustration three graphs are given below which are taken from an OECD publication.[2] These graphs make it possible to estimate the relative size of the aid component if the loan is granted under preestablished financial conditions. The first graph shows the aid component as a percentage of the interest rate, assuming a 10 percent discount rate and alternative conditions with respect to grace periods and terms of the loans. The second graph on the other hand assumes a 6 percent discount rate. The third graph shows the aid component as a function of the discount rate.

In the interests of evaluating the effect of placing conditions on aid, the aid component calculated according to the method mentioned has been called the purely financial aid component of the gross aid component because it reflects only the effect of the interest, amortization period, and grace period of a loan. If the rest of the costs attributable to tied aid are subtracted from the purely financial aid component the remainder is the amount designated in this study as net aid component or adjusted aid component. It should be noted that the cost of tied aid, as understood in this study, is basically the overpayment by the borrower for certain inputs imported when, under the provisions of the loan contract, such imports must come from the lending country even though there is a definite possibility that they could be acquired in the international market at lower prices.

In calculating the cost resulting from tied imports, the study compares the f.o.b. value of the imports in the market of the lending country (or country of origin of the imports, as established in the loan) with the f.o.b. value of the imports according to the lowest possible bids in the international market.[3]

---

[1] J. A. Pincus. *Costs and Benefits of Aid: Quantitative Analysis*, UNCTAD ID/B/C. The formula is constructed as follows:

$$R.V. = \frac{i}{q} L(1-e^{-qG}) + \frac{i}{q}Le^{-qG} + (1 - \frac{i}{q})L\frac{e^{-qG} - e^{-qT}}{q(T-G)}$$

A.C. = L - R.V.

(in which R.V. = real value; q = the discount rate; G = the grace period; i = the interest rate; L = the face value of the loan authorized; T = the term of the loan; and A.C. = the aid component).

[2] OECD, *The Flow of Financial Resources to Less-developed Countries* (Paris, 1967).

[3] A more accurate comparison would be made on a c.i.f. basis, in order to include the probable differential effect of the freight and insurance costs of the most favorable alternative source of the imports.

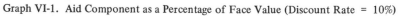

Graph VI-1. Aid Component as a Percentage of Face Value (Discount Rate = 10%)

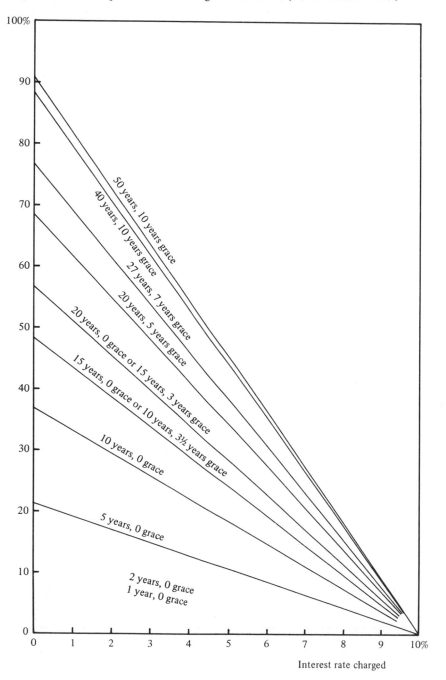

Interest rate charged

Source: OECD.

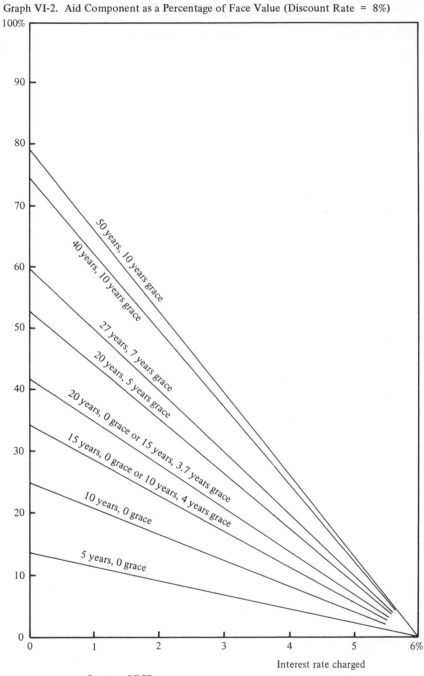

Graph VI-2. Aid Component as a Percentage of Face Value (Discount Rate = 8%)

50 years, 10 years grace

40 years, 10 years grace

27 years, 7 years grace

20 years, 5 years grace

20 years, 0 grace or 15 years, 3.7 years grace

15 years, 0 grace or 10 years, 4 years grace

10 years, 0 grace

5 years, 0 grace

Interest rate charged

Source: OECD.

182

Graph VI-3. Aid Component of Typical Loans as a Function of the Discount Rate

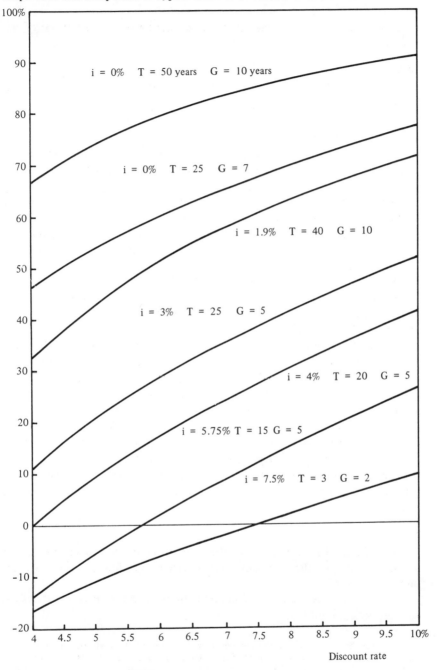

i = 0%   T = 50 years   G = 10 years

i = 0%   T = 25   G = 7

i = 1.9%   T = 40   G = 10

i = 3%   T = 25   G = 5

i = 4%   T = 20   G = 5

i = 5.75% T = 15 G = 5

i = 7.5%   T = 3   G = 2

Discount rate

Source: OECD.

183

Data were provided for the most part by the pertinent authorities of the lending country.

Case I

An $8,000,000 loan granted by EXIMBANK for expanding nine small electric power plants.

The conditions of the loan were: 5.5 percent interest, seventeen years amortization, and three years grace.

In this case it was possible to obtain comparative price information for some products (see table VI-B-1) the cost of which was 19 percent of the total loan.

The cost of tying in the products indicated amounts to 30.7 percent of the value of the purchases from the tying source.

Since no information has been obtained on the rest of the loan, two hypotheses could be used to suggest the lower and upper limits of the total cost of tying.

One hypothesis would assume that the rest of the purchases were made according to the lowest bid on the international market, that is, the cost of the tying would be the same as shown in table VI-B-1 ($468,023), or 5.8 percent of the total loan.

The other hypothesis would assume that the cost of tying of the sample is representative of all of the items purchased, in which case the relative importance of the tying would be 30.7 percent of the value of the loan.

The aid component included in the loan—calculated by considering the loan as a credit bearing a 6 percent interest rate[4]—is 3.8 percent of the value of the loan. As the minimum cost of tying would be 5.8 percent (the first hypothesis), there would not be in this case a positive aid component but rather a net loss equal to 2.1 percent of the value of the loan.

Taking the second hypothesis (with the cost of the tying equal to 30.7 percent of the loan value), the net loss would be equal to 26.9 percent of the loan value.

Case II

A $5,500,000 loan granted by the IDB, from the Social Progress Trust Fund, to construct fifteen potable water systems and four sewerage systems in eighteen cities.

The loan conditions are: 3.5 percent interest, thirty years amortization, and one year grace.

---

[4] Unlike the estimates of the aid component made in the main part of this document, which are based on a 9 percent interest rate, these estimates presume a 6 percent interest rate. The reason is that these project loans could have been financed by supplier credits at this lower rate.

Appendix Table VI-B-1. Case I

Item	Quantity	F.o.b. Value in Tied Source ($) (A)	Lowest Bid in the International Market ($)[a] (B)	(A) − (B) Additional Cost due to Tying ($) (C)	(C) ÷ (A) (%) (D)
1. T-7800 kw electric diesel units	11	1,180,267	725,400	454,867	38.5
2. T-30750 kva power transformers	15	163,377	163,377	–	–
3. Insulators (pulley-type)	47,894	11,567	7,040	4,527	39.1
4. T-10158 kva distribution transformers		129,953	129,953	–	–
5. 25 kva distribution transformers	35	9,905	8,015	1,890	19.1
6. Aluminum cables; example: 2/0 AWG (ACSR)	182,000m	21,039	16,613	4,426	21.0
7. Class 54-1 porcelain insulators	100	49	36	13	26.5
8. No. 6 (3/4") 46-foot round iron	40,000hgs.	6,160	4,640	1,520	24.7
9. 240 volt, 15 amperes, tri-phase, watt-hour meters	50 u.	1,905	1,125	780	40.9
Total		1,524,222	1,056,199	468,023[b]	30.7

[a]This column repeats the amounts for the tied source when that amount was the lowest possible bid obtained on the international market.
[b]Total is 30.7% of total of col. (A).

An analysis is given below of one of the fifteen projects for a potable water system at a total estimated cost of $1,220,000.

It was possible to obtain alternative bids for 68 percent of the total imports (see table VI-B-2), which represent 37.8 percent of the cost of the project. The cost attributable to tying amounts to 36.2 percent of the value of the purchases. If the cost of tying for the rest of the acquisitions were zero, the tying would represent about 13 percent of the project cost.

The aid component of the project would amount to 10 percent of the project cost on the basis of a discount rate of 6 percent, after deducting the cost attributable to tying.

According to data provided by the lender, it is estimated that the ratio of the imported inputs indicated (see table VI-B-2) to the total cost of the fifteen projects considered is 33.7 percent ($1,853,500).

If the cost due to tying for the fifteen projects were equal to that of the project analyzed, i.e., 36.2 percent of the value of the goods in the tied source, this would amount to $670,967, which is 12.2 percent of the total loan.

The aid component of the loan would be 23.5 percent. By subtracting the cost of tying, it is possible to determine the maximum value of the net aid component: 11.3 percent of the loan value.

Case III

A joint loan of AID/IDB/IDA/IBRD to finance a highway program for a total of $39,000,000.

The loan conditions varied according to the institution.

The portion provided by the IBRD was $9,000,000 with a 5.5 percent interest rate, twenty years for amortization, and five years of grace.

The IDB loan was for the amount of $6,000,000, charged against ordinary resources and its terms were: 5.75 percent interest rate, twenty-one years amortization, and four years grace.[5]

AID made two loans for this project. Both were for amortization in thirty years and a period of grace of ten years. In one of these loans, for the amount of $2,700,000, the interest rate was 0.75 percent, and in the other, for $13,300,000, it was 2 percent.

The IDA loan, for a total of $8,000,000, is for a period of fifty years, with ten years grace and without interest.

Tying was felt in the following aspects:

---

[5]The rate of interest in the case of IDB includes a commission of 1 percent. IDA charges a commission of 0.75 percent which has been considered in the determination of the aid component.

Appendix Table VI-B-2. Case II

Item	Quantity	F.o.b. Value in Tied Source ($)		Lowest Bid in the International Market ($)		Additional Cost due to Tying	%
		Amount	Origin	Amount	Origin	(A) − (B)	(C) ÷ (A)
		(A)		(B)		(C)	(D)
1. Asbestos cement pipe ∅ 50 mm.	9,330m.	8,457	Colombia	7,082	Italy	1,375	16.3
2. Asbestos cement pipe ∅ 100	7,745m.	10,843	,,	8,562	,,	2,281	21.0
3. Asbestos cement pipe ∅ 150	4,015m.	10,261	,,	6,956	,,	3,305	32.2
4. Asbestos cement pipe ∅ 200	775m.	3,264	,,	1,965	,,	1,299	39.8
5. Asbestos cement pipe ∅ 250	86m.	506	,,	309	,,	107	21.1
6. Asbestos cement pipe ∅ 300	26,684m.	255,149	,,	147,616	,,	107,533	42.1
7. Asbestos cement pipe ∅ 350	15,383	157,509	,,	109,016	,,	48,493	30.8
8. Asbestos cement pipe ∅ 400	199	2,115	,,	1,811	,,	304	14.4
9. Chlorinator (6–20 lbs./24h.)	3	2,694	USA	2,433	Germany	261	9.7
10. Total output meter (350 mm.)	1	1,852	USA	1,521[a]	,,	331	17.9
11. House meters ∅ 1/2	780	8,424	Mexico	6,903	,,	1,521	18.1
Total		461,074		294,174		166,900	36.2

[a]The capacity of this meter is 400 mm., i.e., larger than the one purchased.

1. All purchases of roadbuilding equipment charged against the AID loan had to be made in the United States.

2. The services of a firm of foreign consultants had to be hired, since it was felt that local firms did not meet all the requirements of the lending agencies.

In regard to point 1, the cost of tying has not been calculated since comparative prices were not requested for the type and quality of equipment to be used.

In relation to point 2, the borrower feels that qualified technical personnel was available locally and that foreign experts would only be required for specific subjects, such as bridges, rigid and flexible pavement, maintenance, construction using heavy machinery, and works administration. It would be necessary in each of these cases to hire an expert in each field.

It is interesting to note that the ratio between the sum paid to consultants and the disbursements of agencies amounted to 14.4 percent during a period of 30 months. Specialized offices of the borrowing government feel that if local consultants were used, this ratio would be reduced by one-half, i.e., 7 percent ($273,000).

The aid component included in these loans, without considering the cost of tying, is approximately 37 percent of the over-all loan.

Case IV

A $650,000 loan from AID for an electrification program leading to the generation of 1.2 megawatts.

The terms of the loan were: 3/4 percent, thirty years amortization, and ten years grace period. Credit also was provided to finance 80 percent of local costs.

In this case the financial aid component would be 65.2 percent of the authorized amount of the loan.

The effects of tying were felt in the hiring of consultants from the lending country and in the purchase and transportation of equipment.

The cost of consulting services over a thirteen-month period was $32,000, representing 25 percent of total disbursements made during the same period.

In this case it has not been possible to obtain alternative prices for the equipment purchased, consequently the cost of tying has not been determined; however, officials of the borrowing country estimate that the cost of American equipment is 15 to 20 percent higher than that of British equipment.

As for transportation, in addition to the higher cost, delays occurred because of the irregular nature of the shipping service provided by United States vessels to the borrowing country.

Case V

A joint loan from AID and EXIMBANK to finance the expansion and equipping of an airport, for a total of $5,050,000.

The terms of the loan authorized by EXIMBANK were: 5.75 percent interest, twelve years amortization period, and three years grace.

The characteristics of the loans authorized by AID were: 3.5 percent interest, eighteen and nineteen years amortization period, and one and two years grace period.

The authorities of the borrowing country believe that the tying of the loan constituted a disadvantage in the following respects:

1. *Design and Supervision*

The lending agencies established the requirements to be met by the consultant firms interested in competing. These conditions were such that, in practice, they prevented local consultant firms and those from neighboring countries from participating.

Nonetheless, the borrower believes that if the services of a local consultant firm with experience in similar projects had been employed, a saving of 20 percent would have been made on the actual cost ($351,997) of foreign consultant services.

2. *Personnel Training*

The lending institutions found it necessary to include this item among the components of the project. However, since in practice personnel training was limited to the issuing of two pamphlets on airport administration and maintenance and did not include training as such, it resulted, in the opinion of the local authorities, in an unnecessary cost.

3. *Special Expenditures*

Lack of knowledge on the part of the consultants regarding the physical and climatic conditions of the site resulted in special expenditures amounting to $258,388. These expenditures were for reconstruction of the building and installation and construction of an adequate drainage system for the runways.

Besides the problems pointed out above, the construction of the landing runway gave rise to greater costs, principally, because of the poor construction and quality of the lighting equipment.

Adding all these factors, the borrowing country concludes that the higher costs resulting from tying were approximately $1,300,000, or about 25 percent of the total amount of the loan.

The aid component of the loan may be calculated on the basis of a 6 percent interest rate (see table VI-B-3).

For the EXIMBANK loan, the aid component would be 1.7 percent of the authorized amount of the loan.

Appendix Table VI-B-3. Case V

Agency	Amount (Thousands of $)	Rate of Interest (%)	Grace Period (Years)	Amortization Period (Years)	Aid Component	Ratio of Aid Component to Amt. of Loan (%)
EXIMBANK	2,650	5.75	3	12	44,600	1.7
AID	800	3.5	1	19	146,067	18.3
AID	1,600	3.5	2	18	400,730	25.1
Total	5,050				591,397	11.7

In the case of the AID loan, the average aid component would be about 22.8 percent of the total authorized, or $546,800.

In total, the aid component of the three loans is $591,397. If this is subtracted from the adverse effects of tying as measured in dollars, the resulting figure is $708,603, which should be interpreted as the additional cost to the borrowing country resulting from tying.

Case VI

An AID loan for the construction and outfitting of thirty-two health stations and eighteen health units in rural areas. The project cost was $1,450,000, of which $700,000 was financed by AID and the remainder, $750,800, by the borrowing country.

The terms of the loan were: 2 percent interest, twenty-eight years amortization, and twelve years grace.

The authorities of the borrowing country estimate that the effects of tying were as follows:

1. *Design and Supervision*

The lending agency required that these stages be carried out by a consulting firm with experience in similar projects. This eliminated the possibility of hiring local consultants.

It has been impossible to quantify the adverse effects of this condition. A quantitative statement is presented below regarding the cost of tying, according to specialists of the borrowing country.

Because of a lack of knowledge of local conditions, it was necessary to correct and rewrite plans several times, hence delaying the initiation of the project, as well as increasing the costs of design and supervision.

2. *Equipment*

The required equipment was classified in four groups; this method of soliciting bids precluded the manufacturers of the items involved from submitting their bids directly, so that bidding was confined to intermediaries.

It is also appropriate to note that the aid was conditioned upon the purchase of equipment in the lending country.

Table VI-B-4 provides a breakdown of the actual total cost of the program, the estimated total cost if it had been carried out with local resources in its entirety, and the cost of tying.

Appendix Table VI-B-4. Case VI

Item	Actual Cost (A)	Estimated Cost (B)	Cost of Tying (A) – (B) (C)	% (A) ÷ (C) (D)
1. Design	56,200	28,000	28,200	50.2
2. Supervision	154,600	96,000	98,000	63.4
3. Construction	920,000	822,000	58,600	6.4
4. Equipment	320,000	224,000	96,000	30.0
Total	1,450,800	1,170,000	280,800	19.4

Based on a discount rate of 6.1 percent,[6] the aid component in this case has been calculated at 51.7 percent of the authorized value of the loan. Adding in the $280,000 corresponding to the cost of tying, it will be seen that the net aid amounted to 11.6 percent ($81,164).

Case VII

An AID loan totaling $1,200,000 for highway construction; the loan was subsequently canceled.

The terms of the loan were: interest rate of 2.5 percent, thirty years amortization, and ten years grace period.

The granting of this loan was conditional upon the grant of another loan from EXIMBANK, which was for $2,533,000, with an interest rate of 5.5 percent and amortization and grace periods of eight and three years, respectively. The draft of the AID contract provides the following:

Conditions prior to the first disbursement for other services relating to the project, excepting construction services for the project, the borrower shall submit, in a form and content acceptable to AID, a national highway maintenance plan, together with satisfactory evidence of arrangements for equipment, organization and financing to implement the plan, including arrangements for personal training and manning of the agency responsible, for the purchase of equipment required and the continuation of financing for the plan.

[6] Average interest rate for suppliers' credits to 46 developing countries. World Bank and IDA, *Annual Report, 1966–67*, p. 34.

Officials of both the borrowing country and of AID stated that this clause referred to the operation proposed by EXIMBANK.

The borrowing government objected to the transaction with EXIMBANK because they considered that the amount of technical assistance offered was too high. In addition, it argued that suppliers of equipment should offer free personnel training and, further, that there were qualified local personnel capable of setting up an adequate maintenance program.

The amount allocated for technical assistance was $250,000, almost 10 percent of the total loan.

If this $250,000 is considered as the cost of tying, the net aid component would become a loss of about $180,000.

The AID loan includes a *gross* aid component of 43.5 percent, which would more than offset the loss on the EXIMBANK operation; but in this case it seems that the very fact that the loan was tied was more significant than the financial cost of the tying.

Case VIII

A $1,100,000 loan from the Social Progress Trust Fund of the IDB for a program to expand the university of the borrowing country.

The terms of the loan are: 2 percent interest rate, twenty years amortization, and one year of grace.

The conditions imposed had their impact in connection with the purchase of equipment charged to the loan, since $600,000 of the total had to be expended in United States markets.

It has not been possible to obtain complete quantitative information regarding the cost of this tying; however, table VI-B-5 lists some items for which it was possible to make price comparisons in other markets.

If this operation is compared with a supplier's loan at an interest rate of 6 percent, the aid component comes to 30 percent of the total amount of the loan.

If it is assumed that the calculated cost of tying (43.5 percent) is representative for all expenditures that must be made in the United States market ($600,000), then the net aid under this loan would be 6.4 percent of its value.

Case IX

An AID loan of $2,000,000 for a housing construction program to eradicate slums.

The terms of the loan were: 3/4 percent interest, twenty-nine years amortization period, and eleven years grace period.

1. *Engineering Services*

Appendix Table VI-B-5. Case VIII

Item	No.	Total Value at Source of Tying			Total Value at Competitive Source			Cost of Tying	
		Equipment	Installation	Total	Equipment	Installation	Total	(A) – (B)	% (C) ÷ (A)
				(A)			(B)	(C)	(D)
Elevators type (a)	3	25,842	140,400	166,242	17,220	78,000	95,220	71,022	42.7
Elevators type (b)	1	7,807	31,517	39,324	5,237	20,000	25,237	14,087	35.8
Elevators type (c)	1	7,807	31,517	38,324	3,820	14,200	18,020	21,304	54.2
Total		41,456	203,434	244,890	26,277	112,200	138,477	106,413	43.5

It was provided that the services of a United States supervisory engineer would be engaged. The technicians of the borrowing country consider that, given the nature of the project, a local consultant firm could have been employed.

2. *Transportation*

Although AID stipulates that a certain percentage of the goods acquired with the proceeds of the loan must be shipped on American bottoms, in this case the borrower was free to contract for a more suitable service since American vessels had no regular service to the country.

3. *Purchase of Materials*

The restriction concerning the origin of materials resulted in the purchase of cement with local funds, since to use loan funds for this purpose would have meant a reduction in the number of houses to be constructed.

To illustrate this point, a comparison of prices is given in table VI-B-6.

Appendix Table VI-B-6. Case IX

| Item | Source of Cement | | Difference ($) |
	U.S. ($)	Other Countries of the Hemisphere ($)	
Price per bag	2.89	1.60	1.29
Total project cost	291,191	161,519	129,672

Total expenditure for cement was 44.5 percent less than it would have been if made with loan funds.

4. *Administrative Conditions*

The AID contract provided that the houses had to be sold, with maximum periods set for payment. Since the project is intended to relocate families in the low-income group, in many cases the monthly payment was incompatible with the level of family income. While this factor has not been quantifiable, it is pointed out as an example of a condition that lowers the level of efficiency that might be expected.

Case X

A loan of $3,500,000 granted by the IDB with funds from the Social Progress Trust Fund for the construction of dwellings.

The conditions of the loan were: 2 percent interest, twenty-five years amortization, and one year grace period.

The IDB limited the market for materials to its member countries. A sample of building materials for which there are comparative figures is shown in table VI-B-7.

Appendix Table VI-B-7. Case X – Comparative Figures

Item	Amount	Tied Source ($) (A)	Most Competitive Bid ($) (B)	Cost of Tying ($) (A) – (B) (C)	Percentage (C) ÷ (A) (D)	Source of Bid
1. Doorknobs 4"	3,123	533.08	448.19	84.89	15.9	Japan and/or Europe
2. 3/4" x 20 m. tape	3,684	3,743.50	890.33	2,853.17	76.2	,,
3. Bathroom shut-off valves	3,062	3,270.09	2,543.96	726.13	22.2	,,
4. Keys	3,086	6,344.41	5,593.96	750.45	11.8	,,
5. 3" latches	8,394	1,940.03	1,901.96	38.07	2.0	,,
6. Reduction from 1/2" to 3/8" galv. iron	3,062	837.16	277.49	559.67	66.8	,,
Total		15,668.27	11,655.89	4,012.38	25.6	

The cost of purchasing these materials on the markets designated under the terms of the loan is, on the average, 25.6 percent higher than if there had been free access to the world market.

If this loan is compared to another one with 6.1 percent interest, the aid component involved would be 34.7 percent. However, it cannot be concluded that this is the amount of aid since only a partial list of materials is given. It might be assumed that the rest of the project behaves in a similar fashion to that observed here, i.e., the tying cost is equal to 25.6 percent of the amount of the loan authorized. This would result in a net aid component of 9.2 percent ($321,155).

In order to determine the aid component included in this loan, the figure shown here has been compared with a supplier's credit having an interest rate of 6.1 percent. The resultant aid component is 66.7 percent. It should be pointed out that the tying relative to consultant services and sale of dwellings has not been quantified.

Unfortunately, it is impossible to quantify the total cost of tying since there is no further information on other materials required to implement the project.

Case XI

A loan of $500,000 from AID to finance a malaria eradication project.

The conditions of the loan were: 2.5 percent interest, twenty-nine years amortization, and eleven years of grace.

The loan is being used to finance local services, hence none of the disadvantages typical of loans for purchase of materials have come up.

In this case, the effect of tying was evidenced in the administrative aspects, which caused a delay of one year and a half in the authorization and disbursement of the loan. At the time the loan was authorized, the epidemiological situation had worsened since the original study on which the application for the loan had been based. It is impossible to quantify the cost of this delay, its significance in terms of the health of the population, the economic aspect of the hours of work lost through sickness, and so on.

This case has been presented in this study to show the importance of processing loans rapidly and efficiently and of streamlining administrative procedures.

Case XII

An IDB loan from the Social Progress Trust Fund for a drainage and sewerage project for $3,020,000.

The conditions of the loan were: 3.5 percent rate of interest, twenty-five years amortization, and three years grace.

No international bids were tendered for the purchase of materials. For this reason, in order to measure the cost of the tying, the prices of materials were compared with those for similar products purchased with local funds in a similar project executed during the same period.

A comparison between the two sources, that is, tied and competitive, is presented in table VI-B-8.

If the sample shown here is representative, that is, if the total cost of the imported materials was 9.5 percent higher than would be the case if they had been purchased with untied funds, the result would be that the aid component of the loan, less the cost of tying, would be 14 percent (in comparison to a loan with 6 percent interest rate).

In this case, the unquantified advantage of being able to amortize the loan in the local currency or currencies in which they were disbursed would have to be added to the aid component indicated above.

Case XIII

A loan of $5,300,000 granted by the IDB from the Social Progress Trust Fund for the construction of rural dwellings.

The conditions of the loan were: 2 percent interest, twenty-seven years amortization, and a four-year grace period; 85 percent could be set aside to cover local costs and could be amortized in local currency.

In this case, tying consisted of the requirement that the goods be purchased in the member countries of the IDB. There are no data for quantifying the cost of tying.

Comparing this credit with another hypothetical loan at an interest rate of 6 percent, the aid component would amount to 40.7 percent of the total loan.

Case XIV

The government of the Federal Republic of Germany granted a loan of DM70 million (approximately $17,500,000) through Kreditsanstalt für Wiederaufbau (KFW) to build a sugar mill; $10 million were earmarked for financing imports and the remainder could be utilized for defraying expenses in the local currency of the borrowing country.

The conditions of the loan were: interest at 4¾ percent, eleven years amortization, and four years grace.

In this case, international bids were invited, the lowest being for $284,101, while the lowest figure in the tying source was $382,531. The latter was selected since the difference between the two ($98,430) could be considered the cost of informal tying.

Appendix Table VI-B-8. Case XII

Description of Item[a]	Number of Meters	Total Value F.o.b. at the Tied Source ($)
2" cast iron pipe	14,900.34	34,221.60
3" " " "	4,301.13	15,099.84
4" " " "	3,549.53	14,487.62
6" " " "	3,598.90	22,080.96
8" " " "	6,402.32	55,602.88
10" " " "	2,348.06	27,657.36
12" " " "	1,799.45	27,276.48
2" cast iron pipe	22,698.14	51,912.86
3" " " "	13,812.49	53,468.16
4" " " "	9,958.45	41,327.55
6" " " "	3,017.70	18,414.00
8" " " "	3,199.38	27,866.57
10" " " "	3,198.60	36,361.71
3" cast iron pipe	1,499.54	5,805.60
4" " " "	2,099.36	9,746.52
6" " " "	3,298.99	21,269.16
2" " " "	39,479.00	92,883.62
3" " " "	33,801.00	131,311.93
4" " " "	16,610.00	101,628.94
6" " " "	8,195.00	71,462.61
8" " " "	6,308.00	73,703.55
10" " " "	1,151.00	23,103.71
2" " " "	27,800.00	57,007.50
3" " " "	34,600.00	102,170.70
4" " " "	14,900.00	52,309.09
6" " " "	23,400.00	119,002.80
6" " " "	800.00	4,068.75
Total		1,291,252.07
Similar material purchased in France, in accordance with bids made		1,169,000.00
Cost of tying		122,252.07
% of total value of tied source		9.5%

[a]Based on four bids.

If this credit is compared with one from suppliers, at an interest rate of 6 percent, the aid component would amount to 8.8 percent, which, after deducting the cost of tying, would amount to 8.37 percent.

The aid component (8.3 percent) would increase if it is considered that about 43 percent of the loan is earmarked for financing local expenses.

Case XV

A loan offered by AID for a telecommunications program. In view of the stipulations of the loan, the authorities of the borrowing country considered a supplier's credit to be preferable.

The bid consisted of financing for three projects of substantial size. The value of the loan was $23 million under relatively favorable financing terms for the borrowing government: 2.5 percent interest, thirty years amortization, and ten years grace. However, in its turn, the government had to make a twenty-year loan to the company at an interest rate of 5.5 percent.

On the other hand, a suppliers' loan, with no tying as to the market in which the goods are purchased, at 6 percent interest for ten years with three years grace, was more suitable for the company, for the following reasons:

1. In a comparison of bids for equipment in various markets, that of the United States was unfavorable, as may be seen from table VI-B-9.

Appendix Table VI-B-9. Case XV

Source of Bid	Price Differential (%)
Japan	0 – 10
Europe	5 – 15
Canada	10 – 20
United States	15 – 25

In view of this background, two projects were awarded to Japanese and Dutch companies. Both operations involved imports for a total value of $4 million.

2. Apart from the price differences indicated above, the United States bid was considered to involve deficiencies in the following areas:

   a. Longer delivery period.

   b. High cost of feasibility study since it had to be carried out by a United States firm in accordance with the requirements of the financing agency.

   c. High cost of equipment maintenance, inspection, and supervision of the project required by AID.

   d. High cost of the training program to be implemented simultaneously with the projects.

The experts of the borrowing country estimate that requirements b, c, and d would give rise to an additional expense of the order of $4 million for the three projects combined.

3. Among other additional points considered to favor supplier's credits were:

 a. That insurance and freight could be locally contracted.

 b. That the equipment and the system in operation were delivered on time.

 c. The quality of the equipment.

 d. The percentage of national components in the project.

Case XVI

A loan of $3.3 million granted by AID for an electrification project. This case forms part of an UNCTAD[7] study in which a sample is presented of imported goods to be used in the projects (see table VI-B-10).

The conditions of the loan were .75 percent interest rate, thirty years amortization, and ten years of grace.

The cost of tying in the sample amounts to 11.3 percent of the value of goods purchased in the tied source. If the sample were representative (if the cost of tying were 11.3 percent of the value of the loan), the added cost of purchasing the total inputs at the tied source would amount to approximately $373,000. On this assumption, the adjusted aid component would amount to 53.9 percent of the total loan.

The added cost of 11.3 percent observed in this case is one of the lowest that has come up in the cases studied by the Secretariat. One possible explanation would be the fact that international bids were invited; it has been observed in other studies on this topic[8] that United States producers lowered the prices of their goods when bids of a substantial size were involved, in which the competition of other industrialized countries had to be met.[9]

[7]UNCTAD, *Growth, Development Financing and Assistance.* TD/7/Supp. 8/Add. 1. 8 December 1967.

[8]Mahbub ul Haq, *Capital Movements and Economic Development* (International Economic Association, St. Martins, 1967).

[9]Officials of various Latin American countries have reported similar experiences in discussion with the Secretariat.

Appendix Table VI-B-10. Case XVI – Some Background

Description of Item	Value F.o.b. Tied Source ($) (A)	Value Lowest International Bid ($) (B)	Source	Cost of Tying (A) – (B) (C)	Cost of Tying in Relation to Value in the Tied Source (%) (C) ÷ (A) (D)
1. 230 kw preconnectors	5,775	2,170	Japan	3,605	62.4
2. Disc insulators	8,425	6,093	Japan	2,332	27.7
3. Steel cable	7,205	7,005	Switzerland	200	2.8
4. 5/16" – 5/8" steel cables	9,490	9,114	Belgium	376	4.0
5. Copperweld type cables and connectors	17,241	15,785	France	1,456	8.4
6. Two Gardner Denver rotary compressors	29,759	24,142	United Kingdom	5,617	18.9
7. One light Ford truck	10,367	8,456	United Kingdom	1,911	18.4
8. Standard electric meters	9,888	8,799	Netherlands	1,089	11.0
9. Purchase of a motor grader	19,360	17,475	Germany (F.R.)	1,885	9.7
10. Two "molinetes" with spare parts	1,795	1,795[a]		—	—

Appendix Table VI-B-10. *Continued*

Description of Item	Value f.o.b. Tied Source ($) (A)	Value Lowest International Bid ($) (B)	Source	Cost of Tying (A) − (B) ($) (C)	Cost of Tying in Relation to Value in the Tied Source (%) (C) ÷ (A) (D)
11. 170 55-gallon drums of insulating oil for transformers	3,321	3,321[a]		—	—
12. 265 55-gallon drums of insulating oil	5,378	4,980	United Kingdom	398	7.4
13. Purchase of 4 tractors	10,915	10,760	United Kingdom	155	1.4
14. Purchase of 252 ampules of 250 kw-mercury gas and 150 ampules of 400 kw-mercury gas	2,687	2,598	Switzerland	89	3.3
15. Purchase of telegraph parts	2,779	2,746	Switzerland	33	1.2
16. One vehicle	10,367	8,456	United Kingdom	1,911	18.4
17. Spare parts for 4 locomotives	24,973	23,780	Germany (F.R.)	1,193	4.8
18. Two tractors	35,924	33,900	United Kingdom	2,024	5.6
Total	215,649	191,375		24,274	11.3

[a]The values of the tied source have been repeated in this column when they are the lowest obtainable bids on the world market.

CHAPTER VII

Summary and Conclusions: External Financing and Development Strategy for Latin America during the Next Decade

MAJOR CHARACTERISTICS OF EXTERNAL FINANCING SINCE 1961

In order to provide a proper basis for evaluating the necessary requisites of external financing with a view to contributing, to the extent and in the form necessary, to the success of the development strategy that should be proposed in Latin America for the next decade, we must first review briefly the main conclusions of the analysis of external financing received by the region under the Alliance for Progress presented in earlier chapters of this report.

The external public financing received by Latin America since 1961 has undoubtedly made a significant contribution to the economic and social development of the region. In some cases, external financing has contributed significantly to satisfactory acceleration of the pace of economic growth and social progress. In others, the external contribution has prevented sizable deteriorations in import capacity and has, consequently, helped to avoid fairly serious balance-of-payments crises. For the region as a whole, it is apparent that this financing has constituted a significant supplement to the domestic effort. Acknowledging, therefore, the net positive contribution of external financial cooperation since 1961—much greater than in the previous decade, when public financing for development was almost nonexistent in the region—we should also point out certain shortcomings whose correction would provide undoubted benefits in consolidating the development process of the Latin American countries.

The total volume of external public financing received since 1961, though significantly higher than in the preceding periods, has nonetheless been less than was expected at the time the Charter of Punta del Este was signed. Furthermore, the financial contribution represented by these public resources was offset to a very considerable extent, especially during the first few years of the decade, by the heavy amortization and interest payments that had to be met by the countries of the region on the sizable short- and medium-term debts contracted in earlier years. In short, the level of external savings transferred to the region in net terms did not expand to the extent that would have been necessary to achieve the goals stated at the time the Alliance for Progress was launched.

Pursuant to the methods and calculations presented in chapter II of this report, the aid component of the external financing received by Latin America amounted to an annual average of nearly $750 million for the period 1961-67. From the standpoint of the United States, the opportunity cost of its financing to Latin America would, by these calculations, amount to about $620 million as an annual average during the period 1961-67. In both cases, a sizable reduction in aid is apparent during the past few years.

Despite the comparatively favorable conditions of financing received from AID and the Social Progress Trust Fund and the Special Operations Fund of the IDB, the average conditions—interest rates and grace and amortization terms—of total public financing received by most of the countries have been hard to such an extent that the structure of external indebtedness has not been adapted to foreseeable payment capacity during the next few years. In other words, the aid component of external public financing should have constituted a higher proportion of the whole, in order to prevent the possible future emergence of bottlenecks in the external sector handicapping the development process.

In the case of bilateral credits, the tied aid procedures employed appear to have significantly reduced the aid component of those credits and, therefore, their effective contribution to development of the recipient countries. Although from the standpoint of the United States, the tied aid method has proved helpful in improving that country's balance-of-payments position, for the Latin American countries it is necessary to find ways of eliminating such tying.

The effects of tied aid have been significantly accentuated in recent years, owing to application by the United States of the principle of additionality, aimed at promoting expansion of United States exports and at least maintaining United States participation in total imports by the recipient countries. This criterion has caused very serious problems in loan operations, resulting in a significant reduction of the prospective benefits of such financing to the recipient countries. At the same time, it does not appear to have exerted sizable favorable effects on the balance-of-payments position of the United States.

The observation contained in this report on the sectoral composition of external financing by external public institutions and on the policies promoted in extending such financing appears to indicate the need for stepping-up efforts toward coordination between the various agencies and for defining financing priorities, with increasing consideration for the specific needs of the development process in each country and the basic objectives of its economic and social policy. This need is even more apparent considering that the international financing agencies and AID are currently and separately programing their future financing operations with each country on the intermediate range.

The net contribution of foreign private investment in financing the transfer of real resources to Latin America has been relatively low in recent years, while the total outflow of foreign exchange for profits and other capital returns has expanded significantly, with both financing currents together determining an increasingly negative flow. Although this fact is not in itself an adequate basis for evaluating the desirability of foreign private investment, it is a circumstance that should be taken into account in defining the region's future policy toward such investment, particularly since this investment appears to have been increasingly channeled during the last few years toward activities with a comparatively limited positive impact on net foreign transactions of nonfinancial goods and services.

With regard to this latter aspect of the sectoral composition of foreign private investment, it should be noted that its contribution to the exporting sectors has declined appreciably in recent years: the portion allocated to traditional exports has dropped significantly as compared to the previous decade, while that earmarked for new export lines does not appear to have expanded at a rapid rate. This is particularly important considering that these new activities are the very ones most urgently requiring the transfer of technological advances from the industrialized countries. This does not necessarily imply that the sole field of action for foreign enterprise acceptable from the balance-of-payments standpoint is the area of new, directly exporting activities, for foreign investment, with its contribution of technology and managerial efficiency, should always contribute to some extent to the replacement of imports and to an increase in the country's general productivity and, consequently, its competitive position abroad. But it does indicate that these new export activities, especially in the industrial sector, should, given conditions at the current stage of development of most of the Latin American countries, be the highest priority area in channeling the financial and technological contribution of external private capital.

FUTURE EXTERNAL FINANCING REQUIREMENTS

In order to appreciate the scope of future external funding requirements of Latin America, as well as the conditions on which such resources must be extended, the Secretariat has prepared projections of the trade and savings gaps for each country in the region during the period 1970–85 which are shown in chapter IV. In an initial approximation based on the continuity of historic trends observed in the major economic variables, these projections indicate that Latin America could not achieve during the next decade the minimum growth rate proposed in the Charter of Punta del Este unless substantial changes were made with a view to intensifying the domestic effort and external cooperation. This initial approximation also tends to suggest that, in most countries of the region, the trade gap rather than the savings gap is the major factor restricting growth possibilities.

The initial approximation referred to in the preceding paragraph also indicates that, in order to achieve the growth rate without appreciably intensifying domestic efforts—mainly with regard to promotion of exports and generation of savings—the external financing required would be extremely high and the amount would increase rapidly throughout the entire period. These amounts reach much higher levels than can be expected to be available, even under the best of international circumstances, during the next few years. Moreover, the Latin American countries could not, for economic reasons and for sociological and political considerations as well, allow their development to be subordinate to a growing dependence on external aid over the course of several decades.

Consequently, a second approximation projected that the domestic effort should be raised to levels that can be considered reasonable in terms of circumstances in each country, providing for fairly rapid expansion of exports and national savings and, consequently, a sizable reduction in the external resources required. Nevertheless, these requirements would still be too high—given currently prevailing conditions with regard to interest rate and grace and amortization periods—to ensure that service on the external debt would not in the future create serious liquidity problems in the balance of payments for most of the countries in the region.

The solutions suggested to these problems in this study are based on the view that, during a period that could cover up to about the middle of the next decade, it would be necessary to secure a substantial increase in the total amount of external resources received by the region. Moreover, most of the countries would have to limit significantly their external indebtedness on hard conditions and also significantly increase the resources obtained on concessional terms, in order to expand the aid component of external financing received by the region to the extent required, that is, in order to reduce interest rates and expand grace and amortization terms on the average. In subsequent years, over-all net external resources requirements would gradually decline, although gross financing should remain at very high levels in order to meet payments of amortization and interest on the previous debt. It would also be possible to regularize gradually the conditions on which financing is contracted.

The strategy outlined in the previous paragraph can obviously be implemented through various combinations of volumes and conditions of financing from the different external sources. In order to illustrate quantitatively one alternative that would meet the necessary requisites and that would appear to have some possibilities of implementation, chapter IV of this report contains an additional projection on procurement of external resources for the region as a whole, based on the following hypotheses with regard to the amounts to be obtained:

a. During the period 1970–75, Latin America would restrict its indebtedness for credits from suppliers and EXIMBANK—both categories are comparatively hard—to amounts equivalent to amortization on earlier debts for the same purposes. Beginning in 1976, net indebtedness of this type would gradually increase to become, together with IDB credits, a major source of external credit resources for the region.

b. Financing from the World Bank would increase significantly throughout the entire period, according to a recent statement by the president of that institution.

c. Financing by European governments was projected assuming a moderate growth above current levels and the same has been done for foreign private investment.

d. Financing granted under the Alliance for Progress itself, that is, from the IDB, AID and P.L. 480, which have a larger aid component, would increase substantially, taken as a whole, during the period 1970–75, through a sizable expansion of IDB operations to an average annual total of about $1.5 billion—a little more than double the average annual total disbursements received during the years 1961–68 from the three previously mentioned sources. After 1975, the aid component of such financing and the portion corresponding to United States contributions would gradually decline to fairly low levels about the end of the period.

With regard to conditions of interest and grace and amortization terms, this projection has taken as a basis, for credits from the World Bank, European governments, EXIMBANK, and suppliers, the average of those conditions in the year 1967–68, with the changes explained in the following paragraph. This implies, first of all, the assumption that these conditions will evolve during the near future in the manner and to the extent required to offset any deterioration occurring during the final months of 1968 and the beginning of 1969.

Furthermore, with regard to credits from suppliers and EXIMBANK, it has been assumed that the interest rate will drop from the average levels observed in recent years, between 6 and 6.5 percent, to around 5 percent. This would imply that the supplier countries would probably subsidize interest rates on these export credits in some way. Moreover, it has been assumed that the average grace and amortization terms for suppliers' credits will be extended slightly to three years of grace and thirteen for amortization—that is, terms similar to those granted by the EXIMBANK.

Considered as a whole, the financing granted during the period 1970–76 by AID and IDB would have to improve its average conditions to levels like the following: interest rate of 3.1 percent, ten years of grace, and forty years for amortization. These conditions would gradually harden during subsequent years, as the aid component of this type of financing and contributions by the United States declined.

The essential factors in the external financing strategy presented in these pages are, on the one hand, a substantial increase in external financing granted during the next few years, during the period 1970–75, by the financing institutions of the Alliance for Progress: AID, IDB, and possibly other multinational agencies such as subregional development banks.[1] The other basic factors of this strategy would be an intensification of domestic efforts, especially to expand exports of national savings, which would make it possible beginning in 1975 to decrease gradually net transfers of external resources and the net amount and aid component of financing granted under the Alliance for Progress.

In order to secure the necessary increase in financing under the Alliance for Progress—mainly the IDB and AID—over the next few years, various alternatives might be considered. Since those years coincide with the period in which a solution can be expected to be found to the United States balance-of-payments problems but during which these difficulties will probably continue to restrict United States financial cooperation severely, these various solutions will have to take this consideration into account. The United States balance-of-payments problems will be discussed at a later point in this analysis; the following paragraphs present one of several possible solutions, with a subsequent indication of other alternatives that could modify or supplement the proposal made here.

According to the most widespread current criterion on foreign aid in the United States, financial cooperation extended abroad by that country in the future should be channeled, more fully than in the past, through multinational institutions, thereby reducing the ratios of bilateral assistance. Since this is also apparently the majority opinion in Latin America, it would be advisable to consider the possibility of implementing this approach for the region in the immediate future. Therefore, in the quantitative aspects of the solution suggested in this report, it is provided that bilateral financing by the

---

[1] The observations made in the rest of this section with regard to the IDB are also applicable to the other multinational institutions already in operation or to be set up in the near future.

United States to Latin America be limited, beginning in 1970, to a level approximately equivalent to 20 percent of total gross contributions by that country to regional development financing. In the projection presented in chapter IV, it is assumed that these resources will be granted on average conditions similar to those prevailing for AID credits up to 1968 and partially for operations under P.L. 480. It is also projected that all such bilateral aid will decline in the closing years of the period 1970-85 and will be totally eliminated in 1985. Meanwhile, total financing to be granted by the IDB would rise by an annual average of a little over $1.3 billion during the five years 1970-75.

The proposed solution calls for a substantial increase in nonreimbursable contributions by the United States to the IDB. These contributions would increase from an annual average of $250 million for the years 1965-67 to more than $650 million in the period 1970-75, declining gradually in subsequent years almost to the vanishing point in 1985. This projection, together with that for bilateral financing through AID and P.L.480, would imply that gross United States financing to Latin America during the period 1970-75, not including EXIMBANK, would total $825 million a year, that is, a level similar to the annual average in the period 1961-67[2]—including AID, P.L. 480, and IDB contributions—but with a higher aid component: about $775 million a year in the period 1970-75 as compared to slightly over $600 million in the period 1961-67.[3] If we add to that component the figure corresponding to the aid component of financing by EXIMBANK—which was negative in the period 1961-67 and is projected as positive for the period 1970-75, as a result of the subsidized interest rates proposed on p. 208—we would have a total aid component for United States financing of about $850 million on an annual average during the period 1970-75, as compared to slightly less than $600 million as an annual average in the period 1961-67. It should be kept in mind that this projection represents an even more significant improvement with regard to the prevailing situation beginning in 1967, since in the last two years both the total authorizations of United States

---

[2] The actual United States *disbursements* during the period 1961-67 were slightly less—around $700 million yearly. Nevertheless, the total United States resources at the disposal of the region under concessional terms—i.e., the *authorizations* of credits and grants from AID, P.L. 480, and IDB contributions—are a little higher, reaching an annual average of nearly $900 million.

[3] The difference between the aid component for 1961-67 and that projected is actually still greater than shown, since the historic figure set forth here—a yearly aid component of $600 million—refers to *authorizations*, whereas strictly speaking, the comparison should have been made with the component corresponding to disbursements, which was undoubtedly less. For the reasons set forth in chap. II, the calculation of the aid component for disbursements is not available.

financing, excluding EXIMBANK, and its aid component have fallen well below the 1961-67 average.

In order to ensure that average conditions of total external financing received by Latin America in the period 1970-75 are consistent with the long-range payment capacity of the regional countries, it would be necessary, within the framework of the quantitative solution proposed in this study, to have the $1.35 billion in annual financing proposed by the IDB during the period extended on an average of 3.1 percent interest, with a grace period of ten years and an amortization term of forty. This could be achieved on the basis of the nonreimbursable United States contributions already mentioned for half of this financing ($600 million) and an equal amount of other resources. The latter amount would be composed—in a portion not accurately determined in this report but which is stated by way of example at about $50 million a year—of the resources of the IDB itself and about $600 million to be obtained by that institution on the international capital markets at an average interest rate, around 7 percent a year, similar to that prevailing in 1967-68 and somewhat less than the prevailing rate for IDB operations in those markets in the first months of 1969.

In order to facilitate proper programing of IDB operations, as well as of the development policy of the Latin American countries, it would be most advisable for the United States Congress to authorize in a lump sum, for terms of more than one year—and if possible for the entire 1970-75 period—the contributions to be made by that country to the IDB.

Taking into account the experience of the recent past, it would appear difficult at first glance for the IDB to obtain the amounts indicated in the preceding paragraph on the international capital markets, particularly if the aim were to attract these funds for the most part outside the United States. However, it should be pointed out that the industrialized countries, excluding the United States, could be encouraged to permit and promote this attraction of resources by the IDB if it were combined with a liberalization of tied aid procedures. This procurement of resources on the international capital markets could also be facilitated if all the IDB member governments jointly guaranteed the bond issues of that agency.

The proposal outlined very briefly in this study is not, obviously, the only one possible for attaining the desired objectives. Consideration could be given to such possibilities as the following, which would to some extent alter the assumptions suggested here:

    a. The cost of resources obtained by the IDB on the international capital markets could be sizably reduced if the industrialized countries would exempt earnings on securities of that institution from domestic taxes, which would in practice represent a subsidy of the interest rates at which those resources were obtained.

b. The requirements for financing on concessional conditions would also be significantly reduced if the developing countries were assigned a high percentage of the special drawing rights (SDRs) to be established in the International Monetary Fund.

c. Furthermore, a significant improvement in export prospects for Latin America and in the trade policy of the industrialized countries could lead to a reduction in the region's external financing requirements, on the assumptions of total economic growth adopted in the calculations presented in this report.

d. Naturally, it would also be possible to evolve various other combinations of volumes and conditions of external financing—grants, concessional credits, subsidies on interest rates, and hard credits in proportions that would vary according to the hypotheses adopted—which would give a result similar in terms of total amounts and average conditions to the proposal suggested here. The main purpose of this proposal is to illustrate a series of requisites that would be consistent with future demands for external resources by the Latin American countries and with the aim of multilateralizing hemispheric financial cooperation.

TIED AID: PROBLEMS AND SUGGESTIONS

Considering that the most acute problem currently existing in the field of tied aid is application of the principle of additionality by the United States,[4] due primarily to the innumerable difficulties caused by that principle in the recipient countries, and further considering that this procedure does not appear to be exerting the positive effects on the United States balance of payments predicted at the time it was established, the Secretariat considers that it would be beneficial to all the interested parties for the United States government to abolish immediately the measures issued to implement this additionality principle.

The general existence of tied aid procedures causes significant difficulties for the recipient countries and constitutes a sizable reduction in the aid component of external financing received by Latin America. From the United States standpoint—contrary to the case of the principle of additionality—it can be concluded that the general tying of financing granted by the United States does appear to have been an important factor in the behavior of the

[4] See chap. V, pp. 143-57.

United States balance of payments during the present decade, by preventing a further worsening in that country's net external position. However, taking into account the fact that the Latin American balance of payments with the United States[5] has deteriorated significantly during the decade, it does not seem fair to retain procedures that penalize the Latin American countries by making them pay for an appreciable share of the cost of the difficulties encountered by the United States in its external transactions with other regions of the world. Emphasis should, therefore, be placed on the need to adopt formulas that will also eliminate in the near future all tied aid proceedings in the financial cooperation offered by the United States to Latin America under the Alliance for Progress.

The Secretariat considers it possible to encounter such formulas, especially since the current position of the United States balance of payments can be viewed as transitory and susceptible to significant improvement during the near future if current efforts aimed at controlling domestic price rises in that country are successful. Consideration should also be given to alternatives that would reduce, and might even eliminate, the probable impact on the United States balance of payments of the general untying of its aid as proposed here.

According to the calculations reproduced in chapter V, if financing granted through AID were not tied, only about 50 percent of this financing could be expected to return to the United States in the form of payments for exports of goods and services from that country.[6] Consequently, it can be assumed that if an over-all amount of financing was delivered to Latin America composed equally of United States contributions and contributions from other sources, the net short-term effect of that contribution by the United States on its balance of payments would be wholly offset by an equivalent amount of payments to the United States for additional imports of goods and services from that country. In the proposal suggested in this study, the IDB, as we have seen, would be financed by a 50 percent United States contribution combined with 50 percent in other resources.[7] It would therefore be possible to untie the United States contribution without any harm to that country's balance of payments, if the remaining 50 percent, which would also be untied, were obtained through utilization of the IDB's own resources and funds from other capital markets. In turn, the other DAC member countries, and any others wishing to participate in the system, would be encour-

[5] See the report of the Secretariat.

[6] In a study carried out in 1963 (*The U.S. Balance of Payments in 1968*), the Brookings Institution calculated that the proportion in export payments returning to the United States would be 55 percent, if the aid granted to Latin America was untied.

[7] In effect, in this quantitative illustration, United States participation in future IDB resources was determined in terms of this possibility of untying its aid.

aged to permit the sale if IDB bonds on their respective markets because (*a*) this would be a condition for untying United Stated aid; (*b*) this system would significantly expand the region's "free" capacity to import—and consequently Latin America's prospects for exporting to all DAC members—and, (*c*) the IDB could refuse to finance imports from countries failing to contribute public and private resources in the required amounts.[8]

It is possible that the IDB will be unable to obtain in those other industrialized countries all the resources required annually to reach the levels of US$600 million suggested in this report. But at any rate it appears likely that a high proportion of these funds can indeed by secured especially if this step is linked, as indicated, to the incentive of untying United States aid to Latin American countries. At the same time, the United States, taking into account the improvement reported in its balance of payments with Latin America during this decade, could also permit certain sales of IDB bonds on its domestic capital market.

In the event that difficulties should arise making it impossible to completely untie the aid—whether on the basis of the proposed or an alternative plan—it is considered an immediate necessity to find at least a compromise formula to alleviate to some extent the disadvantages of the present tying conditions on United States loans. While stressing the need to continue efforts designed to achieve complete untying of aid, it is appropriate to consider another compromise solution outlined in the previous chapter. This would consist in adopting, with respect to the Latin American countries as a whole, a criterion similar to the one now in effect for loans to member countries of the Central American Common Market. In these operations, which are already an exception to the usual practices of economic assistance, it is contemplated that credits may also be utilized in payment of goods and services from other countries of the CAMV. In view of this precedent of regionalization of financing conditions, and considering that in Latin America the marginal propensity to import from the United States seems higher than that existing in other areas receiving United States economic assistance, it is reasonable to expect that, if complete elimination of conditions for tying financing granted under the Alliance for Progress is not achieved, at least there should be an extension to LAFTA countries of the possibility of supplying the demand for goods and services generated by such financing.[9] The

[8]This could also constitute some tying for all IDB financing, but in a much more flexible manner and less prejudicial to the recipient countries, than the bilateral tying. The required amounts could be determined, for example, on the basis of the participation of exports from each industrialized country in total Latin American imports.

[9]Of course, if the purpose is to effectively promote the participation of Latin American producers in the demand originating in the flow of Alliance resources, given

adverse impact of this measure on the United States balance of payments will undoubtedly be small; nevertheless it could certainly result in a considerable stimulus to the process of integration and to the development of Latin America—particularly in sectors involving advanced technology—and would likewise contribute in large measure to perfecting hemispheric solidarity. In spite of this, it should be noted that although the effect of the measure itself would not be too significant in terms of the United States balance of payments, it could, within the context of the proposal set forth on p. 212, have a major short-term impact. Thus, it seems reasonable to expect that, by choosing the system of partial untying, a considerable portion of the loan funds to be obtained in capital markets would have to be obtained from the United States, since without the stimulus offered by a complete untying of financing, it would be difficult to obtain from the other industrial countries levels of financial cooperation substantially higher than those they now grant to Latin America. This cooperation, as pointed out above, should consist basically in providing adequate means for access to capital markets in order to make it possible to obtain from such markets the largest share of the resources required.

In order to promote industrial development of the Latin American countries and the integration of their economies, it would be advisable for the IBRD, in the bidding convoked for its project loans, to extend to all Latin American producers the margin of preference it currently grants for such bidding to producers of the recipient countries, and for the IDB to adopt a similar procedure.

It should again be noted that the amounts, conditions, proportions assigned to each source, the proposals for untying aid, and other aspects of the suggestions presented in this study attempt only to illustrate an apparently feasible solution to some of the problems outlined here. Additional studies to improve the quality of results obtained here and take into account other aspects not explicitly considered in this proposal, as well as other possible alternatives, would be necessary before this solution could be adopted.

NATIONAL PRIORITIES AND EXTERNAL FINANCING

Most of the Latin American countries do not as yet have fully operational development plans. This fact, together with the lack of coordination, at both the internal level of each country and within the international framework, of

---

the productivity differences existing with regard to United States products, such producers should be granted, on a regional level, adequate margins of preference. For a detailed study of this aspect as well as of other aspects involved in the implementation of this system of partial untying, see chap. VI.

operations by external financing institutions, emphasize the need for encountering formulas aimed at securing external financing in an increasingly more orderly fashion and more fully consistent with the basic objectives of the development process in each country.

This study proposes that the Latin American countries requiring financing on concessional conditions prepare an annual program of external financing that would include—in great detail for the immediately following year and more generally for two and three subsequent years—the following data:

 a. Total external financing requirements in accordance with over-all projections, and projections for the public sector and the balance of payments.

 b. Detailed projections of disbursements on credits obtained earlier.

 c. Detailed and properly documented lists of new projects eligible for external financing.

 d. Residual needs to be covered by program credits—over-all and/or sectoral—and, where necessary, balance-of-payments financing as such.

 e. Policies for procurement in the relevant fields of the required financing.

To attain its objectives, the external financing program must be coordinated with the various aspects of domestic policy that determine in each case the national efforts which the external resources should serve to supplement. Such coordination is necessary with fiscal, monetary, and credit policies, together with policies on foreign trade and development of priority sectors. In short, the external financing program must form part of a general process of operational programing of the economic and social policy, although in many cases such programing cannot yet be formally concerted in annual operating plans.

It would also be advisable for these external financing programs to be drafted with a view to long-range strategies determining the factors that limit the country's development outlook and the general guidelines of policies to be adopted in order to remove these limitations, in a manner consistent with the basic objectives set forth in the Charter of Punta del Este and in the Declaration of the Presidents of America. In order for that strategy to provide a proper framework for the programing of external financing, its definition should give special attention to the country's prospects for external debt capacity.

As the Secretariat has observed on the basis of its continuing contacts with the Latin American governments within the framework of the CIAP country reviews, most countries in the region are able to prepare such external financing programs adequately. To this end, they could also receive external technical cooperation whenever necessary; the OAS General Secretariat, for example, would be willing to assign the highest priority to requests for cooperation presented by the countries,[10] and the same can be expected from other international institutions.

Following their completion, these external financing programs could serve as the main basis for the annual review conducted by CIAP of each country and for negotiations with the various institutions and countries participating in the financing received by Latin America. These studies and negotiations would, accordingly, use the priorities and policies defined by each country as a point of departure.

The benefits to the countries of having their external financing granted, insofar as possible, in terms of the basic development objectives of each can be better appreciated if certain effects of this financing are considered. For example, concentration in the past of the resources of some international financing institutions on credits for economic infrastructure projects—construction of highways, hydroelectric plants, etc.—has significantly helped several countries of the region to develop adequate technical capacity for preparing and executing projects in these fields by themselves, since such external financing has been accompanied by high-level technical cooperation. If this same contribution of technical and financial resources was concentrated in the highest priority fields in each country—for example, for several countries of the region in export industries, with fuller collaboration than in the past with the national development institutions—significant results could be achieved in resolving the basic balance-of-payments bottlenecks in many countries, in the acquisition by those countries of technical know-how not always directly linked to the direct operation of foreign companies, and in the strengthening of national public and private enterprises operating in the goods-producing sectors.

PROGRAM LOANS IN THE FUTURE FINANCING
OF REGIONAL DEVELOPMENT

The two major objections made in recent years to continuation and expansion of the use of over-all program credits to help finance development of the Latin American countries are: (a) the lack of adequate programs in the recipient countries which would ensure acceptable use of the resources contributed; and (b) the fact that, in the absence of such programs and in order to ensure acceptable utilization, it would be necessary, in order for over-all credits to be extended bilaterally, for the recipient country to agree to discuss and arrange with the country contributing the funds domestic policies that should rightfully be oriented and defined by the country applying them. The

[10] In fact, the Secretariat is already beginning to collaborate on this aspect with three countries whose governments have so requested.

proposal presented in preceding pages has been designed for the express purpose of providing an adequate response to both difficulties.

In the first place, the preparation of the external financing programs proposed in this study would be consistent with the current orientation of the Latin American planning process.[11] The external financing program would constitute an essential part of the operating plans which are today the major focus of planning tasks in various countries of the region, thus facilitating their preparation and eventual execution. These programs could, in the opinion of the Secretariat, provide adequate and sufficient expression of the development policy—provided they relate to the guidelines of the long-range strategy—to serve as a basis on which over-all credits not directly connected with specific investment projects could be granted.

Moreover, definition of the pertinent policies under those programs by the governments, and discussion and evaluation of results within the multilateral framework of the CIAP subcommittees, would be an adequate means of overcoming the objections that can justifiably be made to bilateral discussion of those policies. This would supplement and improve, in a manner consistent with the free determination by governments of the goals of their economic and social policy, the procedure initiated by AID in partially basing the granting of its program credits on the conclusions and recommendations of the CIAP subcommittee meetings and on the presentation to the CIAP chairman by the respective governments of statements outlining their intentions in certain fields of economic and social policy.

The proposal presented here calls for a significantly higher utilization of program credits than in the past, without, of course, excluding continued use of the other means of financing—project credits, sectoral credits, contributions to development banks, etc. The essential consideration in this respect is that the external resources should finance all of the needs for programs utilizing the external resources projected by Latin American governments for each year. In this respect, more flexible procedures for project financing—for example, with increasing percentages allocated to finance local costs—can be as important as the granting of program credits. At any rate, considering that many of the policies to be adopted for development promotion are not linked to the execution of specific industrial projects eligible for external financing, and that, despite this fact, these policies can exert an expansive effect on foreign exchange requirements, it appears likely that many countries will need over-all financing.

The proposal put forth in this report provides that a large share of the program credit requirements will be covered by the new sources to be as-

---

[11] See "Estado de la Planificación en América Latina" (CIES/1383).

signed to the IDB. The financing to be continued bilaterally through AID could also include program credits of this type and it would be desirable for other institutions, such as IBRD, to incorporate similar credits within their financing operations with Latin America.

CONTRIBUTION OF EXTERNAL PRIVATE FINANCING

The external financing strategy described above should be supplemented by as precise a definition as possible of the proper role of external private enterprise in transferring to the region the resources—financial, technological, and management ability—required for development of the Latin American countries. The Secretariat does not intend to present such a definition here, since it will be the subject of a special report to be submitted by CIAP shortly.

However, mention should be made of the need for this definition to give special attention to the over-all impact of foreign investment on the balance of payments of the Latin American countries. It would be advisable to channel this investment in the future into new export activities, particularly in the industrial sector, where the technological and financial contribution of external enterprise could be beneficial. It would also be advisable to define the other areas in which the technological requirements of development suggest participation by the foreign investor in the future growth of production.

It also appears necessary for the schemes adopted with regard to foreign investment to take into account the urgent need to promote expansion and modernization of the national entrepreneurial class in the Latin American countries. A Latin American strategy for development of the entrepreneurial sector should consider the comparative importance to be assigned to systems of joint enterprises in which, under certain conditions, national and foreign capital collaborate. Systems could also be evolved with a view to gradual transfer of the ownership of foreign companies to national interests.

The possibility of setting up new financial mechanisms at the regional or subregional level to promote development of Latin American national and multinational enterprises should also be considered. A study might be made, for example, of the various requirements for formation of a Latin American financing corporation with close ties to the IDB and subregional banks, designed primarily to strengthen the Latin American companies by facilitating the transfer of capital and technology from abroad to those enterprises.

CONCLUSIONS

In these closing paragraphs it should be repeated that the quantitative aspects of the proposals presented in this study are aimed solely at illustrating the extent of the domestic effort and external cooperation that would be required in order for each country to maintain, during the next decade and thereafter, the minimum 2.5 percent per capita growth goal proposed in the Charter of Punta del Este. These quantitative aspects may vary, especially at the level of individual countries, because of the very many circumstances that cannot be anticipated in a report of this type, but the basic elements of the strategy proposed here would, in the opinion of the Secretariat, remain valid within the framework of the estimates included in this report. It should be stressed again that various countries in the region could exceed the minimum annual growth goal of 2.5 percent of the per capita product which serves as a basis for the estimates given here. If the countries are willing to undertake the greater domestic efforts required for this purpose, external cooperation should also be expanded above the levels projected in this report.

The basic factors in the strategy outlined above can be summarized as follows:

a. The Latin American countries will have to accentuate their domestic efforts significantly during the next few years, especially those aimed, first, at expanding exports, and, second, at generating the required volume of national savings.

b. The financial cooperation of the United States should increase significantly, in terms of quantity and quality, during the next few years, declining substantially thereafter beginning in the second half of the 1970's.

c. This increased cooperation from the United States, which would include elimination of the tied aid systems, could be undertaken without significantly prejudicing the United States balance-of-payments position through procedures such as that illustrated in this study.

d. At the same time, it is essential to secure greater financial cooperation from the other industrialized countries.

e. Just as important as procurement of increasing amounts of external credit, or more so, is a substantial improvement in the conditions of the financing received by the region, with regard to interest rates and grace and amortization terms that determine the real aid component of such financing.

f. The multilateralization of financing granted under the Alliance for Progress suggested in this report implies a sizable expansion of IDB credits. This will probably require that agency to expand its entire operating structure, adapting it to the new responsibilities assigned, and to redefine and coordinate closely the functions of the IDB and those of the mechanisms of the Inter-American system.

Finally, it must be emphasized that the domestic effort and external financing cooperation outlined here might fail to achieve the desired results if the conditions of international trade should again evolve along lines unfavorable to Latin America. To provide for this eventuality, the Secretariat considers, in addition to all the suggestions presented in this report, that a study should be made of the prospects for establishing at the regional level, in view of the difficulties involved in its application at the world level, a system of supplementary financing to offset any deterioration that may occur in exports by the Latin American countries in relation to the goals of their development and financing programs.

Appendix to Chapter VII

APPENDIX VII-A: MEASURES PROPOSED FOR EXPANDING THE VOLUME OF RESOURCES FOR DEVELOPMENT FINANCING

Owing to a variety of circumstances, there has in recent years been a revival of the concern for encountering formulas and mechanisms designed to expand, on suitable conditions, the flow of financial resources to the developing countries. On the one hand, these countries are confronted by a growing burden of service and amortization on the external debt. On the other, direct bilateral allocation of public resources in some countries providing assistance has met with increasing political difficulties within the framework of budget appropriations, resulting in a substantial absolute reduction in the amounts earmarked for these purposes. Mention should also be made of the trend toward hardening of financing terms in the capital markets and by official and international institutions. Consequently, there is a general consensus on the need for stepping up aid to the developing countries in order to increase the net flow of resources and for granting such financing on more favorable terms.

For the purposes of this study, a brief examination will be made of the main feature of the Horowitz Proposal and of the proposal presented by the IBRD as a modification of the former, followed by a summary exploration of the possibilities of applying such a system to Latin America.

THE HOROWITZ PROPOSAL[1]

The System

The general interest evinced in this scheme is derived from the fact that, accepting the premise that political and budgetary obstacles will maintain the flows of public concessionary financing at insufficient levels, it provides the means of considerably expanding the volume of financing on concessionary terms, on the basis of these comparatively reduced amounts of public financing.

To these ends, it is proposed that development resources be secured in the capital markets of the developed countries and that public financial aid serve to cover the difference between the commercial interest rates at which the resources would be obtained and the concessionary rates at which they would be granted to the developing countries. In this way, a specific amount of

---

[1]*Development Financing Plan*, prepared by D. Horowitz, Governor of the Bank of Israel, and presented by the delegation of that country to UNCTAD in 1964.

public financial assistance would make it possible to place at the disposal of the developing countries a much larger volume of resources than that provided under the aid itself.

The system would operate as follows. An international institution would obtain the funds in the capital markets of the developed countries by selling bonds on commercial conditions. The same international institution, or another of the same type, would loan these funds to the developing countries to finance projects at lower interest rates and on longer terms.[2] The interest margin resulting from the difference between rates—and also presumably administrative costs—would be covered by an "interest equalization fund," which would be set up and maintained by the developed countries through annual budget appropriations; the proposal considers that international financing institutions might also contribute to that fund by assigning part of their net operating profits.

With regard to the necessary basis of guarantees that would be required to attract the funds, the proposal suggests establishment of an *ad hoc* system of government guarantees for capital and interest that would be extended by developed countries.

The participation of each of these countries in contributions to the interest equalization fund and the granting of guarantees would be proportional to their respective quotas in the IMF or their capital subscription to the IBRD; that is, distribution of the effort would be consistent with the comparative economic capacity of the countries but independent of transitory balance-of-payments positions. However, insofar as possible, these conditions would be taken into account in the procurement of funds, which would be aimed preferably at countries with a very favorable balance-of-payments position; this, consequently, implies that absorption of resources in the various national capital markets would not necessarily be proportionate to the economic size of the country but rather to circumstantial prospects.

Problems and Possibilities of Implementation

The Horowitz Proposal has received special consideration from UNCTAD and the World Bank, which at the request of the Conference, conducted a broad study on prospects for its implementation and the problems requiring solution.[3] These aspects were also examined by a group of financial experts,

---

[2] The proposal calls for terms of thirty years.

[3] World Bank, *International Bank for Reconstruction and Development: The Horowitz Proposal, A Staff Report, February 1965.*

at the request of the UNCTAD Secretariat,[4] which in turn also studied the basic problems involved in implementation of the proposal.[5]

A topic that has been the subject of considerable controversy has been the institutional arrangements envisaged in the proposal. Although it is not the aim of this report to examine this particular problem, it appears advisable to present the views expressed in this connection, since they are of undoubted general interest. The proposal calls for the World Bank to procure resources in the capital markets. The World Bank would loan these funds to the IDA which would in turn use these resources for loans on "softer" conditions to the developing countries. According to the original version of the proposal, the governments of the developed countries would particularly guarantee payments of capital and interest on these loans from the World Bank to the IDA by means of *ad hoc* guarantees. Subsequently, Mr. Horowitz presented a new version of the proposal in which, in order to circumvent problems that might emerge in the future with regard to establishing a separate system of guarantees for these operations, it is suggested that the World Bank grant the loans to the IDA on its current basis of guarantees, that is, the bank's callable capital (capital subscribed but not paid in). In the opinion of the World Bank technical staff, the placement of bonds for the purpose of making loans to the IDA would unfavorably affect the bank's credit, even with a new and independent system of guarantees. The group of financial experts felt, in contrast, that if the operations were independently guaranteed, they could by no means be considered as prejudicial to the bank's credit. With regard to the execution of operations without the new system of guarantees, some members of the UNCTAD group of experts believed that the institution's credit would not be harmed if the over-all amount of the operation did not exceed a certain fairly moderate ceiling;[6] to the contrary, other members, high executives of important European banking enterprises, felt that this practice would inevitably undermine the bank's credit. Mention should also be made of the opinion of the financial experts of the group that if the IDA itself should place bonds on the market, the over-all amount that could be procured by this institution and the bank would probably aggregate more

[4] UNCTAD, *The Horowitz Proposal, Report of the Group of Experts* (Document TD/B/C.3/23; May 11, 1966).

[5] *Growth, Development Financing and Aid (Synchronization of International and National Policies): The Horowitz Proposal*, study by the UNCTAD Secretariat (Document TD/7supp. 11; December 6, 1967).

[6] According to some opinions, a volume of loans from the World Bank to the IDA amounting to $200 million a year over a period of five years would be prudent; according to others, the maximum overall quota could not exceed $200 million without serious detriment to the bank's credit.

than what the bank would obtain if it had to float an issue for both its own purposes and for loans to the IDA as well; that is, the entrance of a new borrower into the market could effectively increase the resources for development.

The system of government guarantees that would have to be established in order for the international agency selected to carry out operations in the capital markets on an appreciable scale involves a significant amount, since the cost of the resources and/or their volume would depend largely on the alternative adopted. In this respect, three basic possibilities have been mentioned:

1. A system of joint guarantees, in which each guarantor government would assume responsibility for the total amount of bonds guaranteed, so that if necessary any creditor could demand from any individual guarantor payment of all bonds in his possession; this system does not, of course, exclude ultimate adjustment of the distribution of guarantees to proportional participation by the guarantor governments.
2. A system of joint guarantees, in which each guarantor government would assume responsibility solely for a specific percentage of each bond; that is, if necessary each holder could demand payment from the various governments that had guaranteed the bonds.
3. A system of limited and joint guarantees, as an intermediate possibility, in which each government, by granting only a joint guarantee, would contribute a certain amount, according to the proportion of the percentage of bonds it guaranteed, to establishment of a fund that would be distributed among the creditors if necessary.

The first system of joint guarantees would be the most desirable, since it would undoubtedly make it possible to place the largest volume of bonds at the lowest cost; somewhat less effective would be the system of limited and joint guarantees, and the least favorable would be the strictly joint guarantees. However, it is believed that the system of strictly joint guarantees would be the one which the governments would be most willing to accept, followed in order of possibility by the system of limited and joint guarantees. Naturally, the adoption of either system would represent a significant difference in the cost of the funds procured in the market. For example, it has been estimated that if a certain volume of funds could be obtained at 5 percent with the system of limited and joint guarantees, under the system of joint guarantees, only a smaller volume of bonds at interest rates of from 5½ to 6 percent could be placed.[7] In addition to the effect of this factor on the

[7]World Bank, *International Bank for Reconstruction*. It should be kept in mind that this estimate of the interest rate precedes the recent increase in that rate on the international capital markets.

size of contributions to the interest equalization fund (or on the cost of loans to the developing countries, if it should be decided to subsidize a fixed difference of so many points between interest rates), it should be considered that the need for offering higher returns could lead to difficulties in access to the markets, since it is possible that the countries would be willing to permit this only on the condition that interest rates did not exceed the limits considered advisable.

Among the problems and difficulties projected in implementation of the proposal with regard to procurement of funds, mention is also made of current prospects offered by the capital markets in view of the prevailing excess of demand and the consequently high interest rate; the problems that would be confronted by a new institution entering this field, and the difficulties that would be created by its competition with other international development financing institutions already operating in bond sales. There is, however, a broad consensus that these problems and difficulties are far from insoluble, though it is true that a solution to some of them may require more time than would be desirable. At any rate, it appears that one of the most important aspects to be resolved, in order to permit the procurement of resources at the world level in suitable amounts and conditions, would be an agreement on organization of the best possible system of government guarantees.

With reference to prospects that might exist on the capital markets for securing an adequate volume of resources, preliminary investigations by World Bank experts during preparation of their report in 1964 indicated a fairly moderate outlook. Consultations with leading members of financing circles in New York and Europe suggested that, for an international institution solidly supported by *ad hoc* government guarantees and granted reasonable facilities for market access, the most that could reasonably be procured annually in the United States, Canada, and Europe, would be an additional $600 million a year. This would undoubtedly fall far below the desirable level for meeting requirements on a world scale;[8] however, procurement of an additional volume of resources of this size could justify the implementation of the system. At any rate, possible prospects in the capital markets would undoubtedly deserve more exhaustive exploration through systematic market studies.

With regard to the interest equalization fund, the various studies agreed that its establishment would not involve any serious technical problems. It is noted, nevertheless, that, for countries contributing to the fund, support of the system would signify acceptance of the commitment to make such

---

[8] Mr. Horowitz initially called for the procurement of $2 billion a year.

contributions over a period of many years, since by definition the loans to be extended to the developing countries would be long term. This characteristic has led to certain reservations concerning the feasibility of this system, for it does not appear likely that the industrialized countries, and especially their respective legislatures, would be willing to assume this long-range commitment since, as is most probable, contributions to the fund would derive from budget allocations which, modest though they might be, would be periodically subject to possible political difficulties. This would mean that the system would run the serious risk of possible suspension of contributions to the fund at any time, a risk that obviously could not be assumed by any international banking institution without prejudicing its financial solidity and, consequently, its capacity to attract resources on the international capital markets. Among possible solutions to this serious obstacle, it has been suggested that the industrialized countries should appropriate in one or a very few fiscal years the over-all amount of the budget appropriation corresponding to their contributions to the fund over an extended period of years; these resources could be placed in a special account of the country itself for the international institution administering the fund, and the amounts corresponding to the country's contribution for the period withdrawn each year.

VARIATION ON THE HOROWITZ PROPOSAL
SUGGESTED BY THE WORLD BANK

In examining the Horowitz Proposal, the IBRD staff suggested an operational alternative for procuring funds and subsidizing the interest rates.[9]

Within the context of the scheme evolved for implementation on the world scale, the IBRD proposed that the fund for loan resources be formed by loans from the industrial countries participating in the international institution, on the same terms on which the latter would grant financing to the developing countries, deducting the commission that the institution would have to charge to cover its operating expenses. Each contributing government would collect the funds as it deemed best, either through budget appropriations or by bond sales on the capital markets or a combination of both. The governments opting for bond sales would absorb the interest differential between rates at which the funds were procured and the concessionary rate of the loans to be granted by the international institution.

This operating procedure would undoubtedly offer certain considerable advantages with respect to the original concept of the Horowitz Proposal.

[9]World Bank, *International Bank for Reconstruction.*

Provisionally, it would eliminate the need for establishing an international system of guarantees, forestalling a possible source of problems in reaching agreements if the guarantees should have to be signed by various countries. Under this system, it would also be unnecessary to set up an interest equalization fund and, since the governments would undoubtedly sell their bonds on less burdensome conditions, the cost of the development financing to the contributing countries, in terms of subsidy for the interest rates, could be lower.

Despite the advantages offered by this variation, it would most likely fail to solve one of the very problems that have prompted the search for new mechanisms to attract and channel resources. In effect, unless the governments of the countries providing the resources could secure the funds through an independent financing institution, the placement of bonds and/or allocation of funds—that is, all of the resources for development—might require legislative approval and, therefore, the system would continue to be contingent upon political considerations.

PROSPECTS FOR UTILIZATION OF THE HOROWITZ PROPOSAL SYSTEM FOR LATIN AMERICAN FINANCING

Recently, it has been suggested on several occasions that the Horowitz Proposal system be used for the purpose of expanding the United States contribution to the financing of Latin American economic development on concessionary conditions.

Within the framework of the original concept of the system, and considering the prevailing criteria in the United States that this country's external financial aid should be channeled to a greater extent through multinational institutions, it is logical to assume that the financial institution responsible for attracting and channeling these funds would be the IDB.

The subsidy on interest rates would be essentially a matter for decision by the United States, but this does not exclude the possibility of other industrialized countries—primarily those most interested in expanding their trade with the region—making their own contributions to the interest equalization fund.

Furthermore, it has been suggested[10] that contributions to the interest equalization fund could be distributed among the countries belonging to the IDB in proportion to their participation in the funding of the Special Opera-

---

[10]CIAP, Panel of Experts, *La Brecha Externa de la América Latina 1968-73*, December 1968.

tions Fund.[11] In this way, the region as a whole, excluding the United States, would obtain a reduction in the cost of financing equivalent to two-thirds of the difference between the interest rate at which the funds would be obtained on the market and the loans granted. There would, therefore, be a redistribution of resources among the Latin American countries in favor of the most needy, which, by receiving larger loans, would obtain a net benefit between the subsidy extended on the interest rates and their contributions to the equalization fund. Given the nature of the system, the burden on the countries contributing to the net fund would be very moderate, even for the United States; however, the procedure suggested involves a greater complexity that does not seem strictly necessary in view of the stated goals. Although an intra-Latin American transfer of resources through the cost of credit or by other means should be considered within the schemes for regional financial cooperation, it would not be essential, in this case, where the purpose would be to encounter a mechanism to facilitate an expansion of United States assistance.

In order to evaluate the amounts involved in the interest equalization fund, table VII-A-1 provides an example illustrating what would be entailed in mobilization by this system of a volume of $1.3 billion in one year, an amount similar to that required by Latin America from the financing institutions of the Alliance for Progress during each of the following years, in accordance with the projections given in chapter IV of the main text of this report. For the purposes of this calculation, the following assumptions have been employed:

1. The attraction of funds in the capital markets through bond sales would amount of $1.3 billion, with disbursements for the same amount in that year chargeable to the loans to be granted.
2. The loans would be granted at an interest rate of 3.1 percent a year and grace and amortization terms of ten and forty years, respectively.[12]
3. The bonds would be placed on the market at an interest rate which, together with the commission to be charged by the financing institution, would amount to 7.5 percent, on the same terms as those of the credits to be extended. As this is very probably unworkable—since bonds are usually placed on the capital markets without grace periods

[11] The United States contributes two-thirds of the over-all amount of contributions to the Special Operations Fund of the IDB; the other member countries contribute the remaining one-third in proportion to their comparative economic capacity.

[12] That is, the average conditions required for financing from Alliance for Progress sources during the period 1970–75, pursuant to the assumptions adopted in chapter IV of this report.

and at a shorter term than that considered here—this assumption would actually imply renewal by the financing institution of its debt during the years in which amortization payments exceeded amortization collections through additional issues for amounts equivalent to those differences.

Under these assumptions, the interest differential, which in this case would be 4.4 points on the rates, would represent a margin of $1.745 billion for the entire period between the amounts of interest receivable and payable (see table VII-A-1).

Appendix Table VII-A-1. Resources Required for the Operation of Financing under the Horowitz Plan

Years	Placement of Bond and Loan Disbursements	Amortization	Current Principal	Interest Paid (7.5%)	Interest Charged (3.1%)	Interest Differential[a]
	(1)	(2)	(3)	(4)	(5)	(6)
1	1,300.0	–	1,300.0	97.5	40.3	57.2
2		–	1,300.0	97.5	40.3	57.2
3		–	1,300.0	97.5	40.3	57.2
4		–	1,300.0	97.5	40.3	57.2
5		–	1,300.0	97.5	40.3	57.2
6		–	1,300.0	97.5	40.3	57.2
7		–	1,300.0	97.5	40.3	57.2
8		–	1,300.0	97.5	40.3	57.2
9		–	1,300.0	97.5	40.3	57.2
10		–	1,300.0	97.5	40.3	57.2
11		32.5	1,300.0	97.5	40.3	57.2
12		32.5	1,267.5	95.1	39.3	55.8
13		32.5	1,235.0	92.6	38.3	54.3
14		32.5	1,202.5	90.2	37.3	52.9
15		32.5	1,170.0	87.8	36.3	51.5
16		32.5	1,137.5	85.3	35.3	50.0
17		32.5	1,105.0	82.9	34.3	48.6
18		32.5	1,072.5	80.4	33.2	47.2
19		32.5	1,040.0	78.0	32.2	45.8
20		32.5	1,007.5	75.6	31.2	44.4
21		32.5	975.0	73.1	30.2	42.9
22		32.5	942.5	70.7	29.2	41.5
23		32.5	910.0	68.3	28.2	40.1
24		32.5	877.5	65.8	27.2	38.6
25		32.5	845.0	63.4	26.2	37.2
26		32.5	812.5	60.9	25.2	35.7
27		32.5	780.0	58.5	24.2	34.3
28		32.5	747.5	56.1	23.2	32.9
29		32.5	715.0	53.6	22.2	31.4
30		32.5	682.5	51.2	21.2	30.0
31		32.5	650.0	48.8	20.2	28.6

Appendix Table VII-A-1. *Continued*

Years	Placement of Bond and Loan Disbursements (1)	Amortization (2)	Current Principal (3)	Interest Paid (7.5%) (4)	Interest Charged (3.1%) (5)	Interest Differential[a] (6)
32		32.5	617.5	46.3	19.1	27.2
33		32.5	585.0	43.9	18.1	25.8
34		32.5	552.5	41.4	17.1	24.3
35		32.5	520.0	39.0	16.1	22.9
36		32.5	487.5	36.6	15.1	21.5
37		32.5	455.0	34.1	14.1	20.0
38		32.5	422.5	31.7	13.1	18.6
39		32.5	390.0	29.3	12.1	17.2
40		32.5	357.5	26.8	11.1	15.7
41		32.5	325.0	24.4	10.1	14.3
42		32.5	292.5	21.9	9.1	12.8
43		32.5	260.0	19.5	8.1	11.4
44		32.5	227.5	17.1	7.1	10.0
45		32.5	195.0	14.6	6.0	8.6
46		32.5	162.5	12.2	5.0	7.2
47		32.5	130.0	9.8	4.0	5.8
48		32.5	97.5	7.3	3.0	4.3
49		32.5	65.0	4.9	2.0	2.9
50		32.5	32.5	2.4	1.0	1.4
Total	1,300.0	1,300.0	—	2,974.2	1,229.2	1,745.0

[a]Interest differential that would exist if the bond terms were the same as the loan terms. See assumption 2 in the text.

Bases: See text.

Assuming that the system would operate on the basis of subsidies covering that difference to be contributed by the United States to the IDB, the amount mentioned, $1.745 billion, would be the sum of the contributions to be made during the fifty years following the year in which the IDB grants the loans for $1.3 billion and obtains an equal amount in the capital markets.

Two alternatives might be considered here within the context of this possibility. The first would call for the United States Congress to approve a budget authorization of $1.745 billion, to be disbursed over the next fifty years in the amounts listed in column 6 of table VII-A-1. There is a possibility that this alternative would encounter political difficulties preventing its approval, in view of the high level of the budget authorization required and the fact that a similar authorization would have to be approved in each of the years included in the 1970–75 period, according to the projections presented in chapter IV of this report.

The second alternative would be a contribution in each year of the period to a fund which, invested by the institution administering the system, would yield resources sufficient to cover the interest differentials. If this fund were invested at 6 percent, the amounts needed in each of those years would be about $750 million. If the yield were 7.5 percent, the annual contribution required would be about $650 million. It should be noted that establishment of such a fund for investment at 7.5 percent—that is, the same rate as the cost of loans to the IDB in the example discussed—would be virtually the equivalent of utilizing the amount of this fund directly in IDB operations and reducing by the same amount the attraction of funds in the capital markets.[13] This possibility, which is suggested as the most feasible alternative in this report, is examined briefly in the following section.

AN ALTERNATIVE TO THE HOROWITZ PROPOSAL
SYSTEM FOR LATIN AMERICA

In order to avoid the difficulties that might arise in selling large volumes of bonds on the capital markets and in arranging commitments for contributions to the interest equalization fund over many years, this report suggests a system which, to some extent, combines the current practices of public financing with the attraction of resources in the capital markets. The system would operate as follows. The financial aid to be provided by government sources would be entirely in the form of "aid," that is, nonreimbursable contributions, to an international financing institution, in this case the IDB. The latter, for its part, following receipt of the contributions, would secure a similar amount on the capital markets by placing bonds on commercial terms. The over-all volume of funds deriving from both sources would be used to grant credits on concessionary terms to the Latin American countries. Under the same assumed conditions as in the preceding example—$1.3 billion a year in loans granted by the IDB at 3.1 percent and a total cost to the IDB of 7.5 percent—and the same grace and amortization terms, this system could function if the IDB received nonreimbursable contributions, presumably from the United States, for about $650 million a year and had available the remaining $650 million from utilization of its own resources and issues of securities

---

[13]The difference between the two alternatives, in terms of costs to the IDB, derives from the fact that the 7.5 percent taken here as representative of the total cost to the IDB includes not only the interest rate paid but also a commission to cover operating costs, which would still have to be charged even though the amount to be procured on the capital markets were reduced to one-half.

on international capital markets. Assuming that the IDB can count on fairly sizable resources of its own over the next few years—for example, $50 million a year—the amount to be procured on the capital markets would be $600 million. Feasible interest rates within the context of this example would be nearly 7 percent, assuming that the commission charged by the IDB would range between 0.50 and 0.75 percent.

It will be observed that the system suggested here includes features very similar to those of the Horowitz Proposal, with the advantage that the amount to be attracted in the capital markets is reduced to about one-half. In both cases, the aid component would be approximately equal and the same conditions could be maintained for credits granted by the IDB to the Latin American countries.

Operation of this system would undoubtedly be simpler than that proposed by Mr. Horowitz. Provisionally, the fact already noted that it would only be necessary to procure in the capital markets slightly over half of the development financing would, in addition to solving many of the questions concerning the absorption capacity of those markets, undoubtedly facilitate the placement of bonds and reduce the costs of this financing. Furthermore, the system precludes formation of an interest equalization fund, wholly eliminating any uncertainty with regard to continuity of the contributions to subsidize interest rates; in this case, in contrast to what could have occurred under a system such as the Horowitz Proposal, eventual suspension of public contributions would in no way affect functioning of the system with regard to operations already concluded.

With reference to the system of guarantees that would necessarily have to support the placement of bonds on the capital markets in order to attract sizable volumes of funds, the views expressed at UNCTAD provide various indications. In the first place, assuming that the institute of issue would be the IDB, it would probably be necessary to set up an additional system of guarantees for these operations in order to facilitate sales of the institution's securities at the lowest possible interest rate. In the special case of Latin America, the possibility of a joint system of guarantees should be explored, for this would undoubtedly contribute to the success of a system such as the one suggested here.

With reference to the prospects for obtaining significant volumes of resources in the market, the most pessimistic views expressed at UNCTAD would indicate a favorable outlook with regard to Latin American needs, at least so long as the market were not disputed by another institution working toward the same end. Assuming these circumstances and considering that the IDB would operate under the protection of a system of guarantees possibly more satisfactory for the market than what could be obtained to set up the system on a world scale, it is conceivable that the institution could attract $650 million a year, an amount similar to that projected in 1965 for operations of IDA or the World Bank for these purposes,[14] assuming that the governments of the industrial countries provide adequate facilities for access to their markets.

Appendix Table VII-A-2. Yield on Central Government Bonds (in Percentages)

Country	1968				1969	
	September	October	November	December	January	February
United States	5.09	5.24	5.36	5.65	5.74	5.86
Canada	6.60	6.99	7.16	7.34	7.31	7.32
Germany[a]	6.30	6.30	6.30	6.30	6.30	n.a.
Belgium	5.49	5.66	5.64	5.56	5.58	5.64
France	5.95	5.81	5.77	6.00	5.93	n.a.
Netherlands	6.25	6.20	6.18	6.34	6.53	6.52
Italy	5.86	5.94	6.10	6.11	5.98	n.a.
United Kingdom	7.43	7.44	7.63	7.99	8.24	8.40
Sweden	5.91	5.88	5.87	5.88	5.97	6.09
Switzerland	4.34	4.38	4.33	4.33	4.38	4.40

[a]Bonds of local authorities.

Source: IMF, International Financial Statistics.

With reference to the interest rates at which bonds could be placed in the amounts and on the terms desired, only conjectures can be made in the absence of a market study. As a general criterion based on the experience of the World Bank,[15] it could be expected that under current circumstances bonds placed by the IDB should provide a yield one-half percent higher than government issues and perhaps even higher, given the present conditions on the international capital markets and the amounts involved in this proposal.[16] Recent conditions of annual average yield on central government bonds for issues at a term of at least twelve years are shown in table VII-A-2.

[14]Considering that the capital markets have undergone an appreciable expansion that explains the current comparative shortage of capital as a result of a surplus growth of demand over supply, the estimates mentioned can be taken as still relevant at present.

[15]IBRD, *op cit.*

[16]This excess over current rates for government bonds could be substantially reduced if a system of guarantees designed for this purpose were adopted, as explained in earlier paragraphs of the text.

List of Abbreviations

AID	Agency for International Development
AIF	Asociación Internacional de Fomento (International Development Association of the IBRD)
CACM	Central American Common Market
CIAP	Comité Interamericano de la Alianza para el Progreso (Inter-American Committee on the Alliance for Progress)
CIES	Consejo Interamericano Económico y Social
CORFO	Corporación de Fomento de la Producción
DAC	Development Assistance Committee (OECD)
ECLA	Economic Commission for Latin America (UN)
EXIMBANK	Export-Import Bank of the United States Government
IA-ECOSOC	Inter-American Economic and Social Council
IBRD	International Bank for Reconstruction and Development
IDA	International Development Association of the IBRD
IDB	Inter-American Development Bank
IFC	International Finance Corporation
ILPES	Instituto Latinoamericano de Planificación Económico y Social
KREDITANSTALT (KFW)	KREDITANSTALT für Wiederaufbau
LAFTA	Latin American Free Trade Association
OECD	Organization for Economic Cooperation and Development
SPTF	Social Progress Trust Fund
UNCTAD	United Nations Conference on Trade and Development

List of Tables and Graphs

Text tables

Text tables

Text tables

Index

Action Program of Viña del Mar, 162n
Additionality, 144, 146–57, 161, 178, 204, 211
Adelman, I., 114
Africa, aid component of, 49n
Agency for International Development (AID), ix; additionality and, 146n, 147, 150n, 156–57; aid component of, 47, 53, 56, 109; case studies of joint loans involving, 186, 188–90; case studies of loans from, 188, 190–92, 194, 196, 199–200, 200–202; credits and grants from, x, 2, 47; criteria for the selection of projects of, 159; effective interest rate of, 55; and the financing gap, 103; gross disbursements of, to Latin America, 20; "letters of commitment" of, 149; letters of credit of, 145; loans from, 1, 4–6, 8–13, 18–19, 29–32, 37, 40, 43–44, 46; loans to Central America, terms of, 174; local currency operations of, 58–59; method of operation of, 145–46, 152, 159–61; and the need for coordination of financing agencies, 204–5; projected financing from, 99–101, 106–7, 207; projected terms of, 102, 208; recommendations regarding, 218; specialization of, 159; terms of, 22–24, 53, 144, 154, 160–61, 169; tying practices of, 163–64, 170, 172–73
Agriculture: aid component for, 51–52; liquidation value of surpluses of, 39n; loans for, 6–9, 12–13, 28–29, 32, 44
AID. *See* Agency for International Development
Aid: measurement of, 34–37; distribution of, by country, 49; proposal for, 232
Aid component, 35–36, 38–39; in case studies of tied financing, 164–66, 179–80, 184, 186–92, 196–97, 199; in external financing received by Latin America, 44–56, 204; graphs illustrating, 181–83; of local currency operations, 58–59; mathematical formulas for deter-

mining, 60–62; projected, 94–95, 103, 106, 109, 207; of recommended financing from the United States, 209; reduced by additionality, 154; relationship of, to degree of development, 97; relationship of, to effective interest rates, 56; by sector, 52; and tied financing, 53–56, 144, 151, 157, 173; of United States aid, 210
Airport, case study of financing of, 189–90
Alliance for Progress, 34; goods stamped with the emblem of, 145; increased financing by institutions of, recommended, 207–8; projected financing through, 99, 106; proposal for, ix
Amortization periods, 22–26
Argentina: aid component of, 50–53; debt refinancing of, 3; distribution of development funds for, 17; exports of, 82, 156n; external financing of, 12, 14–16, 33; growth of GNP of, 81; parameters used for, 114; placements of government bonds by, 44n; private U.S. investment in, 64–65; projected resource and financing gaps for, 83–84, 118–22; projected surplus resources of, 85–86; surplus resources of, 89–90, 115–16; terms of loans to, 25–26; U.S.-owned manufacturing companies in, 72

Balance of payments: of Latin American countries, 218; and tying, 152, 171–74; U.S., and additionality, 151–53
Bilateral financing: reduction of, proposed, 106–7, 208–9; tied condition of, 143–44, 178–79, 204
Bolivia: aid component of, 49–50, 52–53; debt refinancing of, 3; distribution of development funds for, 17; external financing of, 12, 14–16, 33; financing needs of, 93; growth of exports of, 82; growth of GNP of, 81; parameters used for, 115; procedure used in study to re-